LITTLE PHIL

ALSO BY ERIC J. WITTENBERG

Protecting the Flank:
The Battles for Brinkerhoff's Ridge and East Cavalry Field,
Battle of Gettysburg, July 2–3, 1863

Glory Enough for All:
Sheridan's Second Raid and the Battle of Trevilian Station

At Custer's Side:
The Civil War Writings of Bvt. Brig. Gen. James H. Kidd,
6th Michigan Cavalry

Under Custer's Command:
The Civil War Journal of James Henry Avery

One of Custer's Wolverines:
The Civil War Letters of Bvt. Brig. Gen. James H. Kidd,
6th Michigan Cavalry

We Have It Damn Hard Out Here:
The Civil War Letters of Sergeant Thomas W. Smith,
6th Pennsylvania Cavalry

Gettysburg's Forgotten Cavalry Actions

LITTLE PHIL

A Reassessment
of the Civil War Leadership of
Gen. Philip H. Sheridan

ERIC J. WITTENBERG

Foreword by
JEFFRY D. WERT

POTOMAC BOOKS, INC.
Washington, D.C.

Library of Congress Cataloging-in-Publication Data
Wittenberg, Eric J., 1961–
   Little Phil : a reassessment of the Civil War leadership of Gen. Philip H. Sheridan / Eric J. Wittenberg ; foreword by Jeffry D. Wert.
      p. cm.
Includes bibliographical references and index.
   ISBN 1-57488-385-2 (acid-free paper)
   1. Sheridan, Philip Henry, 1831–1888—Military Leadership. 2. United States—History—Civil War, 1861–1865—Campaigns. 3. Command of troops—Case studies. 4. Generals—United States—Biography. 5. United States. Army—Biography. I. Title.
   E467.1.S54 W58 2002
   973.7'3'092—dc21

                                                            2002002657

ISBN 1-57488-548-0   (paper)

Potomac Books, Inc.
22841 Quicksilver Drive
Dulles, Virginia 20166

First Edition

10 9 8 7 6 5 4 3 2 1

This book is respectfully dedicated to the
men of the Calvary Corps of the Army of the Potomac
and the Army of the Shenandoah who followed
Philip H. Sheridan into battle.

It is also respectfully dedicated to the
memories of Generals William Woods Averell and Gouveneur
K. Warren, both of whom suffered
terrible injustices at Sheridan's hand.

⤙ SHERIDAN'S RIDE ⤚

by Thomas Buchanan Read
(1822–1872)

Up from the South, at break of day,
Bringing to Winchester fresh dismay,
The affrighted air with a shudder bore,
Like a herald in haste to the chieftain's door,
The terrible grumble, and rumble, and roar,
Telling the battle was on once more,
   And Sheridan twenty miles away.

And wider still those billows of war
Thundered along the horizon's bar;
And louder yet into Winchester rolled
The roar of that red sea uncontrolled,
Making the blood of the listener cold,
As he thought of the stake in that fiery fray,
   With Sheridan twenty miles away.

But there is a road from Winchester town,
A good, broad highway leading down:
And there, through the flush of the morning
 light,
A steed as black as the steeds of night
Was seen to pass, as with eagle flight;
As if he knew the terrible need,
He stretched away with his utmost speed.
Hills rose and fell, but his heart was gay,
   With Sheridan fifteen miles away.

Still sprang from those swift hoofs, thundering
    south,
The dust like smoke from the cannon's mouth,
Or the trail of a comet, sweeping faster and faster,
Foreboding to traitors the doom of disaster.
The heart of the steed and the heart of the master
Were beating like prisoners assaulting their walls,
Impatient to be where the battle-field calls;
Every nerve of the charger was strained to full play,
       With Sheridan only ten miles away.

Under his spurning feet, the road
Like an arrowy Alpine river flowed,
And the landscape sped away behind
Like an ocean flying before the wind;
And the steed, like a barque fed with furnace ire,
Swept on, with his wild eye full of fire;
But, lo! he is nearing his heart's desire;
He is snuffing the smoke of the roaring fray,
       With Sheridan only five miles away.

The first that the general saw were the groups
Of stragglers, and then the retreating troops;
What was to be done? what to do?—a glance told
    him both.
Then striking his spurs with a terrible oath,
He dashed down the line, 'mid a storm of huzzas,
And the wave of retreat checked its course there,
    because
The sight of the master compelled it to pause.
With foam and with dust the black charger was
    gray;
By the flash of his eye, and his red nostril's play,
He seemed to the whole great army to say:
"I have brought you Sheridan all the way
       From Winchester down to save the day."

Hurrah! hurrah for Sheridan!
Hurrah! hurrah for horse and man!
And when their statues are placed on high
Under the dome of the Union sky,
The American soldier's Temple of Fame,
There, with the glorious general's name,
Be it said, in letters both bold and bright:
"Here is the steed that saved the day
By carrying Sheridan into the fight,
From Winchester—twenty miles away!"

✦ CONTENTS ✦

MAPS

✦ FOREWORD ✦

When the silence returned to a divided nation at Appomattox, Philip H. Sheridan stood with Ulysses S. Grant and William T. Sherman as the Union's most renowned generals. Four years of conflict had taken them from obscurity to national prominence. While Sheridan's stature as a general did not equal either Grant's or Sherman's, his achievements, particularly in the Shenandoah Valley in 1864, had vaulted him into this front rank of Union generals. His popularity had been insured by Thomas Buchanan Read's poem, "Sheridan's Ride."

With the peace the three heroes added more accomplishments to their records—Grant, the presidency; Sherman and Sheridan, General of the Army. In time they would belong to history. Each of them penned a memoir, framing the outline of history's judgment upon their records. But history possesses a long reach, and Grant's and Sherman's Civil War careers have been controversial until the present day. Sheridan, however, has been spared from much of this contentiousness. His record has remained relatively solid.

Eric J. Wittenberg reexamines Sheridan's Civil War successes and failures in this book. An attorney and a historian of Union cavalry in the Army of the Potomac, Wittenberg has written a scathing indictment of Sheridan's record. He focuses primarily on Sheridan's generalship during the war's final year, when he commanded the cavalry in the East and later the Army of the Shenandoah during the 1864 Valley Campaign. Wittenberg finds little to praise about Sheridan and much to condemn. In these pages, "Little Phil" is neither a gifted tactician nor strategist, and is an unlikable man. The author's judgments are provocative and will engender much debate.

Although I disagree with some of Wittenberg's conclusions, history should be unblinking, unsettling, and if necessary, argumentative. His work is all of these. It will rile admirers of Sheridan and reassure those who prefer to remember him only as the general who torched the Shenandoah Valley and cashiered Gouverneur Warren at Five Forks. Wittenberg has challenged the accepted judgments about Sheridan's generalship. He seeks to lead us to a different interpretation, and by doing so, has written a stimulating book that is well worth reading.

JEFFRY D. WERT
Centre Hall, Pennsylvania

⇥ PREFACE ⇤

Settled history remembers Philip Henry Sheridan kindly. He is considered one of the four great captains of the Union cause, along with Ulysses S. Grant, William T. Sherman, and George H. Thomas. Sheridan owed this lofty position to his great benefactor and friend, Grant. "As a soldier, as a commander of troops, as a man capable of doing all that is possible with any number of men, there is no man living greater than Sheridan," crowed Grant. "I rank Sheridan with Napoleon and Frederick and the great commanders of history. No man ever had such a faculty of finding things out as Sheridan, or of knowing all about the enemy," Grant claimed years after the Civil War. "Then he had that magnetic quality of swaying men which I wish I had—a rare quality in a general. I don't think anyone can give Sheridan too high praise."[1]

Grant became Phil Sheridan's most ardent and most consistent supporter. A newspaper correspondent who traveled with Grant's headquarters for most of the Civil War had many opportunities to observe the lieutenant general's conduct. According to the correspondent, Grant overlooked Sheridan's many faults. "His attachment for Sheridan sprang from his unbounded belief in his abilities as a great commander. He thought Sheridan free from many of Sherman's infirmities of temper, and cooler in judgment," recorded the correspondent, "It was well known to Grant's intimates that he considered Sheridan the ablest general of the war on either side."[2]

Sherman echoed a similar sentiment. "General Sheridan impressed me as a typical Irishman, impulsive, enthusiastic, social and pleasant," he wrote. "With all of his impulsiveness, however, he was a deep thinker. So much stress has been laid upon his dash as an officer that the public did not give him credit for the mental concentration he was capable of. He was a man of brains as well as heart, of thought as well as action." Sherman lavished high praise on his former subordinate after the Irish bantam's early demise. "He was a great soldier and a noble man, and deserved all of the honors bestowed upon him. General Sheridan's services to his country could scarcely be overestimated," claimed the great warrior. "He was a man of quick perception, and as a commander had the faculty of grasping the whole situation on a field of battle intuitively, and history already records the valuable work he did in his country's defense."[3]

Nothing tops Victorian prose for florid descriptions. "Full of the magnificent passion of battle, as everyone knows, riding around with his sword drawn, rising in his stirrups, grasping a battle-flag, turning disaster into victory, or pursuing the enemy with the terror and speed of a Nemesis he was also abundant in caution, wily as an Indian, original and astounding in his strategy—always deceiving as well as overwhelming the enemy," raved one of Little Phil's enthusiastic admirers. "It was not only his personal courage and magnetic bearing, his chivalric presence and intense enthusiasm, which produced his great results. He was a great commander of modern times; learned in the maneuvers and practice which require intellectual keenness and comprehensive calculation. The combination which he employed in all his greatest battles are strokes of military genius almost matchless in our time."[4]

Sheridan's death brought about intense national mourning. "Few men of our day are so secure of renown in the generations to come as the great soldier who rose from humble circumstances to the command of the Army of the United States and has now just passed away," eulogized the *New York Times* in 1888. "The brilliant Lieutenant, on whom Grant so confidently relied, and whom he loved to praise, possessed those qualities of dashing soldiership which always command the enthusiasm of mankind."[5] Such was the esteem his countrymen held him in, and they publicly poured out their grief when he died. They lamented the loss of one of the great heroes of the Civil War. With Sheridan's passing, only one of those great heroes—William T. Sherman—remained.

Traditionally, we remember Sheridan as the aggressive, outstanding cavalry commander who whipped the underachieving Federal cavalry into shape, and then wielded its mighty sword to win the war. According to most accounts,

Sheridan destroyed the army of Lt. Gen. Jubal A. Early in the Shenandoah Valley through the feisty Irishman's superior generalship. By all accounts, any flaws in his character are subsumed by the luster of Sheridan's record as a commander of men. In the minds of most, the results garnered are paramount, not the means used to achieve those results, or the lives he destroyed along the way.

Few have ever questioned the traditional view of Sheridan's generalship. One who did observed, "In what relates to the Army of the Potomac, [Sheridan's] memoirs add but little to the volume of statements . . . but they invite attention by furnishing explanation of much that hitherto has seemed to many anomalous and perplexing." The same writer, a former staff officer of the Cavalry Corps, correctly pointed out, "For a quarter of a century past, all criticism, or argument, or narration, tending to support, or defend, the reputations of the veterans of the Virginia battlefields, as against statements, or implications, or claims, made by, or on behalf of Generals Grant and Sheridan, has been met by clamorous charges of jealousy." He concluded, "General Sheridan's Memoirs are interesting commentary upon this line of argument."[6]

The passage of more than a century from the death of Sheridan permits the modern historian to examine his life and career in an objective context, free of fears of recriminations. Phil Sheridan cast a long shadow over the second half of the nineteenth century, so it is no surprise that people were afraid to criticize him publicly.

Expensive, larger than life monuments to this man dot the American landscape. There are handsome monuments to Sheridan in Greenwich Village in New York City, in Chicago, on the grounds of Fort Sheridan, Illinois, in front of the state capitol building in his alleged birthplace of Albany, New York, in the middle of Embassy Row in Washington, D.C., and in his hometown of Somerset, Ohio. Another monument to Sheridan graces the front lawn of the Ohio State House in Columbus. Formerly, the Sheridan Gate guarded the grounds of Arlington National Cemetery, near the general's final resting place, perhaps the ultimate tribute. There are at least four cities named for him, and countless roads.[7]

How accurate are these perceptions of Sheridan? Does he really deserve a place in the pantheon of the immortals of the Civil War? If he does deserve such a place, what sort of place should it be?

This book will answer those questions. Nearly 140 years after the end of the Civil War, Sheridan's performance in that conflict is long overdue for a full assessment. The answers to these questions are complex, and there are many issues to explore. Undoubtedly, many will be angered by the conclusions drawn, and many will disagree with them. My purpose is to encourage the reader to draw his or her own conclusions. Whether the reader agrees with me is not the important thing. What is important is that the reader should tackle these difficult questions for himself or herself. If that happens, then I will have accomplished my goal.

Six years ago, I began researching Sheridan's second raid, and the resulting Battle of Trevilian Station, fought on June 11 and 12, 1864. Trevilian Station, the largest all-cavalry battle of the Civil War, resulted in a major defeat for Sheridan's horsemen. When that process began, I had no preconceived notions other than what I knew of Sheridan's reputation as one of the great commanders of the American Civil War. I had read a couple of the fawning early biographies of Sheridan, only reinforcing the traditional notions of Little Phil's generalship. In the course of researching the Trevilian Station book, I had to tackle the questions of Sheridan's legacy, and of his record as commander of the Cavalry Corps of the Army of the Potomac. I was disappointed to learn that the official record does not match Sheridan's historic reputation. Then, I had to face the question of Sheridan's conduct at the Battle of Five Forks while editing a new edition of Frederic C. Newhall's *With General Sheridan in Lee's Last Campaign.* Newhall's book is an impassioned defense of the injustice done to Maj. Gen. Gouverneur K. Warren by Sheridan on the night of April 1, 1865. After a great deal of research and reflection, I realized that this man's life and career required serious reevaluation.

This book will provide a sketch of Sheridan's life and military career up to his appointment to command the Army of the Potomac's Cavalry Corps in the spring of 1864. Up to this time Sheridan was still a subordinate commander whose actions had less of an impact on the outcome of battles. As a result, the sketch of Sheridan's career before his appointment to command the Cavalry Corps does not go into great detail, and is provided to set the stage for the analysis of his performance in 1864–1865. The critical analysis begins in 1864, when Sheridan came east to assume command of the Army of the Potomac's Cavalry Corps. I then examine Sheridan's record and achievements as commander of the Cavalry Corps and the Middle Military District. Next, I look at some of Sheridan's personality traits, including his treatment of the officers who served under him, his inconsistent treatment of the men who served under him, and his inability to tell the truth about the performance of his command. I also address his favorable personality traits in an effort to provide balance to the analysis. Sheridan was, after all, a human being, filled with strengths, weaknesses, and the usual human frailties. He definitely had some positive attributes. Because of the nature of this project, some of the topics will overlap, meaning that some of the same subjects may be addressed in more than one chapter. To minimize redundancy, I have tried to avoid repeating the same information as much as possible. However, in some instances it cannot be helped, as the facts must be spelled out for the analysis to make sense. I apologize in advance for any such redundancy, and hope that you, as the reader, will allow me some latitude with it.

For readers to assess Sheridan's credibility, they should be able to read Sheridan's own words. To that end, I have included Sheridan's official reports of the Overland, Shenandoah Valley, and Appomattox Campaigns as appendices to this book. I encourage the reader to take the time to read them and to evaluate his words in light of my analysis. The reader is cautioned, though, to remember that two of these three reports were written in the spring of 1866, after the successful conclusion of the Civil War. They clearly demonstrate the wisdom of twenty-twenty hindsight. When all of these things are assessed, I conclude that Sheridan does not deserve the lofty reputation bestowed upon him by history.

A detailed analysis of Sheridan's record indicates that he lost most of the Cavalry Corps' fights during his stewardship. It also shows that any competent general should have dispatched Lt. Gen. Jubal A. Early's Confederate army in the fall of 1864. Indeed, the odds were so overwhelming that even an incompetent commander should have defeated Early's tenacious little army. While Sheridan displayed some skill against Early, any reasonably capable general with such a large numeric advantage should have prevailed in the Valley Campaign. As it was, Early actually outgeneralled Sheridan at Winchester and Cedar Creek, two of their three major engagements. I also came to understand that his peers viewed Sheridan as a petty, hypocritical, and mendacious man whose primary agenda was self-promotion. While he possessed a unique ability to motivate men, and a true gift for commanding combined arms operations, the final conclusion can only be that history has been far more kind to this man than he deserves.

I am, by training and experience, a trial lawyer. I have spent years evaluating and presenting evidence, and I have done so here. While I have tried to be neutral and objective, I have written this book along the lines of a legal brief. I lay out my thesis, and defend it with the evidence before me. Although I assume the role of an advocate here, rest assured that I take my responsibility as an historian seriously, and that I have ample evidence to support each of my assertions. Like any good lawyer, I understand that there are two sides to every case, and I fully expect equally competent defense counsel to rush to Sheridan's defense. I not only encourage that, I look forward to the dialogue.

My friend and fellow lawyer Jamie Ryan reviewed this manuscript and gave me some outstanding feedback that pointed out the weaknesses in my arguments.

I used Professor Joseph L. Harsh of George Mason University as a sounding board for my theories, and he helped me to flesh out many of these ideas. Professor Mark Kwasny of Ohio State University–Newark also gave my work a thoughtful review and analysis. I am especially indebted to my good friend and fellow historian Jeffry D. Wert of Centre Hall, Pennsylvania. Not only did Jeff review my work for accuracy and content, but he also kindly agreed to write the foreword. Likewise, Scott C. Patchan, who has spent years studying Sheridan's Shenandoah Valley Campaign, and whose work I admire, reviewed an early draft of this manuscript and made some very useful suggestions that greatly improved the quality of this work. Dave Powell of Chicago reviewed and commented on the manuscript and provided photographs of the monuments to Sheridan in Chicago and Fort Sheridan, Illinois. J. D. Petruzzi also gave me the benefit of his thoughts and comments, reading two different drafts of this manuscript.

My friend Blake A. Magner drew the maps that grace these pages. As always, his maps make my work better. I have also included relevant photographs so that the reader can put faces with the words.

This is the third book that I have done with the good folks at Brassey's. I deeply appreciate the faith in my work demonstrated by Don McKeon, the publisher, and I also appreciate the patience and guidance shown me by my editor, David Arthur. The process of bringing an idea into print can be long and frustrating, but I have found that the editorial and production staff at Brassey's have a real gift for making the process as painless as possible. I value the good relationship that I have developed with Brassey's, and I look forward to continuing that relationship in the foreseeable future.

Finally, and as always, I owe the greatest debt of all to my most wonderful and loving wife, Susan Skilken Wittenberg, without whose unflinching tolerance and support, none of my work on the American Civil War would be possible.

NOTES

1. Quoted in Frank A. Burr and Richard J. Hinton, *"Little Phil" and His Troopers: The Life of Gen. Philip H. Sheridan* (Providence, R.I.: J. A. & R. A. Reid, 1888), 17–18.
2. Sylvanus Cadwallader, *Three Years with Grant, as Recalled by War Correspondent Sylvanus Cadwallader,* ed. Benjamin P. Thomas (New York: Alfred A. Knopf, 1955), 342.
3. Quoted in Richard O'Connor, *Sheridan the Inevitable* (Indianapolis: Bobbs-Merrill Co., 1953), 355.
4. Sheridan Monument Commission, *Unveiling of the Equestrian Statue of General Philip H. Sheridan* (Albany, N.Y.: Sheridan Monument Commission, 1916), 19.

5. *New York Times,* August 5, 1888.
6. Carswell McClellan, *Notes on the Personal Memoirs of P. H. Sheridan* (St. Paul, Minn.: Press of William S. Banning Jr., 1889), 2.
7. Ironically, on the grounds of one military base, Fort Bliss, formerly a U.S. Army cavalry base, Sheridan Road intersects with Stuart Road, named for the great Confederate cavalry chieftain who was one of Sheridan's principal rivals.

CHAPTER 1

PHILIP HENRY SHERIDAN: A SKETCH OF HIS LIFE AND CAREER IN THE CIVIL WAR

An examination of Sheridan's life and career during the Civil War is necessary to properly assess his role in history. He came from humble roots that had an impact on his life and career. In some ways, his is the classic American success story—a poor boy who succeeded against the odds. That struggle framed his life and influenced the way he treated the men who served with him.

No one actually knows where Philip Henry Sheridan was born. Some say he was born in Ireland, and others say he was born in Boston, Massachusetts. His parents were in the process of immigrating to the United States when the boy was born, and the baby may have been born at sea. Sheridan claimed that he was born in Albany, New York.[1] Roy Morris Jr., Sheridan's most recent biographer, points out that Sheridan harbored presidential ambitions. "He purposely obscured his foreign birth to protect his putative presidential aspirations, in which case he must have been unusually ambitious, since by this reasoning he began to lie when he was seventeen," observed Morris, "and unusually persistent, since he stood by the story in his posthumous memoirs, long after he had passed beyond such transient glories."[2]

The mystery of Sheridan's birth will be discussed in detail in chapter 6. Irrespective of where he was born, the boy came into the world in 1831 as the third child in a family of six.

The Sheridan family settled in the rugged crossroads town of Somerset, Ohio, which had a large Catholic population and good access to the nearby National Road. John Sheridan, the boy's father, worked as a laborer and construction sub-contractor. His mother, Meenagh (Mary), raised the children and ruled the roost with an iron fist. The boy had a typical childhood, playing and adventuring in the nearby countryside. In 1846, the Mexican War broke out. "The Mexican War, then going on, furnished, of course, a never-ending theme for controversy, and although I was too young to enter the military service when volunteers were mustering in our section," he later wrote, "yet the stirring events of the times so much impressed and absorbed me that my sole wish was to become a soldier, and my highest aspiration to go to West Point as a cadet from my Congressional district."[3]

Getting that appointment became the focus of the boy's efforts. When the original candidate failed the rigorous entrance examinations at West Point, fortune smiled on Phil Sheridan, who received the appointment to the Military Academy in 1848. He immediately set about preparing for the entrance exams, and with the help of his roommate, a scholarly New Yorker named Henry W. Slocum, passed them on the first attempt, becoming a provisional cadet.[4] While his academic performance was unspectacular, his conduct cost him dearly. In September 1851, Cadet Sgt. William R. Terrill, an upperclassman, barked an order at Sheridan on the parade ground. Sheridan did not believe that he had done anything wrong, and "fancied I had a grievance and made toward him with a lowered bayonet, but my better judgment recalled me before actual contact could take place."[5] Terrill, of course, reported the episode, further offending Sheridan. The next time that the hotheaded Sheridan saw Terrill, he attacked him, "and a fisti-cuff engagement in front of barracks followed, which was stopped by an officer approaching the scene." Sheridan admitted that he had been the aggressor, and he was quickly suspended from the academy for a year.[6]

After a year in Somerset, Sheridan returned to West Point and graduated with the class of 1853. His own classmates, including his good friend and roommate George Crook, had graduated in 1852, leaving Sheridan behind. The new brevet second lieutenant's lackluster academic performance prohibited him from choosing his branch of service, and he was assigned to Company D, 1st Infantry Regiment, in Texas. Not long after, he received a promotion to second lieutenant.[7]

Now an adult, Phil Sheridan was short in stature, standing five feet, three inches tall, and weighed no more than 130 pounds.[8] In the spring of 1864, when he assumed command of the Army of the Potomac's Cavalry Corps, Maj. James H. Kidd, commander of the 6th Michigan Cavalry, recorded his observations. Sheridan "was square of shoulder and there was plenty of room for the display of a major general's buttons on his broad chest. His face was strong, with a firm jaw, a keen eye, and extraordinary firmness in every lineament. In his manner there was an alertness, evinced rather in look than in movement. Nothing escaped his eye, which was brilliant and searching and at the same time emitted flashes of kindly good nature," Kidd wrote. "When riding past or among his troopers, he had a way of casting quick, comprehensive glances to the right and left and in all directions. He overlooked nothing. One had a feeling that he was under close and critical observation, that Sheridan had his eye on him, was mentally taking his measure and would remember and recognize him the next time. No introduction was needed."⁹

Lt. Col. Theodore H. Lyman, a staff officer at headquarters of the Army of the Potomac, described Sheridan as "a small broad-shouldered, squat man, with black hair and a square head. He is of Irish parents, but looks very like a Piedmontese."¹⁰ The bandy-legged little general did not make a good first impression on President Abraham Lincoln, who commented that Sheridan was "a brown, chunky little chap, with a long body, short legs, not enough neck to hang him, and such long arms that if his ankles itch he can scratch them without stooping." Lt. Gen. Ulysses S. Grant, who had arranged for Sheridan to be brought east, quickly replied, "You will find him big enough for the purpose before we get through with him."¹¹ Thus was born the legend of Philip H. Sheridan.

He had a true gift for profanity. "Little Phil was no tongue-tied angel when the spirit of battle was on him," observed correspondent James E. Taylor. "Stupidity, cowardice, incompetence, and panic would enrage him to such a pitch that strange, novel, picturesque oaths, made up on the spot, would burst from him spontaneously." Sheridan's legendary profanity echoed over many a battlefield, and helped to ruin many men's lives.¹²

These events were far off in the future, though. In 1853, the young officer's prospects were not bright. The life of a soldier on garrison duty in the far West was not a pleasant one. Peacetime duty in the Regular Army was tedious, with the officers receiving poor pay. They had little prospect of promotion and suffered with poor living accommodations. Many of the best officers—including Ulysses S. Grant and William T. Sherman—resigned their commissions when they found they could no longer bear the vicissitudes of army life. Many others escaped the tedium by drinking themselves into oblivion.¹³

The young officer's regiment fought Indians along the frontier and he did his duty faithfully. By 1857, he was stationed in the far Pacific Northwest, and had taken up with an Indian woman, although he never mentioned her in his memoirs. He spent his days trying to tame the Rogue River Indians, and his nights seeking solace in the arms of his Indian lover. Early in his life, the first of the many paradoxes that marked this man's career emerged. Sheridan spent four long years in this post.[14]

In March 1861, he was promoted to first lieutenant after eight years as a second lieutenant. "At the outbreak of the civil war there were probably few officers in the army whose chances of obtaining high command and future distinction were so remote as those of the solitary and friendless young second lieutenant of foot then occupying a lonely and remote post in Oregon," wrote one of Sheridan's early biographers.[15] Although he had finally gotten a promotion, his prospects for further advancement appeared dim until South Carolinians shelled Fort Sumter. Three months later, in the aftermath of Fort Sumter, Sheridan unexpectedly received a promotion to captain, his second advance in rank in ninety days. Like so many other ambitious young men, the coming of war provided abundant opportunities for rapid career advancement, and Sheridan made the most of those chances. His meteoric rise to high rank was almost unprecedented when compared to the careers of most prewar Regular Army officers.

In the fall of 1861, Capt. Sheridan was summoned to the headquarters of the Army of Southwest Missouri, where he spent several months auditing the books of accounts of the quartermaster's office. It was not interesting work, but the diligent officer immersed himself in the task. He must have done well in that position, for on December 26, 1861, he received an appointment as the department's chief commissary officer. Seeing an opportunity, Sheridan approached the department commander, Maj. Gen. Henry W. Halleck, and suggested that he also be appointed quartermaster general. Halleck did not like the idea, but Sheridan persuaded the general that he should fill both positions, and the appointment followed.

In January 1862, Sheridan reported to Brig. Gen. Samuel Curtis and assumed his post. When Curtis's army marched, Sheridan went with it. That spring, Curtis soundly defeated a Confederate army in the crucial battle of Pea Ridge, in northwest Arkansas. After Pea Ridge, Sheridan had a falling out with Curtis, who wanted to replace Sheridan with a crony. Curtis prevailed, and a forlorn Sheridan reported to Jefferson Barracks in St. Louis, looking for work. Sheridan did not want to join his regiment, which was recruiting and training at Jefferson Barracks. He felt that he could be more useful elsewhere and was not afraid to say so. Like most of his peers, he sought active service in the field where the road to promotion lay wide open.[16]

Not long after the bloody battle of Shiloh in April 1862, at the suggestion of Col. John Kelton, Halleck's assistant adjutant general, Halleck summoned Sheridan to his headquarters at Pittsburg Landing in Tennessee. "This I consider the turning-point in my military career," claimed Sheridan.[17] Halleck assigned the captain to serve as an assistant to the Army of the Tennessee's chief topographical engineer. While serving at Halleck's headquarters, Sheridan encountered his fellow Ohioan, Maj. Gen. William T. Sherman. Sherman asked Sheridan whether he would accept the colonelcy of an Ohio infantry regiment, and Sheridan readily agreed, itching for service in the field. However, to Sheridan's great disappointment, the appointment did not come through. He continued serving as a topographical engineer while he waited for another opportunity to come along.

Capt. Russell A. Alger, a talented young lawyer from Detroit, commanded a company of the 2nd Michigan Cavalry. Alger had a long and productive life, including commanding the 5th Michigan Cavalry and serving as secretary of war under President William McKinley. Alger's good friend Frank Walbridge served as the 2nd Michigan's regimental quartermaster. Walbridge, a New Yorker, also knew Sheridan well. Together, Walbridge and Alger lobbied Michigan Gov. Austin Blair for Sheridan's appointment as colonel of the 2nd Michigan, and they prevailed. On May 27, 1862, Blair appointed Sheridan colonel of the 2nd Michigan Cavalry, and Sheridan eagerly accepted the appointment, even though he had never served in the mounted arm. At first Halleck would not permit the ambitious captain to accept the appointment. When a crestfallen Sheridan reported this news to Alger, Alger persuaded Sheridan to try again. This time Halleck relented, and Sheridan eagerly pinned on the insignia of his new rank. He replaced Col. Gordon Granger, who later served as Sheridan's infantry corps commander.[18]

Sheridan led his new command on a successful expedition to Booneville in northeastern Mississippi a few weeks later. The regiment then participated in Halleck's snail-like advance on Corinth. On June 11, when the incumbent brigade commander received a promotion, Sheridan assumed command of the two-regiment demibrigade, even though he had only a few weeks' experience in commanding horse soldiers. Along the way, Sheridan met a quiet and unassuming soldier named Ulysses S. Grant, whose friendship permitted Sheridan to achieve the heights of army command later in the war. "Although but a few days had elapsed from the date of my appointment as colonel of the Second Michigan to that of my succeeding to the command of the brigade," claimed Sheridan, "I believe I can say with propriety that I had firmly established myself in the confidence of the officers and men of the regiment, and won their regard with thoughtful care."[19]

On July 1, 1862, the new brigade commander led his troopers into battle against a large force of Confederate cavalry at Booneville. Sheridan's little brigade—fewer than a thousand strong—defeated an enemy force of nearly four thousand in a spirited engagement. To his credit, Sheridan masterfully handled his small force against the larger Confederate command. The enemy troopers had drawn Sheridan's command out with a feint and then had struck a hard blow against his brigade. Sheridan successfully masked a crushing flank attack with a noisy diversion. In the process, his men captured important intelligence about the strength and disposition of the Confederate forces. As a reward, Halleck's division commanders, including Brig. Gen. William S. Rosecrans, recommended that Little Phil be promoted to brigadier general, writing, "Brigadiers scarce; good ones scarce. . . . The undersigned respectfully beg that you will obtain the promotion of Sheridan. He is worth his weight in gold."[20] The request was granted, and in September the promotion came through, made effective as of July 1, as a reward for the stunning victory at Booneville. His tenure commanding horse soldiers lasted about ninety days. Until the spring of 1864, these ninety days constituted his entire experience with the cavalry. That inexperience showed when he took command of the Army of the Potomac's Cavalry Corps.

Grant assumed command of the Department of the Mississippi when Halleck went east to become general in chief of the Union armies. Sheridan's zeal and aggressive nature had impressed Grant when they had met at Halleck's headquarters, and Grant marked him as a man to watch. Confederate Gen. Braxton Bragg had invaded Kentucky with a large army, and Sheridan had reported to Louisville, where he received command of a division of infantry in Maj. Gen. Don Carlos Buell's Army of the Ohio. Bragg appeared to be heading toward Louisville, but then veered to the east, threatening Frankfort and Lexington. Buell's army pursued, and the two forces collided near Perryville on October 8.

Buell had chased Bragg's army through Kentucky that hot, dry fall, hoping to prevent the Confederates from capturing the state capital at Frankfort. Buell distracted Bragg's attention and successfully blocked the Southerner's route of march to Frankfort. Maj. Gen. Charles Gilbert's corps, which included Sheridan's infantry division, held the center of the Union position. An excessive drought meant that water, always critical to an army in the field, became an even more precious resource during Bragg's invasion. The two forces vied for possession of the limited water supplies in the vicinity of Perryville, and the quest for fresh water from Doctor's Creek brought about a clash. Neither side wanted to fight a major battle that day. In fact, Gen. Gilbert specifically ordered Sheridan not to bring on a general engagement. Gilbert instructed Little Phil to drive off the enemy, hold, and protect the available water supply.[21]

An aggressive Sheridan "directed Colonel Daniel McCook, with his brigade and Barnett's battery, to occupy the heights in front of Doctor's Creek, so as to secure that water for our men."[22] When McCook successfully took those heights, he brought on a general engagement—Sheridan's advance carried McCook's men far beyond the main Union line of battle, leaving the entire brigade alone with both flanks exposed, offering a ripe target for the determined Confederates. In order to protect McCook's flank, Sheridan also advanced a battery and six regiments of infantry. When they recognized the opportunity presented by McCook's ill-advised movement, the Southerners quickly moved to the attack.

When Gilbert recognized the danger presented by McCook's position, he grew concerned. He found Sheridan and ordered him to recall his men to his original position and to limit himself to its defense unless ordered to attack as part of a general advance. Gilbert again reiterated to Sheridan that Buell did not want to bring on a general engagement unless the entire army had come up.[23] Although Sheridan obeyed Gilbert's order and pulled McCook's brigade back, his rashness committed the entire Army of the Ohio to battle within a few minutes when the Confederates crashed into Little Phil's position on the banks of Doctor's Creek. Not long after, Gen. Alexander McCook's corps marched to the sound of Sheridan's guns and pitched into the fray. The resulting fight raged until dark, when the firing sputtered out along the lines. Sheridan's division had carried the bulk of the day's fighting. At day's end, 4,211 of Buell's men had become casualties, largely as a result of Sheridan's disobedience.

Writing years later, Gilbert downplayed the episode, recounting that Sheridan's "movement was in consequence of some misunderstanding of orders."[24] One of Sheridan's biographers defended Sheridan's conduct. "Gilbert may have thought his orders were clear enough, but he failed to take into account Sheridan's aggressive spirit," wrote Roy Morris Jr. "From the beginning of his career fighting Indians in the Northwest, through the winning of his general's star at Booneville, Sheridan had been governed by his primary instinct to attack. It had always worked in the past, and he had no reason to believe it would fail now." Sheridan simply defended his conduct as being the result of a "misunderstanding."[25]

A bloody, day-long stalemate had taken place, with no clear winner. Sheridan's division was engaged early, and fought long and hard, in spite of Sheridan's having received orders not to bring on a general engagement. Characteristically, he claimed, "I was not bringing on an engagement, but that the enemy evidently intended to do so, and that I believed I should shortly be attacked."[26] Instead, Sheridan pitched into the fray, intensifying the combat and resulting in the general engagement Buell had wanted to avoid. Perryville was far from the last time that the pugnacious general would disobey orders to go looking for a fight. After the indecisive battle, Bragg pulled his army out of Kentucky and

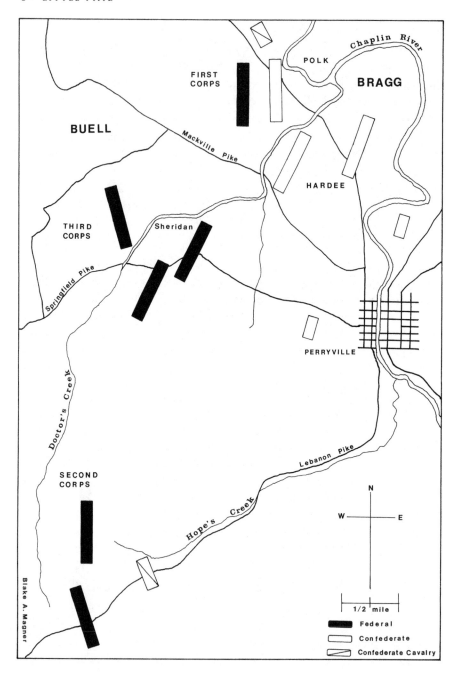

Perryville, October 8, 1862

Buell was relieved of command of the Army of the Ohio. Sheridan's former commanding officer from Mississippi, Maj. Gen. William S. Rosecrans, another Catholic from Ohio, took command of the army. Another of Sheridan's patrons was now in a position to help him advance his career.

As 1862 wound down, Rosecrans fought the bloody Battle of Stones River, which raged as the new year rang in. Sheridan had anticipated Bragg's moves and had made his troop dispositions accordingly. A fierce Confederate attack nearly drove Sheridan's division from the field but, with good advance planning and good execution, his men delayed the enemy assault for more than two hours, giving the rest of the army adequate time to forge a defense. He then broke contact with the Confederates and withdrew his division in good order. Sheridan narrowly missed serious harm when an artillery shell exploded near him, decapitating one of Rosecrans's staff officers, and spraying gore on Sheridan. Grant raved, "It was from all I can hear about it a wonderful bit of fighting. It showed what a great general can do even in a subordinate command; for I believe Sheridan in that battle saved Rosecrans' army."[27] Sheridan had demonstrated that he could conduct a defensive battle. The Army of the Cumberland's victory at Stones River forced Bragg to withdraw from western Tennessee. Rosecrans, in turn, recommended Sheridan's promotion to major general. A scant nine months earlier, Little Phil had been a captain.

The Army of the Cumberland went into its winter encampment needing rest and recuperation. When it emerged in the spring of 1863, Rosecrans led it into middle Tennessee. The Tullahoma Campaign, as it is known, was brilliant. Rosecrans devised and executed a plan for flanking Bragg's army out of the heart of Tennessee, and the plan succeeded. Almost without bloodshed, Rosecrans's advance pushed the Confederates from nearly two-thirds of the state. Rosecrans had planned and executed a spectacular strategic campaign that succeeded almost beyond the Union army's expectations.

In July, during the advance through Tennessee, Sheridan wanted to take a ride on a captured railroad handcar. Sheridan sent for the handcar and, when it did not arrive, the general and several companions set off after it on foot. They trudged on for eleven unpleasant miles before realizing that they were alone and unsupported in hostile country. They knew that continuing was not a good idea. "At every turn we eagerly hoped to meet the hand-car, but it never came, and we jolted on from tie to tie for eleven weary miles," complained Sheridan, "reaching Cowan after midnight, exhausted and sore in every muscle from frequent falls on the rough, unballasted road-bed." Sheridan regretted this excursion for months afterward, as the injuries he sustained nagged him incessantly.[28]

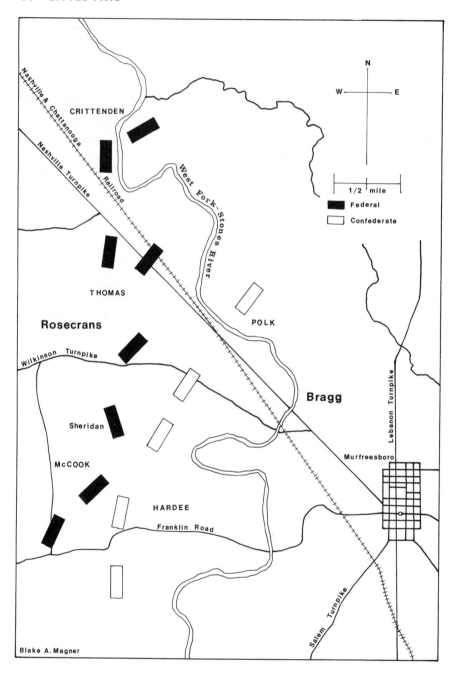

Stones River, December 30, 1862–January 2, 1863

Overconfident as a result of the easy advance across Tennessee, Rosecrans then pushed on into northern Georgia, turned north, and entered the strategic railroad town of Chattanooga almost unmolested. Then Bragg unexpectedly turned on him. Without warning, on September 19, 1863, Bragg launched a savage attack along the banks of Chickamauga Creek. In a harsh two-day battle, the Confederates drove Rosecrans and the Army of the Cumberland back to Chattanooga in wild flight. During the battle, Rosecrans left the battlefield, retreating to the safety of Chattanooga, leaving Maj. Gen. George H. Thomas in command of the battlefield. Thomas's determined stand on Snodgrass Hill earned him the name "Rock of Chickamauga" and prevented Bragg from scoring a decisive victory.

Sheridan's division held the southern end of the battlefield, reflecting Rosecrans's confidence in the pugnacious division commander. Taking heavy casualties, Sheridan managed to stem the tide and halted Bragg's advance on the first day. His division made a gallant stand at Lytle Hill until it was overwhelmed and fled the field with the rest of the Army of the Cumberland on the afternoon of September 20. This was Sheridan's first experience with troops from the Army of Northern Virginia, and with Lt. Gen. James Longstreet, whose troops had delivered the decisive blow in the center of the Union line. When Rosecrans departed, he left his subordinates without orders, and they had to fend for themselves. Unsure of what to do, Sheridan and his division withdrew and began retreating toward Chattanooga, leaving Thomas to his own devices. Sheridan and Rosecrans were later accused of abandoning the fight, but Sheridan had tried to return when Thomas sent a messenger after him. Sheridan's command got lost while trying to make its way to the battlefield, and never made it back to the sound of the fighting. Although the disaster at Chickamauga ruined the military careers of Rosecrans and a number of his subordinates, Sheridan's return to Chickamauga probably saved his from ruin. Bragg's Army of Tennessee had thrashed Rosecrans's army. Sheridan's division had taken heavy losses, and Sheridan himself "was very tired, very hungry, and much discouraged by what had taken place since morning."[29]

After dark, the balance of the Army of the Cumberland safely withdrew to Chattanooga, where it assumed a defensive posture. Rosecrans entrenched around the city and waited for Bragg's pursuit. By September 22, the Confederate army occupied the imposing high ground around Chattanooga, besieging the tired Yankees. Southern infantry held the heights of Missionary Ridge and Lookout Mountain, cutting off Rosecrans's lines of supply and communication. The beleaguered Rosecrans sent for help. Heavy Northern reinforcements from the Army of the Potomac and Grant's Army of the Mississippi began arriving as

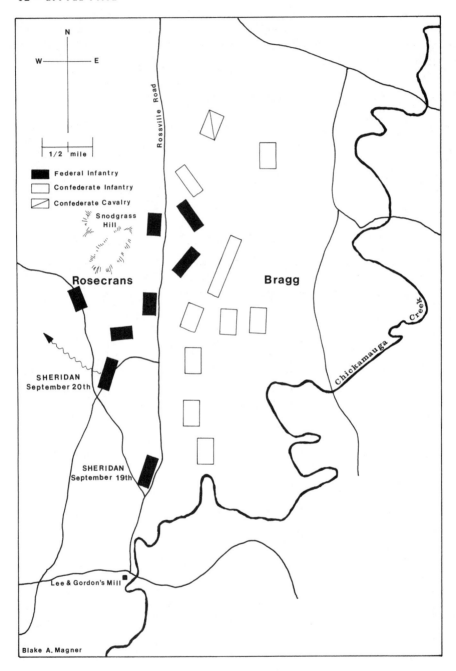

The situation at Chickamauga early on September 20, 1863

September ended. On October 16, 1863, Grant assumed command of all of the Federal forces in Chattanooga, and Thomas succeeded Rosecrans as commander of the Army of the Cumberland. Grant sent for Sherman's Army of the Tennessee to reinforce the beleaguered city, and soon a tenuous supply route known as the Cracker Line was opened, breaking the siege.

Grant believed that the Army of the Cumberland had been demoralized by its defeat at Chickamauga, and wanted to wait until reinforcements from Sherman's army arrived before assaulting Bragg's siege lines. After Sherman's men arrived and an opportunity for an all-out assault presented itself, Grant directed Sherman to attack the enemy stronghold atop Missionary Ridge. Sherman's men fared badly in the attack. At the same time, Federal forces assaulted Lookout Mountain and drove Bragg's Confederates from its slopes in the so-called Battle above the Clouds. Thomas's army connected with Sherman's four divisions and also with those elements from the Army of the Potomac that had carried Lookout Mountain. Bragg's army held only Missionary Ridge.

On November 25, Grant tried again. Under Grant's plan for the battle, the Army of the Cumberland would advance to Orchard Knob and support Sherman's attacks. Its men would attempt to take some rifle pits at the base of Missionary Ridge, diverting Bragg's attention from Sherman's primary attack. Maj. Gen. Gordon Granger's infantry corps would lead the assault on the Confederate stronghold atop Missionary Ridge. Sheridan's division spearheaded the advance with Little Phil at its head. Without firing a shot, they took the enemy rifle pits and held them, coming under fire from the enemy infantry atop the ridge. Sheridan hoisted a flask at the Confederate gunners along Missionary Ridge, proclaiming, "Here's at you!" A shell burst nearby, spraying him with clods of dirt. "That's damned ungenerous," Sheridan proclaimed. "I shall take those guns for that!"[30]

As bullets and artillery fire rained down on them, men of the Army of the Cumberland quickly realized that they could not remain where they were. Without orders to do so and looking to escape the murderous fire from above, Sheridan's division advanced up the hill. Anxiously watching the unplanned assault unfold, Grant turned to Thomas and asked who had ordered the attack. Thomas informed Grant that he had not given the orders, to which the skeptical Grant suggested that someone would suffer if it failed. Sheridan's and Wood's divisions broke Bragg's line and drove the enemy before it. Spotting the guns that had showered him a few minutes earlier, Sheridan climbed astride one, wrapped his stubby legs around the barrel, swung his hat, and cheered his men on as they carried the heights. They led a brief pursuit until darkness closed the day's fighting.

Sheridan got credit for inspiring the unexpected victory that had broken the siege of Chattanooga in less than an hour. A superior officer led away the eleven guns captured by Sheridan's assault, depriving him of his hard-won prizes. However, the high command had noticed Sheridan's role in the victory, and remembered it. "To Sheridan's prompt movement, the Army of the Cumberland and the nation are indebted for the bulk of the capture of prisoners, artillery, and small-arms that day," wrote Grant years after the war. "Except for his prompt pursuit, so much in this way would not have been accomplished."[31]

Grant knew that the day's result had been unlikely. "The victory at Chattanooga was won against great odds," he wrote, "considering the advantage the enemy had of position; and was accomplished more easily than was expected by reason of Bragg's making several grave mistakes."[32] The victorious Grant marked the aggressive Sheridan, to whom he owed the success at Chattanooga, for further advancement. "With his bold and quick-thinking conduct at Missionary Ridge he had put to rest any lingering doubts concerning his uncharacteristic performance at Chickamauga," wrote one of Sheridan's biographers. "Like the much-maligned army in which he served, he had redeemed his honor and avenged his losses. Under the unforgetting eye of Ulysses S. Grant, he had helped to win a mighty victory at Chattanooga, one that confirmed Grant's unrivaled status as the North's preeminent man-at-arms."[33]

After Bragg's beaten army fled, the triumphant Federals enjoyed undisputed possession of the strategic city of Chattanooga. Thus redeemed, the Army of the Cumberland went into its winter camp. Sheridan enjoyed a forty-day furlough, triumphantly returning home to Somerset for the first time since 1853. "This leave I spent in the North with much benefit to my physical condition, for I was much run down by fatiguing service, and not a little troubled by intense pain which I at times still suffered from my experience in the unfortunate hand-car incident on the Cumberland Mountains the previous July," he wrote.[34] Sheridan returned to his division at the end of March 1864, expecting to lead his men into battle again. Instead, he received a summons to Washington, D.C., where he was to report to the adjutant general of the army.

Circumstances had changed significantly during Sheridan's absence from the army. That winter, Grant's political patron, Rep. Elihu Washburne, had introduced legislation to revive the long-dormant rank of lieutenant general in the U.S. army. Washburne and Lincoln intended Grant to hold that lofty rank, making the quiet man from Illinois the highest-ranking officer in Federal service and commander of all the nation's armies. Grant could then shape grand strategy in all the war's theaters.

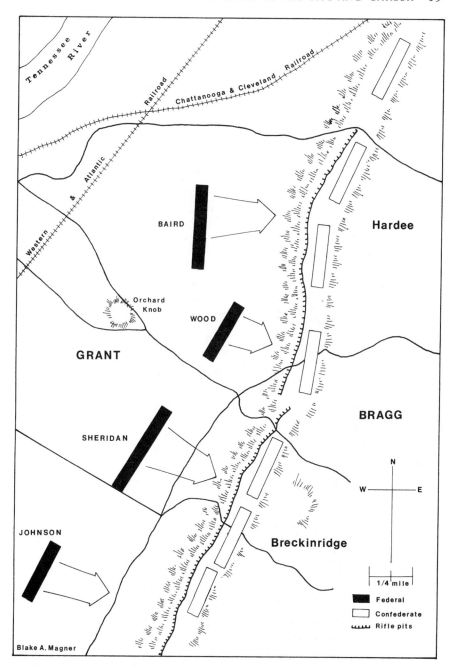

The Union attack on Missionary Ridge breaks the siege at Chattanooga,
November 26, 1863

On March 4, 1864, Grant wrote to Sherman that "the bill reviving the grade of lieutenant general in the army has become a law, and my name has been sent to the Senate." He had received orders "to report at Washington immediately *in person,* which indicates either a confirmation or likelihood of confirmation."[35]

Grant proved correct. Politicians greeted him in the nation's capital as the man who would lead the country to long-awaited victory over the rebellious South. The Army of the Potomac's grizzled quartermaster, Brig. Gen. Rufus Ingalls, Grant's roommate at West Point, told the army's commander, Maj. Gen. George G. Meade, "Grant means business."[36] Grant's old friend, Lt. Gen. James Longstreet, the senior corps commander in the Confederate Army of Northern Virginia, echoed the same sentiment. "That man will fight us every day and every hour until the end of the war," he warned.[37] Lt. Col. Theodore H. Lyman, a staff officer with the Army of the Potomac, described the grim-faced new commanding general eloquently: "He habitually wears an expression as if he had determined to drive his head through a brick wall, and was about to do it."[38] That single-minded determination changed the face of the war.

Congress quickly approved Grant's promotion, and the new lieutenant general set about crafting a plan for the coming campaigns. Grant realized that the only way the North could win the war was to wear out the South, a tactic that required year-round campaigning and constant pressure on a Confederacy already straining its war-making capacity. To that end, Grant decided to coordinate the efforts of all of the Federal armies in the field, bringing all of the Union's resources to bear.[39]

Grant planned a series of simultaneous assaults on all fronts. In the west, Sherman would launch a campaign aimed at preventing Gen. Joseph E. Johnston's Army of Tennessee from reinforcing Lee's army in Virginia. Maj. Gen. Nathaniel P. Banks would lead an expedition designed to capture the important manufacturing town of Shreveport, Louisiana, an operation already planned and approved before Grant's promotion. Banks would then advance on the critical port city of Mobile, Alabama. Other Federal forces would move on Charleston, South Carolina, pinning down the Confederate coastal garrisons.

In the east, Maj. Gen. Franz Sigel, a politically influential German immigrant, was to clear the crucial Shenandoah Valley of Virginia of Confederates, then advance on Richmond from the west. Meanwhile, the Army of the James, commanded by Maj. Gen. Benjamin F. Butler, would advance on Richmond from the east. Grant intended to travel with the main army in the Eastern Theater, the Army of the Potomac, which would bear the brunt of the fighting in the center, flanked by Sigel and Butler.[40]

Meade received peremptory orders from Grant—Lee's army was to be his objective point. Wherever Lee went, Meade would also go.[41] Before the spring's grand campaign began, Meade reorganized the Army of the Potomac into three large corps, the Second, Fifth, and Sixth Army Corps. The Cavalry Corps also underwent major changes in organization and leadership.

During the winter of 1863–1864, the ambitious Brig. Gen. Judson Kilpatrick had taken a large mounted force on a raid toward Richmond to free Union soldiers in the notorious Libby Prison and Belle Isle. Kilpatrick commanded one column of the raid while Col. Ulric Dahlgren, a dashing twenty-one-year-old colonel, led the other. The expedition left Dahlgren dead, fulfilled none of its objectives, and largely wrecked the Army of the Potomac's fine Third Cavalry Division. Maj. Gen. Alfred Pleasonton, commanding the Cavalry Corps, shouldered much of the blame for this failure, even though he had opposed the plan.

The Union high command was dissatisfied with the performance of the army's mounted arm, Pleasonton, with the approval of Secretary of War Edwin M. Stanton, was promptly relieved of command.[42] One cavalry officer noted that "Even [Pleasonton's] success and the proofs he had given of the value of the cavalry, when properly used and led, were not sufficient to overcome the force of traditions and customs, and among higher authorities the idea still prevailed that the mounted force was secondary to, and should be used for the protection, convenience and relief of the infantry." He continued, "Serious differences of opinion on these questions between Generals Meade and Pleasonton had from time to time occurred, and at last had gone so far that the latter . . . could no longer retain his command."[43]

Brig. Gen. John Buford, the Army of the Potomac's most able cavalry officer, had died of typhoid fever in December 1863, and the senior officer, Second Cavalry Division commander Brig. Gen. David M. Gregg, apparently did not have the confidence of the commanding general. Grant seemed unwilling to consider other candidates from within the existing officer cadre.[44] In an early interview with Lincoln, Grant expressed his dissatisfaction with "the little that had been accomplished by the cavalry so far in the war, and the belief that it was capable of accomplishing much more than it had done under a thorough leader. I said I wanted the very best man in the army for that command." The army's chief of staff, Maj. Gen. Henry W. Halleck, asked, "How would Sheridan do?" Grant replied, "The very man I want."[45]

His new command knew nothing about Sheridan. Col. Charles Wainwright, a pithy artillerist, reflected in his diary, "I know nothing . . . of . . . [Sheridan], but a change I think was needed; neither Pleasonton nor [Maj. Gen. George]

Stoneman proved themselves equal to the position."[46] Brig. Gen. Henry E. Davies, who commanded a brigade in the First Cavalry Division, observed that, in the Cavalry Corps, only the fittest leaders survived. This system insured that its prior leadership had come from within the ranks of the Corps. As a result, the men knew little of Sheridan's service in the West. Davies continued, "It was not known that he ever served with or in command of cavalry, and the prejudice . . . among mounted troops against being placed under the orders of an officer whose experiences from which the Army of the Potomac had previously suffered had not induced the belief that the West was the point of the compass from which the advent of wise men bringing rich gifts of victory and success was to confidently be expected."[47] One of Meade's staff officers noted, "If [Sheridan] is an able officer, he will find no difficulty in pushing along this arm, several degrees."[48]

Sheridan reluctantly took leave of his division and caught a train for Washington. He faced a daunting task. The Army of the Potomac's Cavalry Corps had enjoyed success under Pleasonton's leadership in the summer and fall of 1863. With such able subordinates as Buford and Gregg, Pleasonton's horse soldiers scored their first victories over the vaunted Confederate cavalry and gained respect in the eyes of both the infantry and the enemy. With Buford's death, Kilpatrick's exile, and Pleasonton's removal, the Cavalry Corps had to start over. It would do so under the command of a man who had virtually no experience with horse soldiers. Sheridan, whose experience in commanding cavalrymen was limited to those few months in Mississippi, faced a challenge like none that he had faced previously.

The Army of the Potomac's Cavalry Corps consisted of three divisions. Two of those divisions, the Second and Third, had two brigades each, and the First Division had three. With the exception of one brigade, the Reserve Brigade, assigned to the First Division, all of these units were made up of volunteer cavalry. The Reserve Brigade included four small regiments of Regular Army cavalry assigned to service with the Army of the Potomac, providing a solid, professional nucleus to the Cavalry Corps. Batteries of Regular Army horse artillery attached to specific divisions often served regularly with certain brigades. The northern horsemen typically carried pistols, sabers, and a variety of breech-loading carbines, including the seven-shot Spencer repeating carbine.

At Grant's insistence, Sheridan assigned brash, young Brig. Gen. James H. Wilson to command Kilpatrick's Third Cavalry Division. The choice enraged Brig. Gen. George A. Custer, who had briefly commanded the Third Division in the summer and fall of 1863 and outranked Wilson, who had no previous experience commanding troops. The other brigadier general in the Third Division, Henry E. Davies, also outranked Wilson, so he was reassigned a brigade in the Second Division, replacing the injured Col. John B. McIntosh. Custer's brigade moved to the First Division, and Col. George H. Chapman's brigade transferred from the First Division to the Third.

Another outsider, Brig. Gen. Alfred T. A. Torbert of Delaware, a member of the West Point class of 1855, took command of the First Division, displacing its senior brigadier, Wesley Merritt. Torbert's "qualifications as a cavalry commander were not remarkable,"[49] a staff officer recalled. "He was a handsome, dashing fellow . . . a beautiful horseman, and as brave as a lion; but his abilities were hardly equal to such large commands."[50] James E. Taylor, a correspondent for a major magazine, also described Torbert, "With Torbert's physical appearance, I was not favorably impressed for it seemed to lack the characteristics that should constitute a thoroughbred cavalryman, all of which was so well typified in Custer. . . . At a distance he would show to a better advantage, for he affected quite a dandified style in his uniform which gave him quite a picturesque appearance, with his sailor collar, glittering stars, and rakish chapeau."[51] Torbert had commanded New Jersey infantrymen with competence, but he had never commanded cavalry.

Gregg, another professional soldier, commanded the Second Division. Gregg and Torbert were West Point classmates, and the modest Pennsylvanian was a cousin of Andrew Gregg Curtin, the wartime governor of the Keystone State. When war broke out, Gregg was a first lieutenant in the 1st Dragoons. He transferred to the newly formed 6th U.S. Cavalry in the fall of 1861. On January 24, 1862, he became colonel of the 8th Pennsylvania Cavalry, and then was named brigadier general of volunteers on November 29, 1862. By the spring of 1864, at age thirty-one, Gregg had already commanded a division for more than a year. "He was the only division commander I had whose experience had been almost exclusively derived from the cavalry arm," Sheridan noted.[52]

Gregg was remembered fondly as "tall and spare, of notable activity, capable of the greatest exertion and exposure; gentle in manner but bold and resolute in action. Firm and just in discipline he was a favorite of his troopers and ever held, for he deserved, their affection and entire confidence." Gregg knew the principles of war and was always ready and eager to apply them. Endowed "with a natural genius of high order, he [was] universally hailed as the finest type of cavalry leader. A man of unimpeachable personal character, in private life affable and genial but not demonstrative, he fulfilled with modesty and honor all the duties of the citizen and head of an interesting and devoted family."[53] Calm, quiet, modest, and highly competent, Gregg's forethought and good execution led to a spectacular Federal victory over the vaunted Confederate cavalry on the

East Cavalry Field at Gettysburg on July 3, 1863. A former officer later commented that Gregg's "modesty kept him from the notoriety that many gained through the newspapers; but in the army the testimony of all officers who knew him was the same. Brave, prudent, dashing when occasion required dash, and firm as a rock, he was looked upon, both as a regimental commander and afterwards as Major-General, as a man in whose hands any troops were safe."[54]

Thus, Sheridan inherited a command that had been forged in battle and that was led mostly by competent veteran officers who had proven their mettle during months of hard-fought campaigning. The Army of the Potomac's Cavalry Corps had refuted the old cliché, "Whoever saw a dead cavalryman?" The Yankee troopers were reasonably well mounted and superbly equipped. Many of them carried seven-shot, breech-loading Spencer carbines. One Regular Army officer noted of the Spencers: "The workmanship of this gun was indifferent, but it did, notwithstanding, excellent service and gave an immense advantage to the troops armed with it. [They] could throw in a tremendous fire when necessary, with great effect upon the enemy, who was naturally very often deceived in his estimate of the force opposed to him, judging by the unintermitting, incessant rattle along the line that he was contending with at least a division" when only a brigade was involved.[55] Edward Laight Wells of Charleston, South Carolina, later observed that troops armed with Spencers "ought to have been equal to at least double their number carrying only muzzle-loaders."[56] Another Rebel trooper, less elegant in his presentation, described the Spencers, "You'ns load in the morning and fire all day."[57] Compared with the single-shot muzzle-loaders carried by most gray-clad horse soldiers, Yankee troopers had a significant advantage in firepower.

Unlike their Southern counterparts, the Federals also had plenty of supplies, including remounts. But excessive winter picketing, combined with the tribulations of the Kilpatrick–Dahlgren Raid, had taken a severe toll on the Cavalry Corps' mounts. Sheridan quickly noticed the state of the horses in the spring of 1864. Just after the conclusion of the Gettysburg Campaign, the army had created a Cavalry Bureau, which provided plenty of mounts for the burgeoning ranks of the Federal horse soldiers. While not a perfect institution by any means, the Cavalry Bureau successfully supplied ample fresh horseflesh to the Federal mounted arm.

As the spring campaigning season approached, Sheridan had his work cut out for him. Although he had successfully commanded infantry in the Western Theater, he was entirely untested as commander of a large mounted force. Grant had formulated an ambitious plan for the conduct of the war, and he would depend on his mounted arm heavily for the success of that plan.

Would Phil Sheridan be up to the task?

NOTES

1. Philip H. Sheridan, *Personal Memoirs of P. H. Sheridan,* 2 vols. (New York: Charles L. Webster & Co., 1888), 1:2.

2. Roy Morris Jr., *Sheridan: The Life and Wars of General Phil Sheridan* (New York: Crown Publishing, 1992), 10–11. Sheridan's tendency to lie in order to advance his own interests will be examined in detail later in this book.

3. Sheridan, *Personal Memoirs,* 1:7.

4. Slocum went on to become a corps commander in the Army of the Potomac, and later, when his XII Corps was transferred to the Western Theater, of a corps in the West.

5. Sheridan, *Personal Memoirs,* 1:11.

6. Ibid., 1:11–12. Terrill, although a Virginian, remained loyal to the Union. The two officers served together in the Western Theater of the Civil War and resolved their differences. By the time of Terrill's death, they had become friends, reported Sheridan.

7. In fairness, peacetime promotions in the U.S. Army came very slowly, and as a result of attrition among the ranks. It was not unusual for men to serve for more than twenty years and never rise above the rank of captain. Many times, it took men more than forty years of service to achieve the rank of colonel, and by the time those promotions finally came through, the men were too old to be effective regimental commanders.

8. Horace Porter, *Campaigning with Grant* (Bloomington: University of Indiana Press, 1961), 23.

9. James H. Kidd, *Personal Recollections of a Cavalryman in Custer's Michigan Brigade* (Ionia, Mich.: Sentinel Printing Co., 1908), 298.

10. George R. Agassiz, ed., *Meade's Headquarters, 1863–1865: Letters of Colonel Theodore Lyman from the Wilderness to Appomattox* (Boston: Atlantic Monthly Press, 1922), 82.

11. Morris, *Sheridan,* 1.

12. James E. Taylor, *The James E. Taylor Sketchbook—With Sheridan up the Shenandoah Valley in 1864: Leaves from a Special Artist's Sketchbook and Diary* (Dayton, Ohio: Morningside House, 1989), 359.

13. Morris, *Sheridan,* 25.

14. Ibid., 38–39.

15. Henry E. Davies, *General Sheridan* (New York: D. Appleton, 1895), 307.

16. Sheridan, *Personal Memoirs,* 1:133–35.

17. Ibid., 1:136–37.

18. Morris, *Sheridan,* 59. Sheridan's destiny was tied to that of both Granger and Alger. Granger would be Sheridan's corps commander at Chickamauga and Chattanooga, as discussed herein, and Alger would serve under Sheridan's command in the Cavalry Corps. Unfortunately, in an episode that will be addressed later in this book, Alger was forced to resign his commission.

19. Sheridan, *Personal Memoirs,* 1:153.

20. Ibid., 1:166.

21. James Lee McDonough, *War in Kentucky: From Shiloh to Perryville* (Knoxville: University of Tennessee Press, 1994), 210–19. See also, *The War of the Rebellion: A Compilation of the Official Records of the Union and Confederate Armies*, 128 volumes in 3 series (Washington, D.C.: U.S. Government Printing Office, 1880–1891), series 1, vol. 16, part 1, 238. (Further references will be to the "O.R." In addition, unless otherwise noted, all further references will be to series 1 of the O.R.)

22. O.R., vol. 16, part 1, 1081.

23. Charles Gilbert, "On the Field of Perryville," in *Battles and Leaders of the Civil War*, 4 vols., ed. Robert U. Johnson and Clarence C. Buel (New York: Century Publishing Co., 1884–1888), 3:53. (Further references to the *Battles and Leaders* series will be to "*B&L.*")

24. Ibid., 3:53.

25. Morris, *Sheridan*, 90–92.

26. Ibid., 91; Sheridan, *Personal Memoirs*, 1:195.

27. O'Connor, *Sheridan the Inevitable*, 99.

28. Sheridan, *Personal Memoirs*, 1:269.

29. Morris, *Sheridan*, 136.

30. Ibid., 145.

31. Ulysses S. Grant, "Chattanooga," in *B&L*, 3:707.

32. Ibid., 3:709.

33. Morris, *Sheridan*, 148.

34. Sheridan, *Personal Memoirs*, 1:338.

35. William S. McFeely, *Grant: A Biography* (New York: W. W. Norton, 1982), 151.

36. Bruce Catton, *Grant Takes Command* (Boston: Little, Brown, 1968), 163.

37. Porter, *Campaigning with Grant*, 46–47.

38. Agassiz, *Meade's Headquarters*, 81.

39. O.R., vol. 36, part 1, 12.

40. Ibid., 14–18.

41. Ibid., 15.

42. George Meade, ed., *The Life and Letters of General George Gordon Meade*, 2 vols. (New York: Charles Scribner's Sons, 1913), 185. There is some dispute about why Pleasonton was relieved of corps command.

43. Davies, *General Sheridan*, 92–93.

44. Gregg may well have resented being passed over for corps command. When he realized that Sheridan was not competent to command the Cavalry Corps, his resentment may have boiled over. Gregg resigned his commission in the winter of 1865, just before the war's final campaign, and never fully explained his reasons. Exasperation with being passed over for command undoubtedly factored into that decision.

45. Ulysses S. Grant, *Personal Memoirs of U. S. Grant*, 2 vols. (New York: Charles L. Webster & Co., 1885), 2:133.

46. Alan Nevins, ed., *A Diary of Battle: The Personal Journals of Colonel Charles S. Wainwright, 1861–1865* (New York: Harcourt, Brace & World, 1962), 341.
47. Davies, *General Sheridan,* 93–95.
48. Agassiz, *Meade's Headquarters,* 81.
49. Kidd, *Personal Recollections,* 261.
50. E. R. Hagemann, ed., *Fighting Rebels and Redskins: Forty Years of Army Life* (Norman: University of Oklahoma Press, 1968), 224.
51. Taylor, *Sketchbook,* 122.
52. Sheridan, *Personal Memoirs,* 1: 352.
53. "David McMurtrie Gregg," Circular No. 6, Series of 1917, Military Order of the Loyal Legion of the United States, Commandery of Pennsylvania, May 3, 1917, 2.
54. Samuel P. Bates, *Martial Deeds of Pennsylvania* (Philadelphia: T. H. Davis & Co., 1875), 772. Again, there is no satisfactory biography of David M. Gregg available. The only published biography is Milton V. Burgess, *David Gregg: Pennsylvania Cavalryman* (privately published, 1984).
55. Louis H. Carpenter, "Sheridan's Expedition around Richmond, May 9–25, 1864," *Journal of the United States Cavalry Association* 1 (1888), 301.
56. Edward L. Wells, *Hampton and His Cavalry in '64* (Richmond, Va.: B. F. Johnson Co., 1899), 95.
57. Samuel Harris, *Personal Reminiscences of Samuel Harris* (Chicago: The Robinson Press, 1897), 31.

+≡ CHAPTER 2 ≡+

SHERIDAN AS
CAVALRY CORPS COMMANDER:
MEDIOCRITY REIGNS

S heridan assumed command of the Army of the Potomac's cavalry in early
April 1864. Once the reorganization of the Cavalry Corps was completed,
Sheridan assessed the status of the Federal mounted arm. Appalled by the state
of his command and by the wretched condition of its mounts, Sheridan faulted
Meade's tendencies toward excessive picketing during the winter months that
took a severe toll on man and beast. Consequently, the Cavalry Corps' horses
"were thin and very much worn out by excessive, and, it seemed to me, unnecessary picket duty." Sheridan continued, "[H]owever, shortly after my taking
command, much of the picketing was done away with, and we had two weeks of
leisure time to nurse the horses, on which so much depended."[1] As the horses
rested, Sheridan developed a different approach for his troopers.

In his memoirs, Sheridan alleged that he faced resistance from Meade. According to Sheridan, he laid out his "idea as to what the cavalry should do, the main
purport of which was that it ought to be concentrated to fight the enemy's cavalry. Heretofore, the commander of the Cavalry Corps had been, virtually, but
an adjunct at army headquarters—a sort of chief of cavalry—and my proposition
seemed to stagger General Meade not a little." Little Phil continued, "I knew that
it would be difficult to overcome the recognized custom of using the cavalry for
the protection of trains and the establishment of cordons around the infantry

corps, and so far as subordinating its operations to the main movements of the main army that in name was it a corps at all, but I still thought it my duty to try."[2]

Meade disagreed with this approach. Thus began a contentious relationship between the two strong-willed generals. Each time these two men clashed, their conflict would have serious consequences for the rest of the Army of the Potomac. When the army set out for its spring campaign in the first days of May 1864, it had one of the largest and most powerful fighting cavalry commands the world had ever seen. With a well-equipped and well-mounted force of more than ten thousand horsemen, Sheridan champed at the bit to pitch into the Confederate cavalry.

The Army of the Potomac moved out of its winter camps before midnight on May 3. The two armies clashed in the dense thickets of the Wilderness for two days on May 5–6, inflicting massive casualties on each other. Early on the morning of May 5, Wilson's division got its chance when Meade allowed Sheridan to launch an offensive with his horse soldiers. When Meade called Torbert's First Division up to support Sheridan's proposed attack, Wilson shifted his division south of the Catharpin Road to cover the movement of the Second Corps. In his first action commanding troops in the field, Wilson did not do well. Engaging with Confederate Brig. Gen. Thomas L. Rosser's Laurel Brigade, Wilson's troopers had a furious fight. Supported by accurate horse artillery fire, Rosser's Laurels shattered Wilson's line and drove his men from the field, preventing Wilson from warning Meade that the Army of Northern Virginia blocked his path.[3] The new division commander did not have an auspicious debut. Rosser's success permitted Maj. Gen. Fitzhugh Lee to move his division of Confederate cavalry to Todd's Tavern, where it could block the Federal route of march. Thus, Sheridan's aggressiveness caused Wilson's division to suffer a serious defeat at the hands of the Southern horse soldiers.

The terrain of the Wilderness forced the horse soldiers to fight on foot, meaning that Meade's plan for the battle precluded a major role for the cavalry. Instead, the army commander wanted Sheridan to draw in his cavalry and to guard the army's wagon trains. The aggressive cavalryman chafed under the restrictions, complaining, "I cannot do anything with the cavalry except to act on the defensive. Why cannot infantry be sent to guard the trains and let me take the offensive?" Meade gave Sheridan permission to detach portions of his command for secondary operations, such as trying to sever lines of communications, but these orders did not placate his anxious subordinate.[4] With little help from the Northern cavalry, the Confederates defeated Meade's army in brutal, close combat.

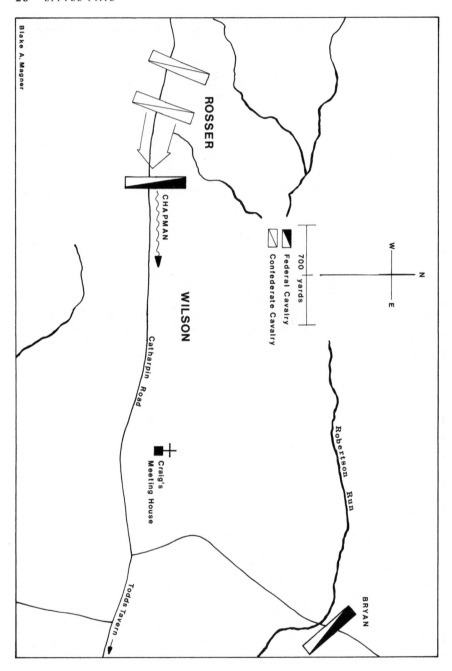

Rosser's Laurels shatter Wilson's line at the Wilderness, May 5, 1864

Instead of pulling back as his predecessors in the east had done, Grant moved around Lee's flank, trying to interpose between Lee and Richmond by occupying the critical crossroads town of Spotsylvania Court House. In the vanguard of the Northern advance, Sheridan's horsemen fought and scouted, and lost crucial engagements along the Plank Road on May 5 and at Todd's Tavern on May 6, 7, and 8. When Sheridan's troopers failed to clear the road from the Wilderness to Spotsylvania, this crucial thoroughfare remained in Confederate hands and permitted the Confederates to seize the crossroads before Grant did.[5] Both Meade and Sheridan issued orders to Brig. Gen. David M. Gregg, infuriating the mercurial Sheridan. Sheridan's failure to act promptly after receiving Meade's orders for May 8 prevented the road to Spotsylvania Court House from being cleared.[6] When Meade failed to beat Lee to Spotsylvania Court House, the two armies fell into a brutal and bloody stalemate, slugging it out there for nearly two weeks.

As a result of the Army of the Potomac's failure to win the race for Spotsylvania Court House, the relationship between Sheridan and Meade fell apart. They had a loud and unpleasant exchange at Meade's headquarters (see chapter 4). As a result, Sheridan received an independent command—something he had craved for a long time—to lead the Cavalry Corps on a raid behind enemy lines.[7]

An elated Sheridan summoned his subordinates on the night of May 8. "We are going out to fight Stuart's cavalry in consequence of a suggestion from me," he said. "[W]e will give him a fair, square fight; we are strong, and I know we can beat him, and in view of my recent representations to General Meade I shall expect nothing but success." The enemy cavalry was to be the primary target. "Our move," he ordered, "would be a challenge to Stuart for a cavalry duel behind Lee's lines, and in his own country."[8] With his entire corps, Sheridan set out on May 9 to whip Jeb Stuart and his vaunted cavalry. Encountering a small force of enemy horsemen, the Federals pushed through their thin ranks. "Keep moving boys," roared Little Phil. "We're going on through. There isn't cavalry enough in the Southern Confederacy to stop us."[9]

When word of Sheridan's departure reached Stuart, he garnered part of his command for a forced march and intercepted Sheridan's line of advance at a place called Yellow Tavern north of Richmond. During a day of intense fighting on May 11, Stuart was mortally wounded. The plumed cavalier died in Richmond the next day while the Army of Northern Virginia fought at the Bloody Angle at Spotsylvania Court House. Sheridan's horsemen drove the Confederate cavalry from their front, and the road to Richmond lay open. After being repulsed, Sheridan did not seize the Southern capital. Instead, he moved toward a linkup with Maj. Gen. Benjamin F. Butler's Army of the James, holding a position on the eastern side of the peninsula. "It is possible that I might have captured the city of Richmond by an assault," he claimed to Meade, "but the want of knowledge of your operations and those of General Butler, and the facility with which the enemy could throw in troops, made me abandon the attempt."[10] Given the strength of the defenses of Richmond it is unlikely that his relatively small force of horsemen could have taken the city, and even if they had taken it, they could not have held it. Instead, he turned northeast.

However, the Southern cavalry had laid a trap for Sheridan at Meadow Bridge, an important crossing over the Chickahominy River, just outside the defenses of Richmond. By May 12, Sheridan's men were nearly out of food, forage, and ammunition, and the gray-clad horse soldiers had hemmed them in. One New Yorker called it "the tightest place in which the corps ever found itself," and another Federal recalled it as "the most foreboding experience of my army life."[11] As Sheridan pushed toward Meadow Bridge, the initial Confederate line, manned largely by clerks from Richmond, broke. But the Confederate resistance soon stiffened. Elements of Brig. Gen. George A. Custer's Michigan Brigade moved out and cleared the causeway over Meadow Bridge, establishing a fragile bridgehead over the Chickahominy.

Sheridan recognized that he had a tenuous position and fretted about his predicament. Maj. Gen. Fitzhugh Lee's Confederate cavalry division had joined the fray, as had more infantry in the defense of Richmond. Custer's Wolverines managed to hold the Confederate horsemen at bay long enough for Federal pioneers to repair the railroad span over the Chickahominy. Northern horsemen streamed across the bridge, and led by the Reserve Brigade, launched a desperate attack that cleared the way for Little Phil's escape. It was, perhaps, Sheridan's finest moment that spring. He proudly watched as his blue-clad horsemen crossed the Chickahominy to safety.[12]

The Cavalry Corps safely made its way to Butler's base of operations at Haxall's Landing on the James River on May 14. They would not rejoin the Army of the Potomac until May 25, leaving Grant and Meade to fumble along blindly, with no cavalry to scout or screen the army's advance, dooming it to fight brutal battles of attrition. Both sides sustained massive casualties as a result of Sheridan's raid.

Stuart's death caused significant problems within the command hierarchy of the Army of Northern Virginia's cavalry. As senior division commander, Wade Hampton was entitled to overall command. However, Gen. Lee did not want to create dissension among the ranks of his mounted arm in the aftermath of Stuart's death, so he instituted a system whereby the three divisions of cavalry constituted independent commands that reported directly to him, and not to a

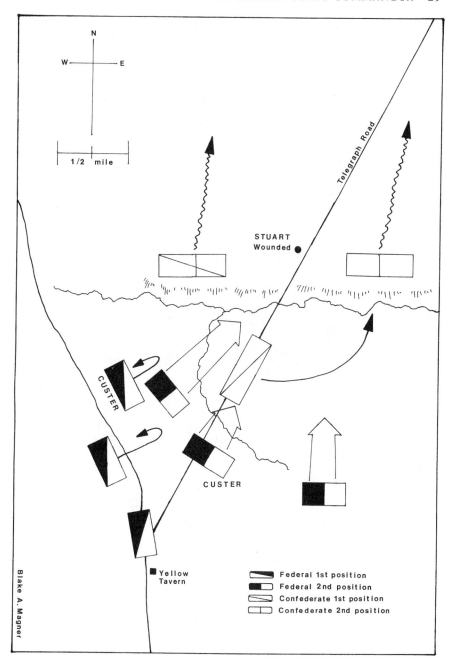

Yellow Tavern, May 11, 1864

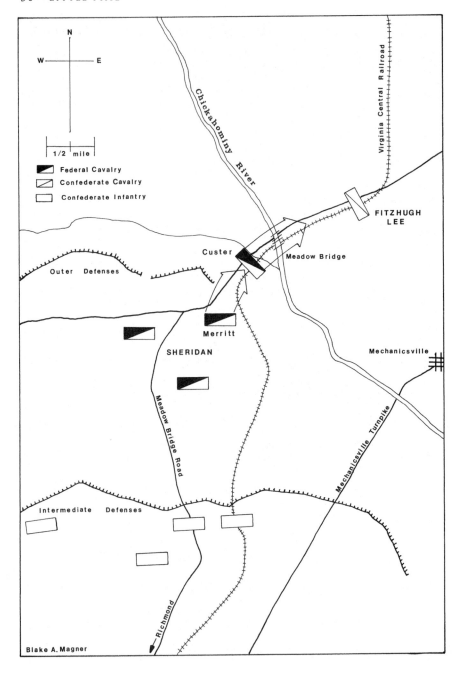

Meadow Bridge, May 12, 1864

central corps commander. It also meant that Robert E. Lee lost his good right arm; he reportedly wept upon hearing the news of his cavalry chieftain's death, lamenting, "He never brought me a piece of false information."[13] William L. Wilson of the 12th Virginia Cavalry of the Laurel Brigade also rued the dashing cavalier's passing, "The Cavalry corps has lost its great leader the unequalled Stuart. We miss him much. Hampton is a good officer but Stuart's equal does not exist."[14]

While the Army of Northern Virginia grimly hung on at Spotsylvania, Sheridan diverted his column onto the peninsula. Though Sheridan won the fight at Yellow Tavern, his raid failed to achieve its objectives: to defeat the Confederate cavalry and enter Richmond. However, in spite of this failure, Sheridan earned a reputation with the Confederates as a "vicious" cavalry leader.[15] Because Sheridan did not rejoin the main body of the Army of the Potomac until May 25, Meade had only five regiments of his cavalry force for more than two weeks. The absence of the Army of the Potomac's Cavalry Corps probably cost Grant a prime opportunity to win the war at the North Anna, for he was left to grope for his adversary.[16]

Sheridan tried to put a positive spin on things when he wrote his memoirs. "Our return to Chesterfield ended the first independent expedition the Cavalry Corps had undertaken since coming under my command," he wrote, "and our success was commended highly by Generals Grant and Meade, both realizing that our operations in the rear of Lee had disconcerted and alarmed that general so much as to aid materially in forcing his retrograde march." He also claimed that "when Stuart was defeated the main purpose of my instructions had been carried out and my thoughts then turned to joining General Butler to get supplies."[17]

In spite of the failure to achieve the raid's objective, the Yankee troopers considered the raid a great success because they had killed Stuart. "With regard to this expedition now at an end, it seemed upon all hands to be taken for granted that it was a brilliant and complete success," reported one Federal. "Whenever in the course of conversation any allusion to it chanced to be made, it was referred to more as a matter which spoke for itself than as one requiring illustration or admitting discussion."[18] Sheridan echoed similar sentiments, claiming that even though his horses were jaded from overwork and lack of forage, his Corps was in "fine spirits with its success."[19] However, the raid was nevertheless ill-advised. "Serious criticism can be leveled against the broader features of Sheridan's campaign," writes historian Gordon C. Rhea. "By taking his cavalry from Spotsylvania Court House, Sheridan severely handicapped Grant in his battles against Lee. The Union army was deprived of its eyes and ears during a

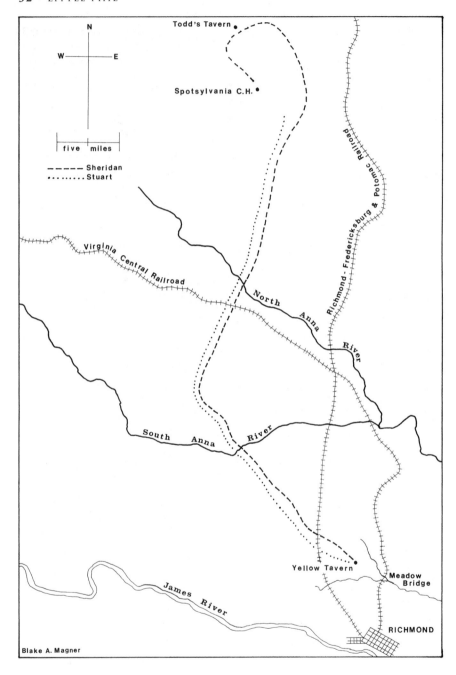

Sheridan's Richmond Raid, May 14–25, 1864

critical juncture in the campaign. And Sheridan's decision to advance boldly to the Richmond defenses smacked of unnecessary showboating that jeopardized his command."[20] In spite of these negative effects, the morale of the Federal horse soldiers reached an all-time high as a result of the May Richmond Raid.

The unusually hot spring of 1864 took a further toll on Sheridan's horses during the lengthy raid. The Cavalry Corps required additional refitting before another major raid could be attempted. Despite a leisurely pace of march, poor worn-out beasts dropped by the score. Rather than allowing broken-down horses to fall into Confederate hands, where they could be nursed back to health and put back into service, the Richmond raid marked a harsher turn to the war. As horses broke down by the side of the road, the Yankee troopers shot them and then trudged off, their saddles and equipment slung over their shoulders.[21] Despite these losses, the Cavalry Bureau provided sufficient remounts and reinforcements to keep a large and effective force in the field.

On May 28, having finally rejoined the Army of the Potomac, Sheridan faced the gray-clad cavalry in the bloody battle of Haw's Shop. It was a long and brutal day of fighting primarily involving Gregg's veterans, and some remembered it as the most severe cavalry fighting of the war. Two newly arrived regiments of South Carolina cavalry commanded by one-legged Brig. Gen. Matthew C. Butler tipped the balance of the fighting for the Confederate victory. The aftermath of the battle effectively removed five brigades of the Army of the Potomac's Cavalry Corps from the war for two days while they rested and refitted. Maj. Gen. Gouverneur K. Warren's Fifth Corps successfully crossed the Totopotomoy Creek on May 29, but a want of cavalry support cost Meade the opportunity to crush Lee's vulnerable right flank the next day. Nevertheless, a few days after Haw's Shop, a Federal staff officer noted, "Our cavalry is full of confidence and does wonders."[22] The new confidence, bordering on arrogance, marked Phil Sheridan's major contribution to the Army of the Potomac's Cavalry Corps.

As part of his grand strategy, Grant had sent Maj. Gen. Franz Sigel's army up the Shenandoah Valley. When a Confederate force defeated Sigel at New Market on May 15, Grant replaced him with Maj. Gen. David "Black Dave" Hunter, a man Confederate cavalry Gen. John D. Imboden derisively described as "a human hyena."[23] Hunter consolidated his command, and then advanced up the Valley toward Staunton, intending to destroy the vital railroad depot there. Once he had completed his mission at Staunton, he would then advance on Charlottesville.[24]

By May 19, the bulk of the fighting at Spotsylvania had ended. That day, Grant ordered Meade to move his entire army to the banks of the North Anna River. On May 21, the Army of the Potomac attempted to cross the North Anna

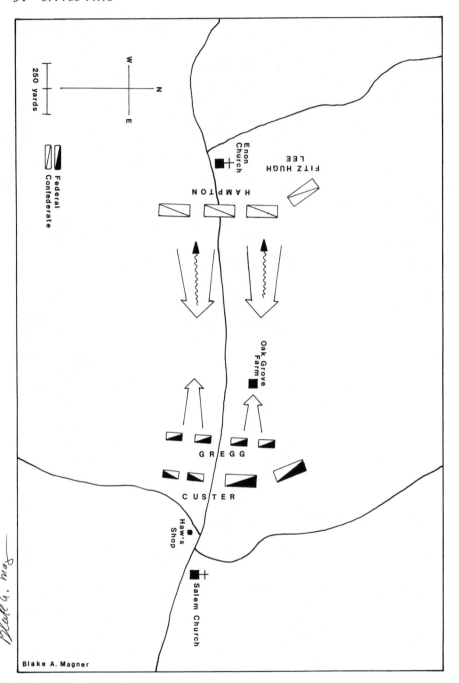

Haw's Shop, May 28, 1864

but was thwarted by a stout Confederate defense. Rebuffed, Grant withdrew, leading to the brutal fight at Haw's Shop. To evaluate the strength of Lee's position, on May 30 Meade ordered all of his corps commanders to sortie. He ordered all corps commanders to move out at dawn on May 31, but Sheridan did not move until nearly four o'clock in the afternoon. When Sheridan did move, his troopers engaged with Fitz Lee's troopers at Old Cold Harbor. This was familiar ground—the Army of the Potomac's 1862 Peninsula Campaign had covered the same terrain.

That afternoon, Brig. Gens. Wesley Merritt and George Custer attacked Fitz Lee's dismounted cavalrymen at Cold Harbor, and a mounted saber charge by Merritt's Regulars and the 1st Michigan Cavalry caught Lee's troopers at the moment that they were withdrawing to deploy Maj. Gen. Robert Hoke's infantry division in line of battle to his rear. Lee's withdrawal left a surprised Sheridan in possession of the crucial crossroads. He recognized that it would be difficult to hold the position and wrote to Meade, "I do not feel able to hold this place. I do not think it prudent to hold on." So Sheridan withdrew to Parsleys Mill, a couple of miles away.

An unhappy Meade ordered Sheridan to hold Old Cold Harbor at all costs.[25] Sheridan later explained his unease. "My isolated position . . . left me a little uneasy," he claimed in his memoirs. "I felt convinced that the enemy would attempt to regain the place, for it was of as much importance to him as to us, and the presence of his infantry disclosed that he fully appreciated this."[26] Obeying Meade's orders, Sheridan and the Cavalry Corps reoccupied Old Cold Harbor in order to hold it until the Army of the Potomac's infantry could come up. The blue-clad troopers, although exhausted from their travails, were determined to hang on. "The morale of the corps was so good and their confidence in Sheridan so great," wrote Capt. Theophilus F. Rodenbough of the 2nd U.S. Cavalry, "that when the order 'to hold at all hazards' was repeated, they never dreamed of leaving the spot."[27]

The dismounted horse soldiers grimly held on until ten in the morning in the face of heavy infantry attacks. Immediately upon the arrival of Maj. Gen. Horatio G. Wright's Sixth Corps, Sheridan withdrew the cavalry nearly four miles, leaving Wright's men unsupported. An afternoon attack by the Sixth Corps nearly succeeded in breaking Hoke's line, and would have if Sheridan had remained in position and his dismounted troopers had joined the attack. Had Sheridan joined Wright's attack, the combined force would have broken through the Confederate line and swept the Army of Northern Virginia back into Richmond. However, Sheridan's refusal to support Wright doomed the Army of the Potomac to two days of intense combat.

Stalemated, the two armies entrenched and fought a protracted and bloody battle. On June 3, Meade ordered a massive unsuccessful frontal assault against the Confederate trenches, costing his army heavy casualties in only a matter of minutes while inflicting only light Confederate losses.[28] "I have always regretted that the last frontal assault at Cold Harbor was ever made," Grant admitted candidly years later. "No advantage whatever was gained to compensate for the heavy loss we sustained. Indeed, the advantages other than those of relative losses, were on the Confederate side."[29]

After his bloody repulse at Cold Harbor, Grant revised his strategy entirely. He decided to cross the James River and advance on the crucial railroad junction town of Petersburg, twenty-five miles south of Richmond. Petersburg had great strategic significance as the junction of the major southern railroads supplying the Confederate capital. If Grant could capture Petersburg and if Hunter could overtake Lynchburg, Lee's army would be entirely cut off from its lines of supply and would have to come out and either fight, surrender, or attempt to flee. Grant believed the move south of the James River had to be hidden from Robert E. Lee's active and vigilant cavalry. With Federal armies on both sides of the river, Grant knew that the safety of the Confederate capital would be "a matter of the first consideration with executive, legislative and judicial branches of the so-called Confederate government, if it was not with the military commanders. But I took all the precaution I knew of to guard against all dangers."[30]

On June 6, Hunter defeated a small Confederate army commanded by Brig. Gen. William E. "Grumble" Jones at Piedmont. Jones was killed in the fighting, and his force withdrew. The next day, before learning of Hunter's victory at Piedmont, Grant ordered Sheridan to lead another audacious strategic raid designed to distract the enemy. Sheridan was to take Torbert's and Gregg's divisions, march along the course of the North Anna River, and fall upon the important rail junction at Gordonsville. The horsemen would then join Hunter's advancing army near Charlottesville. The combined force would march east to join the main body of the Army of the Potomac, which Grant hoped would be safely across the James River and moving on Petersburg.[31] Grant ordered the destruction of the railroad at Charlottesville, Lynchburg, and Gordonsville as the raid's primary mission. On the return trip, Sheridan was to remain on the course of the railroads until "every rail on the road destroyed should be so bent and twisted as to make it impossible to repair the road without supplying new rails," until "driven off by a superior force."[32]

After receiving written orders from Meade, Sheridan and Grant discussed the raid. Sheridan recalled that Grant instructed Hunter to advance as far as Charlottesville, and that Grant expected Sheridan to unite with Hunter there. After joining forces, the two commands were to destroy the James River Canal and the Virginia Central Railroad, and then link up with the Army of the Potomac. Accordingly, Sheridan recounted, "in view of what was anticipated, it would be well to break up the railroad as much as possible on my way westward."[33]

When he penned his report of the 1864 campaigns after the war, Sheridan commented, "There also appeared to be another object, viz, to remove the enemy's cavalry from the south side of the Chickahominy, as, in case we attempted to cross to the James River, this large cavalry force could make such resistance at the difficult crossings as to give the enemy time to transfer his force to oppose the movement."[34] While this statement was the product of hindsight, it nevertheless raises a valid point; drawing off the attention of the Confederate cavalry supported Grant's vision for his strategic cavalry raid. Wilson's division would remain with the main body of the army so that some cavalry could screen the move across the James. Further, Sheridan directed all of his dismounted men, a significant contingent of his command, to report to Wilson.

Grant informed Hunter that the destruction of both the railroad and the canal were of the highest importance to the Federal high command. Hunter was to advance to Lynchburg and then turn east, hopefully taking Lynchburg in a single day. Grant's order suggested that Lynchburg had "so much importance to the enemy, that in attempting to get it such resistance may be met as to defeat your getting onto the road or canal at all." If Hunter did not receive his instructions until his army was already in the valley between Staunton and Lynchburg, he was to turn east by the most practicable road until he struck the Lynchburg branch of the Virginia Central Railroad. Having done that, Hunter was to move east along the line of the railroad, destroying it completely and thoroughly, until his command joined Sheridan's. The orders concluded, "After the work laid out for General Sheridan and yourself is thoroughly done, proceed to join the Army of the Potomac by the route laid out in General Sheridan's instructions."[35]

Sheridan's force was not at full strength. The hard service of the May raid on Richmond and the heavy combat at Haw's Shop cost his command many of its horses, meaning that he had a large number of dismounted men. His command's strength had also been much reduced by men killed and wounded during the same period. He claimed, "The effective mounted force of my two divisions was therefore much diminished, they mustering only about six thousand officers and men when concentrated on June 6 at New Castle Ferry."[36] In reality, Sheridan took more than nine thousand men with him on this raid.

After studying the lay of the land, Sheridan decided to move along the north bank of the North Anna River, marching west nearly sixty miles from Richmond. He would cross the river at Carpenter's Ford, striking the Virginia Central at an obscure stop located at Trevilian Station, six miles west of Louisa Court House, in Louisa County, approximately six miles southeast of Gordonsville. He intended to destroy the railroad between Trevilian Station and Louisa, and bypass Gordonsville, strike the railroad again at Cobham's Station, destroying it from there to Charlottesville, and then link up with Hunter's advancing army. The march west would cover nearly one hundred miles.[37]

Sheridan ordered his command to carry only three days' rations, intended to last five days, and two days' grain for the horses, along with only one hundred rounds of ammunition, of which forty would be carried by the soldiers in their cartridge boxes. Finally, he would take a pontoon train, only one medical wagon, eight ambulances, and one wagon each for division and brigade headquarters, for a total of approximately 125 wagons.[38] They would march early on the morning of June 7.

Word of the impending raid spread quickly among the Federal horse soldiers. Regimental officers received orders to relieve themselves and their men of all unnecessary encumbrances, and all were warned not to expect to find themselves near any depot or other resting place for as many as twelve days.[39] A member of the 6th Ohio Cavalry prophesied, "This means that we are to have some long marches away from our base of supplies, and in all probability some fighting."[40] The two divisions were concentrated at New Castle Ferry, the jumping-off point for the grand raid. A few stray Confederate shells fell on the assembling Yankee troopers, annoying them but causing no harm.[41]

That day, Sheridan left Old Church Tavern and encamped at New Castle Ferry on the Pamunkey River. While riding toward New Castle Ferry, he was joined by soldiers of the 50th New York Engineers, their bridge train in tow. Arriving at New Castle Ferry, the pontoniers laid the bridge across the river in preparation for the coming raid. Gregg's division came up from its position near Bottom's Bridge on the Chickahominy after being relieved by Wilson's men. A *New York Herald* correspondent, traveling with Sheridan's command, noted, "Every one knew now that something was up—another raid probably—and nothing pleases a cavalryman so much as the idea of a raid, if it only be through a country where supplies may be obtained."[42] One Pennsylvanian wrote, "The principal duties which Gen. Sheridan's cavalry are called upon to perform are to make raids into the enemy's country, destroy communications, and harass and annoy the enemy as much as possible."[43] On the night of June 6, Custer scribbled a hasty note to his new bride, writing: "Again I am called on to bid you adieu for a short period. To-morrow morning two Divisions, 1st and 2nd, of this Corps set out on another raid. We may be gone two or three weeks. I will write, the first opportunity. Keep up a stout heart, and remember the successful issue of the past. God and success have hitherto attended us. May we not hope for a continuance of His blessing?"[44]

Sheridan's two divisions departed on June 7, fanning out across Virginia like a plague of locusts, taking everything they could to sustain man and beast. By the next morning, the Confederates knew about the raid. By nightfall on June 8, two divisions of gray-clad cavalry, commanded by Maj. Gens. Wade Hampton and Fitzhugh Lee, along with two battalions of horse artillery, pursued. Hampton, the senior division commander, led the expedition. He performed brilliantly, intercepting Sheridan's line of march at Trevilian Station on June 10. In a grinding battle fought on June 11 and 12, Hampton soundly defeated Sheridan's larger force.

During the first day's fight, four distinct battles occurred. First was a meeting engagement, largely fought mounted. The second phase was a full-scale dismounted engagement that resembled an infantry fight. The third phase was an ill-advised charge by Custer's Wolverines into Hampton's wagon park that led to the Michigan Cavalry Brigade being completely encircled and nearly destroyed. Only good fortune saved Custer's command from annihilation on June 11. The fourth, and final, phase was an all-out assault by the Yankee troopers that drove Hampton's forces from the field, but which left them firmly astride Sheridan's line of march and still full of fight. The second day was a series of seven uncoordinated and unsupported Union assaults against a heavily entrenched enemy position. After repulsing the seventh attack, a coordinated Confederate attack crashed into the Union front and flank simultaneously, breaking the Federal line and driving the blue-clad horsemen from the field in a wild rout.

Despite a terrific effort by the Yankees, Sheridan failed to achieve any of his objectives for the raid: he failed to break the Virginia Central, he failed to link up with Hunter, and he failed to bring Hunter's army back to join the Army of the Potomac. Sheridan did not exercise tactical control over the fight. On both days, he gave Torbert tactical command of the fighting, and while his troopers carried the day on June 11, Torbert's unimaginative tactics on June 12 cost his division heavy casualties and failed to dislodge the Confederates from their position astride the Gordonsville Road. Little Phil also never committed Gregg's division at all on the second day. Sheridan was a nonfactor on both days. In fact, he was strangely absent, perhaps demonstrating his lack of experience in commanding large bodies of mounted men in combat. Trevilian Station was the largest all-cavalry battle of the Civil War, with more than fifteen thousand horsemen engaged. In those two days, Hampton's two divisions suffered 813 casualties out of 6,700 engaged.[45]

After failing to fulfill Grant's objectives for the raid, Sheridan apologized to Grant, writing, "I regret my inability to carry out your instructions."[46] In the process, the two Union divisions lost 1,307 men out of 9,216 engaged. The

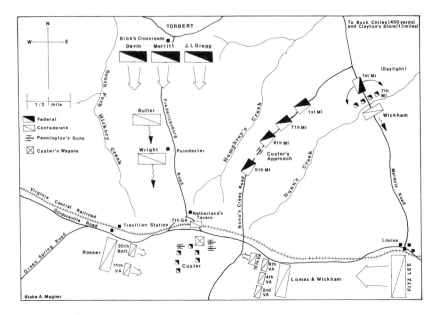

Trevilian Station, Day One, June 11, 1864

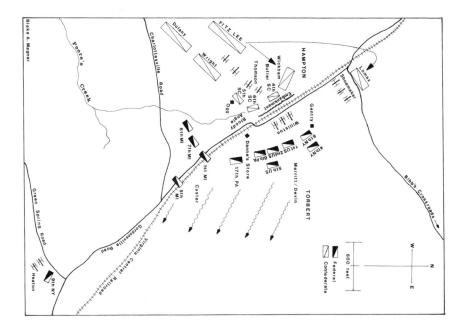

Trevilian Station, Day Two, June 12, 1864

defeat also left Sheridan with a new problem. He now had hundreds of seriously wounded men to transport and approximately five hundred Confederate prisoners to worry about, meaning that the retreat would have to be slow. Sheridan's defeated troopers departed from the area around Trevilian Station about three o'clock on the morning of June 13. They crossed back over the North Anna at Carpenter's Ford.[47] After two long days of intense fighting, the Yankee horse soldiers were tired, and their horses had not had forage for nearly forty-eight hours. A member of Brig. Gen. Henry E. Davies' 6th Ohio Cavalry recalled, "After midnight the withdrawal was skillfully accomplished and with entire secrecy, and a retrograde march commenced, which in some respects was more painful than anything we had before or would hereafter experience."[48]

Confederate Gen. Matthew C. Butler noted: "Pursuit by my command was out of the question. We had been engaged in this bloody encounter from the beginning without food or rest for either men or horses, in the broiling sun of a hot June day, and recuperation was absolutely necessary. As it was, I was not relieved and did not withdraw from my lines until 2 o'clock on the morning of the 13th, and in the meantime had to care for the wounded and bury the dead."[49]

As a result, Sheridan's Yankees got a day's head start on Hampton. Hampton's best opportunity to destroy Sheridan's command slipped away as a result of the wretched condition of his command. "As [Sheridan] had a pontoon train with him which enabled him to cross the river at any point, I was forced to keep on the south of the rivers, so as to interpose my command between him and Grant's army, which he was seeking to rejoin," reported Hampton. "During several days while we marched on parallel lines I constantly offered battle, which he studiously declined."[50]

On June 19, Sheridan finally made contact with the Army of the Potomac. He received orders to march fifteen miles to White House Landing, oversee the dismantling of the supply base there, and escort its garrison and equipment to the new supply base at Harrison's Landing on the James River.[51] There the weary Yankee troopers spotted the welcome sight of the Stars and Stripes waving over the depot at White House Landing.

Hampton did not catch up with Sheridan until June 21, when he attacked White House Landing. Sheridan sent his two divisions out to contest Hampton's advance. Col. Thomas C. Devin's Federal brigade engaged near St. Peter's Church, the site of George Washington's wedding, and a spirited engagement ensued. Sheridan's other four brigades were also committed to the fight, with many of them engaging the Confederates nearly all day. As darkness fell, Hampton withdrew after taking thirty casualties in the day's fighting. "Altogether it was quite a spirited little affair and resulted in nothing particular," observed a trooper of Davies' brigade.[52]

While the two sides skirmished near White House Landing, another Union cavalry raid commenced. On June 21, Grant ordered Meade to send Wilson and the Army of the Potomac's Third Cavalry Division to destroy the principal supply arteries for Petersburg—the Danville and South Side railroads—on another diversionary raid. Brig. Gen. August V. Kautz's small cavalry division of the Army of the James augmented Wilson's division.[53] Departing on June 22, the Wilson-Kautz Raid had no opposition for the first couple of days. Nearly the entire Confederate cavalry force had concentrated near White House Landing, looking to destroy Sheridan's command.[54] While planning his raid, Wilson predicted, "If Sheridan will look after Hampton, I apprehend no difficulty."[55] Unfortunately, Sheridan disappointed Wilson, claiming that he had no clue about the purpose or objectives of the Wilson-Kautz Raid.[56]

As Wilson and Kautz set off, Sheridan's two divisions and Hampton's troopers both enjoyed their first complete day of rest in two weeks. Troopers of both sides spent a pleasant day resting, bathing, and caring for their horses. Many found their first opportunity in weeks to let their loved ones know that they were all right. Sheridan's column advanced again on June 23, this time with nearly nine hundred wagons and a brigade of infantry swelling his ranks. The long, ponderous column snaked slowly across the countryside, aiming for Charles City Court House on the James River. "It was a very serious matter for two divisions, worn down by such excessive labors to less than five thousand men, to escort nine hundred wagons across the Peninsula to the James River; but the necessity was urgent and had to be undertaken," a New Jersey trooper observed.[57] "When strung out it made a line ten miles long and was a very tempting prize for . . . General Hampton with his cavalry corps, who were hovering on our flanks ready to swoop down on us at the first chance of success," observed one of Merritt's men.[58]

Hampton's troopers buzzed around the edges of the column. Reinforced by Brig. Gen. John Chambliss's brigade of Maj. Gen. W. H. F. Lee's division and Brig. Gen. Martin W. Gary's independent cavalry brigade, Hampton looked for an opportunity to fall upon the train. On June 23, the two forces briefly clashed near Nance's Shop, six miles north of Charles City Court House. The horse soldiers of Devin's brigade of the First Cavalry Division held their ground after a spirited engagement, finally driving off Chambliss's men.[59] Gregg's Second Division came up and held the ground around Nance's Shop, protecting the rear of the long wagon train, which safely crossed the James on pontoons that night. Sheridan had successfully shepherded the long wagon train to safety in the face of nearly overwhelming odds. A Pennsylvanian noted, "In performing this duty General Sheridan displayed great generalship, preserving the trains and delivering them safely inside our lines."[60] However, Gregg's men faced a final ordeal.

While Hampton moved on David Gregg's division near Samaria (St. Mary's) Church, he detached Brig. Gen. Lunsford L. Lomax's brigade and sent it to make a desperate, unsuccessful effort to destroy the wagon train. Devin's 9th New York Cavalry charged the Virginians and drove them for nearly a mile and a half. Lomax frowned as he watched the opportunity to bag the vast Federal wagon train slip through his fingers.[61] A member of the 6th Virginia Cavalry complained, "The enemy declining to attack us well back a mile or more . . . but they still refused to attack us." Taking up position behind a crude breastwork, Lomax's Virginians held their position until the next morning.[62]

Hampton planned to go into battle on June 24 with six full brigades of cavalry. Although the big South Carolinian did not know it, the arrival of Sheridan's wagon train at Wilcox's Landing left Gregg's Second Division alone and unsupported. Davies' brigade, Sheridan's rear guard, was especially vulnerable. Sheridan reported to David Gregg at about ten o'clock that morning, "There is some skirmishing in front of Charles City Court House, on the road to Harrison's Landing. . . . I am now moving the infantry down, and will move Torbert's division. Look out for Davies. Support him if necessary."[63] Hampton's force surrounded Gregg's division, still maintaining its lonely vigil guarding Sheridan's flank near Samaria (St. Mary's) Church.[64]

Hampton knew that Davies' brigade was alone and exposed near Nance's Shop, and that Col. J. I. Gregg's brigade was deployed near Samaria Church. Hampton saw an opportunity to destroy David Gregg's isolated division, and he intended to capitalize on that chance. Samaria Church sat about twenty miles from Richmond, about eight miles north of the James River. The terrain was mostly flat, featuring only a few gentle folds and a low ridge to the west of Samaria Church. Hampton deployed his brigades along the ridge, with four regiments held in reserve. Gary's brigade made a flank march around Nance's Shop.

David Gregg's severely outnumbered brigades faced several major problems. First, his flank was in the air, with a wide open field in front and heavy woods behind. Second, he knew that a large enemy force faced him and that he would not get much help from Torbert, who was still shepherding the massive wagon train to safety near Charles City Court House. Thus, David Gregg faced long odds and a heavy task. Nevertheless, he made "every disposition . . . to resist an attack of the enemy should it be made."[65] One of Chambliss's officers recalled, "These regiments, numbering eleven, with three batteries, were placed in a strong position, which they at once proceeded to fortify with breastworks of logs, rails and felled trees."[66]

While the two sides traded potshots for several hours, Matthew Butler surveyed the Federal line for weaknesses. He realized that a flank attack would "strike [Gen.] Gregg a fatal blow without a great loss to our side." Butler reported his findings to Hampton and waited for a response. While he waited, Fitz Lee rode up to Butler's headquarters. When Butler informed Lee that Gregg's flank lay exposed, Lee sent a staff officer to ask Hampton for permission to take command of the field. Hampton granted the request and instructed Butler to take his orders from Lee.[67]

About three o'clock that afternoon, Gary kicked off his attack. His men moved through the fields near Nance's Shop and into a swale, where Gregg's troopers could not see them. With a ringing Rebel yell, the Confederate troopers then attacked on foot. A member of the 1st Maine Cavalry watched them come on, and scrawled in his diary: "Instantly all our men were on their feet and everybody alert. As for myself, I confess my heart was in my mouth."[68]

As Gary engaged, so did Brig. Gen. Williams C. Wickham and then Chambliss. Soon, heavy firing rang out all along the line. The raking volleys from Gregg's breastworks broke the momentum of the initial Confederate attacks, and the gray-clad horse soldiers fell back to regroup. Wickham's men advanced rapidly across the open field and crashed into Gregg's line anew. A severe firefight raged, with the Rebels charging "in the face of a very heavy fire of artillery and musketry, and it was most handsomely accomplished."[69] A Maine trooper described the massed Southern assault as falling upon the Federals "like a thunderbolt."[70]

Gregg's veterans hung on doggedly, repulsing attack after attack. "Savagely the Rebels fight, clubbing their muskets and closely in their rear can be seen Wade Hampton and Fitz Hugh Lee, Gen. Chambliss and Gen. Butler driving their men on. The train! The train! is their rallying cry," observed a member of the 1st Maine Cavalry.[71] An officer of the 1st Pennsylvania Cavalry had an apt description of the action: "We came together like two battering rams, then backed off for vantage-ground, and went at each other again and again."[72]

Finally, the dogged Confederates shattered Gregg's line and sent his men reeling back in a panic. "Our men on the line were out of ammunition, and in ten minutes the whole line was on the skedaddle. The batteries' ammunition soon gave out, too, and we were seven miles from our trains, and there was nothing to do but run for it. We saved the guns with difficulty. . . . We were the last off the field, and I think it was as hot a place as I ever got into," recounted an officer of the 1st Massachusetts Cavalry.[73] Another blue-back noted, "It was the most disorderly retreat I ever have seen since I have been in the service. If the rebels had pushed hard just then they would have gobbled the whole thing."[74]

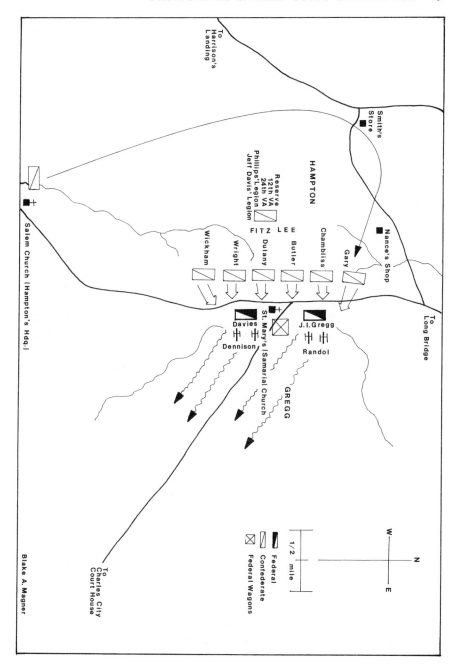

Samaria Church, June 24, 1864

The victorious Confederates pursued for several miles until the extreme heat and exhaustion finally ended the chase. In the process, they swept up many retreating Union troopers, and almost snatched Gregg himself. Only the prescience of Capt. Henry C. Weir, one of Gregg's staff officers, saved the commanding general from being captured. Weir warned Gregg of danger just in time, then turned and made a stand, armed only with his pistol, long enough for Gregg to escape. Weir received the Medal of Honor for his valor.[75]

Lucky to escape, Gregg's routed troopers rallied near Charles City Court House. In an engagement that lasted more than two hours, Gregg's division suffered 357 casualties out of 2,157 engaged, for 17 percent of his total force lost.[76] The 1st Maine Cavalry, which bore the brunt of the fighting, went into battle with approximately 260 officers and men. It lost ten officers and fifty-six enlisted men killed, wounded, or captured, for losses of 26 percent.[77] Hampton lost about two hundred men in the fighting.[78]

While Gregg's men suffered, Torbert's division spent a quiet day relaxing on the banks of the river. On June 25, Sheridan's exhausted Yankees finally made their way across the James River to safety. Their long ordeal had finally ended. "Here closed General Sheridan's second grand raid," noted the historian of the 1st Pennsylvania Cavalry, "the corps having been absent from the army nineteen days, and engaged in either marching or fighting the entire period, without a single day's respite."[79] An officer of the 1st Massachusetts Cavalry summed up the feelings of the Federal troopers quite well, "I don't think these great raids amount to much."[80]

On June 25, Robert E. Lee wrote to Hampton: "I am rejoiced at your success. I thank you and the officers and men of your command for the gallantry and determination with which they have assaulted Sheridan's forces and caused his expedition to end in defeat. So soon as Sheridan crosses the river, I wish you to join me." A proud Hampton consulted with the Confederate high command, and Lee decided that after a brief rest, Hampton's weary troopers would set off after Wilson's and Kautz's raiders.[81] One of Fitz Lee's men gloated, "Having settled accounts with Sheridan, we next moved to pay our attention to the great raiders on the south side."[82] Another of the Southerners was less eloquent: "We have whipped the Enemy's Cav'ly so badly that they are back recruiting new horses."[83]

On June 23, two days into the Wilson-Kautz Raid, Col. George H. Chapman's Federal brigade encountered enemy cavalry near Blacks and Whites Station in an engagement known as the Battle of the Grove. After Chapman's men enjoyed some initial success, Brig. Gen. Rufus Barringer's brigade of North Carolina cavalry arrived, dismounted, and drove off the Yankee raiders, forcing Wilson to withdraw. A Confederate force of infantry and home guards then repulsed the Northern raiders at the Staunton River Bridge on June 25, much to Wilson's embarrassment.

Finally, on June 29, Maj. Gen. William Mahone's Southern infantry division, along with the entire Confederate cavalry force—three divisions strong—fell upon Wilson and Kautz. Soon, they had encircled Kautz's entire force, and the raiders had to cut their way out, narrowly avoiding total destruction. "I have to report that my division and a portion of General Wilson's division have just arrived here. Our expedition was very successful until this afternoon, when we were surrounded and overpowered and had to abandon our transportation, wounded and prisoners," reported a visibly relieved Kautz. "I escaped with my division by taking it through the woods and charging across the railroad."[84]

Wilson lost all of his artillery and his wagon trains. The surviving raiders finally reached the safety of the Federal lines around Petersburg on July 2. Wilson and Kautz had set out with approximately 4,500 men, and they had lost about a third of them along the way. When it became obvious that Wilson and Kautz were in trouble, Meade ordered Sheridan to reinforce the raiders. "The moment I received orders from General Meade to go to the relief of Wilson," claimed Sheridan, "I hastened with Torbert and Gregg by way of Prince George Court House and Lee's Mills to Reams Station . . . but I was too late to render any material assistance, Wilson having already disappeared, followed by the enemy."[85] Meade later reprimanded Sheridan for his lackadaisical movement to support Wilson and Kautz. In short, the raid was an unmitigated disaster, and Sheridan did nothing to help rescue Wilson from his predicament.[86]

While the Trevilian and Wilson-Kautz raids wound down, the Army of the Potomac, again moving without the benefit of any cavalry screen, bogged down in the trenches around Petersburg, and the war rapidly devolved into a tedious siege. With little to do, the Federal cavalry went into camp, doing little more than picket duty for three weeks. However, Sheridan would have one more major test as commander of the Army of the Potomac's Cavalry Corps, and he would be found wanting once again.

On June 13, Robert E. Lee gambled and sent the Army of Northern Virginia's Second Corps after Hunter's army, just as Grant was crossing the James River, precisely what Grant had wanted to avoid. Lt. Gen. Jubal A. Early's Second Corps arrived at Charlottesville on June 16, boarded trains to Lynchburg, and arrived on the night of June 17. Realizing that a strong force of enemy infantry lay in front of him, Hunter declined to attack on July 18 and withdrew. With no enemy force to block his way, Early advanced down the Shenandoah Valley to the banks of the Potomac River. The Confederates then invaded Maryland and sent a cavalry raid into Pennsylvania. On July 25, after several days of heavy skirmishing, and in response to Early's invasion of Maryland, Grant

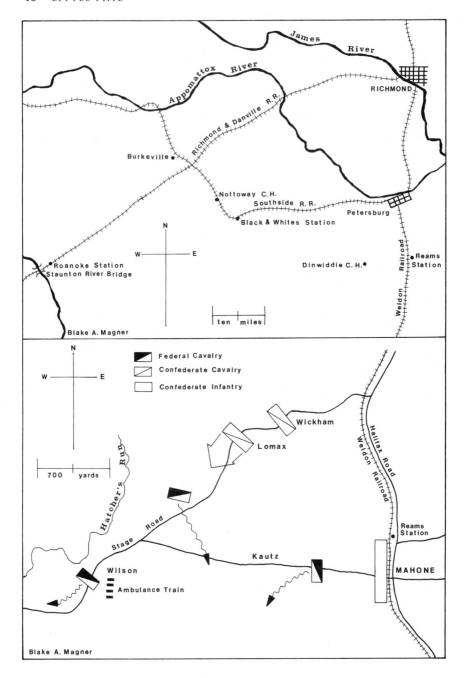

Wilson-Kautz Raid/First Reams Station, June 29, 1864

decided to make a foray north of the James River. He dispatched Maj. Gen. Winfield Scott Hancock's Second Corps, nearly twenty-five thousand men strong, Kautz's cavalry division, and two divisions of Sheridan's Cavalry Corps to advance from Petersburg to Deep Bottom, move northwest toward Richmond, and threaten the enemy garrison at Chaffin's Bluff. Sheridan would cross the Chickahominy, destroy the Virginia Central Railroad north of Richmond, and then return to the Army of the Potomac. If the opportunity presented, Sheridan might even make a dash into Richmond.[87] It was an ambitious plan.

The infantry, commanded by Hancock, would make the primary thrust, and the plan depended on his good execution. Hancock's Corps moved out on July 27, while Gary's small brigade of cavalry, less than one thousand men strong, made one of the bravest and most remarkable stands of the Civil War. Torbert's division also moved out, but made little progress that first day. Merritt's Regulars engaged Gary's men near Fussell's Mill and drove them off. A reconnaissance determined that Confederate infantry blocked Sheridan's route of march and that the flank could not be turned. Torbert, instead of pressing the attack, camped for the night. "General Lee had anticipated the movement around his left flank by transferring to the north side of the James a large portion of his infantry and W.H.F. Lee's division of cavalry," claimed Little Phil in rationalizing the cavalry's failure.[88]

On July 28, Gregg and Kautz were to try to turn the Confederate flank while Torbert's brigades held the enemy in place by demonstrating in their front. Hancock's cautious advance impeded Gregg and Kautz, but the attack by the horsemen bogged down when it encountered infantry. When Torbert's attack on the left drove back the enemy line, Hancock failed to break through the strong Confederate line at Darby Town and pulled back. With the infantry bogged down at Fussell's Mill, a frustrated Meade recognized the futility of further attacks and called off the expedition on July 29. The Battle of Deep Bottom ended as a failure.

Sheridan was supposed to cross the Chickahominy, move west, and destroy the railroad bridges over the river. Once again, Sheridan had left his subordinate commanders to fend for themselves, meaning that their attacks were uncoordinated and ineffective. One historian noted, "None of the Union commanders did well at First Deep Bottom. . . . Sheridan delivered a dismal performance . . . [and] seems to have . . . genuinely feared an attack by overwhelming Confederate numbers."[89] Sheridan later claimed that he did not push the attack because the presence of the Confederate infantry "rendered useless any further effort on Hancock's part or mine to carry out the plan of the expedition."[90] However, these rationalizations ring hollow.

Sheridan claimed that the combination of the failure of Hancock's attack, and the failure of the infantry attack at the Crater in Petersburg, caused Meade to cancel the cavalry's expedition along the Virginia Central.[91] The cavalry then went into camp, and its role in Grant's grand campaign ended with a whimper and not with a bang. On August 8, 1864, Grant ordered Sheridan to take two divisions of the Cavalry Corps to the Shenandoah Valley, where he would assume temporary command of the Middle Military Division. His tenure as commander of the Army of the Potomac's Cavalry Corps ended just ninety days after Sheridan led it into the field, and just over 120 days after Sheridan came east to assume command of the Corps.

Years later, Sheridan made a number of claims in his memoirs. "In the campaign we were almost always on the march, night and day, often unable to care properly for our wounded, and obliged to bury our dead where they fell," he claimed. "Innumerable combats attest the part the cavalry played in Grant's march from the Rapidan to Petersburg. In nearly all of these our casualties were heavy, particularly so when, as was often the case, we had to engage the Confederate infantry; but the enemy returned such a full equivalent in dead and wounded in every instance, that finally his mounted power, which from the beginning of the war had been nurtured with a wise appreciation of its value, was utterly broken."[92]

In reality, Sheridan did poorly in command of the Cavalry Corps. During his four months of leadership, the Corps conducted three major raids and fought thirteen major engagements. Of those engagements—the Wilderness (on May 5), Todd's Tavern, Yellow Tavern, Meadow Bridge, Haw's Shop, Cold Harbor, Trevilian Station, White House Landing, Samaria Church, Nottoway Court House, Staunton River Bridge, Reams Station, and Deep Bottom—only Yellow Tavern can be considered a victory for the Yankee horse soldiers, and the rest were losses. At Haw's Shop, Hampton had set out to develop the strength of Sheridan's force, and Sheridan's task was to prevent Hampton from doing so. Sheridan failed. Trevilian Station was a decisive defeat, one that influenced the future course of the war. In several of these fights, the Federals were lucky to get out intact—Sheridan's command could have been destroyed at Meadow Bridge or Trevilian Station. Gregg's division was nearly destroyed at Samaria Church. Kautz and Wilson were extremely fortunate to have escaped from their raid intact.

Confederate Brig. Gen. Thomas L. Rosser, commander of the Laurel Brigade, observed of Sheridan's performance at Trevilian, "Sheridan displayed no skill in maneuvering; it was simply a square stand up fight, man to man, and Hampton whipped him—defeated his purposes and turned him back." Prophetically, Rosser concluded, "The history writers of the North are endeavoring to make a great general of Sheridan, but the impartial historian, who will write for future generations to read, will overturn their feeble and foundationless structure."[93] While Rosser's analysis was correct, the reputation has stood far longer than the Southerner might have guessed.

Grant had designed four major strategic raids: the Richmond, Trevilian, Wilson-Kautz, and First Deep Bottom. These raids also failed. In each instance, the cavalry's absence left the Union armies groping blindly for the enemy. Dennis Hart Mahan, who taught military science at West Point, wrote the manual of doctrine that served as the basis for all of the army's operations. The primary role of the cavalry, wrote Mahan, was "to secure the front and flanks of the position occupied by the main body, from any attempt to reconnoiter or attack it."[94] In short, the cavalry was to scout and screen the advance of the infantry, not fight battles, irrespective of Sheridan's claims to have invented a new paradigm. And it did so on Grant's orders. The lieutenant general created the problem that cost his armies dearly.

The Federal cavalry utterly failed in this role. The cavalry's continued absence meant that the Army of the Potomac fumbled into Robert E. Lee's trap at Ox Ford on the North Anna, and only good luck prevented its destruction there. Although the combination of the Trevilian Raid and an excellent tactical plan by Maj. Gen. Andrew A. Humphreys made it easier for Grant to slip across the James River unmolested, the absence of his horse soldiers, combined with a clever and effective defense by Gen. P. G. T. Beauregard, kept him from being able to capture Petersburg and force the bloodless evacuation of Richmond. In short, the failure of these two raids prolonged the war in the misery-ridden trenches of Petersburg for nearly ten months. Further, these raids sapped the strength of the Cavalry Corps, bleeding the ranks of men and horses and leaving the Corps *hors de combat* for extended periods of time.

In 1866, when he wrote his report of the Cavalry Corps' actions in the Overland Campaign, Sheridan claimed: "It will be seen by the foregoing narrative that the idea advanced by me at the commencement of the campaign, viz, 'that our cavalry ought to fight the enemy's cavalry, and our infantry the enemy's infantry,' was carried into effect immediately after the battle of the Wilderness. The result was constant success and the almost total annihilation of the rebel cavalry. We marched when and where we pleased; were always the attacking party, and always successful."[95] These claims simply are untrue. The Confederate cavalry remained a formidable opponent, and it seldom lost a fight against the Army of the Potomac's Cavalry Corps. This was not wishful thinking on Little Phil's part, or rationalization of the hardships he subjected his horsemen to. It was a lie. The facts do not support Sheridan's claims of constant success.

According to history's judgment, Phil Sheridan was a great cavalry commander. Again, the historical record does not support this reputation. Aside from his dubious record of success, Sheridan employed unimaginative tactics. His cavalry often fought as infantry, and he rarely demonstrated a true understanding of the nature of mounted combat. Further, his troopers had a significant advantage in both manpower and firepower as a result of their repeating weapons. They should have bested their Southern adversaries on almost every battlefield, but poor tactics often negated these advantages, as at Trevilian Station on June 12. Given Sheridan's limited experience in commanding horse soldiers, this is not surprising. Torbert's seven disjointed, unsupported, and unsuccessful dismounted attacks on the second day of the Battle of Trevilian Station demonstrate this trend plainly. A strong flanking move could have forced Hampton's Confederates out of a seemingly impregnable position, but Torbert instead insisted on making frontal attacks that had no real prospect of success. Sheridan should have taken personal command of the field, recognized the fruitlessness of these attacks, and tried to outflank Hampton. Instead, his tactics showed no imagination or expertise, costing his command heavy casualties again and again.

Sheridan commanded three full divisions of cavalry during this campaign. With the exceptions of Samaria Church and Reams's Station, his mounted forces substantially outnumbered the Confederate cavalry, sometimes by margins of more than two to one. In May, with the coming of the Wilderness Campaign, the Army of the Potomac went into battle with more than ten thousand horsemen, and the Kautz's cavalry division of the Army of the James had nearly twenty-five hundred. By Sheridan's own estimate, his Cavalry Corps suffered five thousand to six thousand casualties, enormous losses by any standard, and previously unheard of in the Army of the Potomac's mounted arm.[96] In short, Sheridan's leadership resulted in casualties of nearly half of his total strength. Any other commander would have been called a butcher for that magnitude of losses, not a great captain. By way of comparison, when the Army of the Potomac's infantry suffered similar casualties during the Overland Campaign, Northern newspapers lambasted Grant for the same proportions of losses. Perhaps the moniker of "butcher" should also have been applied to Phil Sheridan.

Further, Sheridan was not a hands-on commander of his cavalry. As was his habit on nearly every battlefield of the war, Sheridan usually left tactical command of the various battles to his subordinates, most often to Torbert. Torbert was no better as a commander of mounted troops than Sheridan, as he was also an infantryman by training. As a result, fights were often uncoordinated and poorly executed.

A good Civil War general led from the front and led by example. Sheridan almost never exercised tactical command of his cavalry, and it showed. By permitting his division commanders to operate in a vacuum, he doomed his attacks to failure. Sheridan deserves censure for his failure to direct personally the actions of his Cavalry Corps. Great cavalry leaders such as John Buford, Jeb Stuart, and Wade Hampton knew when to do so and often exercised personal command of their troopers. Hampton, in fact, regularly led charges, including one at Trevilian Station where he personally killed two Yankee troopers in close combat.

Although history remembers Philip H. Sheridan as the greatest cavalry commander of the Civil War, the evidence simply does not support the conclusion. In fact, Alfred Pleasonton's record as Cavalry Corps commander was better than Sheridan's, and Pleasonton was a better all-around leader of horse soldiers. Unlike Sheridan, Pleasonton had no powerful patrons in positions of power within the army's hierarchy. Accordingly, Pleasonton has been dismissed as a cavalry commander, even though the Army of the Potomac's Cavalry Corps owes much of its success to him. While Sheridan generally receives credit for the prominent role that the Army of the Potomac's Cavalry Corps played in winning the Civil War, his record as its commander does not warrant that lofty reputation.

NOTES

1. O.R., vol. 36, part 1, 787.
2. Sheridan, *Personal Memoirs,* 1:354–55.
3. Gordon C. Rhea, *The Battle of the Wilderness, May 5–6, 1864* (Baton Rouge: Louisiana State University Press, 1994), 115–17.
4. O.R., vol. 33, part 2, 428, 513, and 515.
5. Little has been written on the critical fighting at and near Todd's Tavern, the substance of which goes far beyond the scope of this work. For the most comprehensive treatment done to date, see Rhea, *The Battle of the Wilderness.*
6. Andrew A. Humphreys, *The Virginia Campaign of 1864 and 1865,* 2 vols. (New York: Charles Scribner's Sons, 1881), 1:60–72.
7. Morris, *Sheridan,* 164.
8. Sheridan, *Personal Memoirs,* 1:370–71.
9. Stephen Z. Starr, *The Union Cavalry in the Civil War,* 3 vols. (Baton Rouge: Louisiana State University Press, 1981), 2:97.
10. O.R., vol. 36, part 1, 778.
11. Alonzo V. Foster, *Reminiscences and Record of the 6th New York V.V. Cavalry* (Brooklyn, N.Y.: privately published, 1892), 75; Edward P. Tobie, *History of the First Maine Cavalry* (Boston: Press of Emery & Hughes, 1887), 266.
12. Gordon C. Rhea, *To the North Anna River: Grant and Lee, May 13–25, 1864* (Baton Rouge: Louisiana State University Press, 2000), 46–56. Rhea's account is the only detailed tactical treatment of the important engagement at the Meadow Bridge.

13. Emory M. Thomas, *Bold Dragoon: The Life of J. E. B. Stuart* (New York: Random House, 1986), 297. For a detailed study of Sheridan's Richmond Raid and the Battle of Yellow Tavern, see Carpenter, "Sheridan's Expedition around Richmond," *Journal of the United States Cavalry Association* 1 (1888), and Theophilus F. Rodenbough, "Sheridan's Richmond Raid," *B&L*, 4:188–93.

14. Festus P. Summers, ed., *A Borderland Confederate* (Pittsburgh, Pa.: University of Pittsburgh Press, 1962), 80; Tracy Power, *Lee's Miserables: Life in the Army of Northern Virginia from the Wilderness to Appomattox* (Chapel Hill: University of North Carolina Press, 1998), 57.

15. Thomas Nelson Conrad, *The Rebel Scout: A Thrilling History of Scouting Life in the Southern Army* (Washington, D.C.: The National Publishing Co., 1904), 109.

16. For a detailed study of the opportunity lost at the North Anna, see Rhea, *To the North Anna River.*

17. Sheridan, *Personal Memoirs,* 1:390–92.

18. Charles E. Phelps, "Recollections of the Wilderness Campaign," Charles E. Phelps Papers, Maryland Historical Society, Baltimore.

19. O.R.. vol. 36, part 1, 777.

20. Rhea, *To the North Anna River,* 62.

21. Carpenter, "Sheridan's Expedition around Richmond," 321.

22. Agassiz, *Meade's Headquarters,* 131.

23. John D. Imboden to I. Marshall McCue, October 1, 1883, Imboden Papers, Museum of the Confederacy, Richmond, Virginia. For more on the campaign in the Valley, see Richard R. Duncan, *Lee's Endangered Left: The Civil War in Western Virginia, Spring of 1864* (Baton Rouge: Louisiana State University Press, 1998).

24. O.R., vol. 37, part 1, 485–86.

25. Ibid., vol. 36, part 3, 411.

26. Sheridan, *Personal Memoirs,* 1:406–7.

27. Rodenbough, "Sheridan's Richmond Raid," 4:193.

28. Ibid., 4:18–22. The fighting at Cold Harbor and Petersburg foreshadowed the ghastly trench warfare of World War I, featuring direct frontal assaults against strongly entrenched enemy positions marked by appalling casualties.

29. Grant, *Personal Memoirs,* 588.

30. Ibid., 591.

31. O.R., vol. 36, part 1, 22.

32. Ibid., part 3, 598.

33. Sheridan, *Personal Memoirs,* 1:415.

34. O.R., vol. 36, part 1, 795. This may be a bit of twenty-twenty hindsight on Sheridan's part.

35. Ibid., vol. 37, part 1, 598.

36. Sheridan, *Personal Memoirs,* 1:417.

37. Ibid., 1:417–18. The precise location of Carpenter's Ford is impossible to pin down today, as that crossing is now under water, part of the Lake Anna dam

complex built for flood control, reservoir, and recreational purposes during the latter half of the twentieth century.

38. O.R., vol. 36, part 1, 795; *New York Herald,* June 21, 1864.

39. Henry Pyne, *Ride to War: The History of the First New Jersey Cavalry* (New Brunswick, N.J.: Rutgers University Press, 1961), 217.

40. Carlos McDonald, "Diary," in *Report of the Forty-Sixth Annual Reunion of the Sixth Ohio Veteran Volunteer Cavalry Association* (Warren, Ohio: Wm. Ritezel & Co., 1911), 54.

41. William P. Lloyd, *History of the First Regiment Pennsylvania Reserve Cavalry, from Its Organization, August 1861, to September 1864, with List of Names of All Officers and Enlisted Men Who Have Ever Belonged to the Regiment, and Remarks Attached to Each Name, Noting Change* (Philadelphia: King & Baird, 1864), 97.

42. *New York Herald,* June 21, 1864.

43. *Philadelphia Press,* July 4, 1864.

44. George A. Custer to Elizabeth B. Custer, June 6, 1864, in *The Custer Story: The Life and Letters of General George A. Custer and His Wife Elizabeth,* ed. Marguerite Merington (New York: Devin-Adair Co., 1950), 193.

45. For a detailed description of the Trevilian Raid and the Battle of Trevilian Station, see Eric J. Wittenberg, *Glory Enough for All: Sheridan's Second Raid and the Battle of Trevilian Station* (Washington, D.C.: Brassey's, Inc., 2001).

46. O.R., vol. 36, part 1, 785.

47. Diary of William G. Hills, entry for June 13, 1864, William G. Hills Papers, Manuscripts Division, Library of Congress, Washington, D.C.

48. A. D. Rockwell, M.D., *Rambling Recollections: An Autobiography* (New York: Paul B. Hoeber, 1920), 150.

49. Matthew C. Butler, "The Cavalry Fight at Trevilian Station," in *B&L,* 4:239.

50. O.R., vol. 36, part 1, 1096.

51. Ibid., 781–82, 784.

52. Diary of Nathan Webb, entry for June 21, 1864, Schoff Civil War Collection, Clements Library, University of Michigan, Ann Arbor.

53. O.R., vol. 40, part 2, 285.

54. Grant, *Personal Memoirs,* 604.

55. O.R., vol. 40, part 2, 286. For further information, see Wilson's report, found at O.R., vol. 40, part 1, 20.

56. Sheridan, *Personal Memoirs,* 1:390.

57. Pyne, *Ride to War,* 224.

58. Edgar B. Strang, *Sunshine and Shadows of the Late Civil War* (Philadelphia: privately published, 1898), 53.

59. O.R., vol. 36, part 1, 810, 844.

60. Hampton S. Thomas, *Personal Reminiscences of Service in the Cavalry of the Army of the Potomac* (Philadelphia: L. R. Hamersly & Co., 1889), 19.

61. O.R., vol. 36, part 3, 791.

62. John C. Donohoe diary, entry for June 24, 1864, Virginia State Archives, Richmond.

63. O.R., vol. 36, part 3, 791.
64. Union accounts of this battle call the church St. Mary's Church. However, the Confederate accounts all refer to it as Samaria Church. The actual name of the church is Samaria Church, which is the name that will be used in this account.
65. O.R., vol. 36, part 1, 855.
66. George W. Beale, *A Lieutenant of Cavalry in Lee's Army* (Boston: Gorham Press, 1918), 162.
67. Ulysses R. Brooks, *Butler and His Cavalry in the War of Secession* (Columbia, S.C.: State Publishing Co., 1912), 268–69.
68. Webb diary, entry for June 24, 1864.
69. O.R., vol. 36, part 1, 1097.
70. Tobie, *First Maine Cavalry,* 294.
71. Webb diary, entry for June 24, 1864.
72. Thomas, *Personal Reminiscences,* 19.
73. Benjamin W. Crowninshield, *A History of the First Regiment of Massachusetts Volunteer Cavalry* (Boston: Houghton-Mifflin Co., 1891), 225–26.
74. William Hyndman, *History of a Cavalry Company: A Complete Record of Company A, Fourth Pennsylvania Cavalry* (Philadelphia: James B. Rogers Co., 1870), 131.
75. David M. Gregg to Russell A. Alger, August 22, 1898, Henry C. Weir Medal of Honor file, RG94, File No. 1465CB1866, The National Archives, Washington, D.C.
76. This number is an estimate based on Gregg's strengths and losses at Trevilian Station. The strength estimate may well be high, given the losses to straggling and horses shot. Nevertheless, the losses are staggering, and the percentage of men lost may actually be a good bit higher, depending on Gregg's true strength on June 24. Unfortunately, we will probably never know the true size of his force, as no records exist to document his strength that day.
77. Torlief S. Holmes, *Horse Soldiers in Blue: First Maine Cavalry* (Gaithersburg, Md.: Butternut Press, 1985), 176.
78. *Richmond Examiner,* June 27, 1864.
79. Lloyd, *First Pennsylvania Cavalry,* 104.
80. Crowninshield, *A History of the First Regiment,* 227.
81. O.R., vol. 36, part 3, 903.
82. "Narrative of Cavalry Operations," *Richmond Sentinel,* July 13, 1864.
83. Horace M. Wade to his sister, July 3, 1864, Lewis Leigh Collection, U.S. Army Military History Institute, Carlisle, Pennsylvania.
84. O.R., vol. 40, part 2, 512.
85. Sheridan, *Personal Memoirs,* 1:444.
86. The most detailed treatment of the Wilson-Kautz Raid done to date is Capt. Greg Eanes, *Wilson-Kautz Raid: Battle for the Staunton River Bridge* (Lynchburg, Va.: H. E. Howard Co., 1999).
87. O.R., vol. 40, part 3, 437–38, 505, 532.

88. Sheridan, *Personal Memoirs,* 1:448. There is no comprehensive study of the First Battle of Deep Bottom, and one is needed. For the best treatment to date, see Bryce A. Suderow, "Glory Denied: The First Battle of Deep Bottom, July 27th–29th, 1864," *North & South* 3, no. 7 (September 2000): 17–33.
89. Suderow, "Glory Denied," 31.
90. Sheridan, *Personal Memoirs,* 1:448.
91. Ibid., 1:451.
92. Ibid., 1:454–55.
93. Quoted in Brooks, *Butler and His Cavalry,* 256–57.
94. Dennis Hart Mahan, *An Elementary Treatise on Advanced-Guard, Out-Post, and Detachment Service of Troops, and the Manner of Posting and Handling Them in the Presence of an Enemy* (New York: J. Wiley, 1861), 87.
95. O.R., vol. 36, part 1, 801.
96. Ibid., 802.

✦══ CHAPTER 3 ══✦

LITTLE PHIL IN
THE SHENANDOAH VALLEY:
A VICTORIOUS CAMPAIGN
BEREFT OF DECISION

With the armies deadlocked at Cold Harbor, Robert E. Lee gambled. Remembering that Maj. Gen. Thomas J. "Stonewall" Jackson's Army of the Valley wreaked sufficient havoc in Maj. Gen. George B. McClellan's rear to draw forces away from Richmond in the summer of 1862, Lee decided to try the same ploy again. Lee sent Lt. Gen. Jubal A. Early's Second Army Corps away from his lines at Cold Harbor. Early marched his men to Charlottesville, where he put his force on trains of the Orange & Alexandria Railroad and transported them to Lynchburg. They arrived just in time to repulse the advance of Maj. Gen. David Hunter's army, moving up the Shenandoah Valley.[1] Early's troops joined forces with the small command of Maj. Gen. John C. Breckinridge at Lynchburg. This combined force, newly dubbed the Army of the Valley, advanced down the Valley toward the Potomac River.

Early crossed the Potomac, defeated a small force of Union troops under Maj. Gen. Lew Wallace at Monocacy Junction, Maryland, and marched on Washington, D.C. Grant had dispatched the 6th Army Corps from Petersburg, which arrived just in time to prevent Early from entering Washington on July 12. On July 24, Early defeated a force under Brig. Gen. George Crook at Kernstown, just south of Winchester. On July 30, Early sent a cavalry force under the command of Brig. Gen. John McCausland into Pennsylvania. McCausland's troopers burned the town of Chambersburg, and then rejoined Early in the Shenandoah Valley. With a force of less than twenty thousand men, Early waited for the Yankee army to come after him.

Grant had originally wanted to send Meade to the Valley to deal with Early, but he decided not to do that, fearing it would appear that Meade had been relieved of command of the Army of the Potomac after the debacle at The Crater at Petersburg. Grant's next idea was to make Maj. Gen. William B. Franklin department commander, with Sheridan as tactical commander. When the War Department rejected Franklin, Grant proposed Hunter as department commander. On August 1, Grant wrote to Halleck, "I want Sheridan put in command of all the troops in the field, with instructions to put himself south of the enemy and follow him to the death. Wherever the enemy goes let our troops go also."[2] Secretary of War Edwin M. Stanton originally opposed the appointment, believing Sheridan was too young for such a high level of command. He eventually agreed, provided that the appointment be a temporary one.[3] Hunter suggested that if Halleck mistrusted him, the best thing for the service would be for him to decline to take the appointment, which he did. Thus, Sheridan ended up in overall command of the Middle Military District in spite of Stanton's objections.[4] "I am glad that you have given Sheridan the command of the forces to defend Washington," wrote Sherman in a letter to Grant. "He will worry Early to death."[5]

The next day, Sheridan reported to Grant at Monocacy Junction, where he took command of the 6th and two divisions of the 19th Army Corps, the Army of West Virginia, and the available cavalry forces. He had good subordinate commanders—the steady Maj. Gen. Horatio G. Wright commanded the Sixth Corps, Maj. Gen. William H. Emory commanded the Nineteenth Corps detachment, which had served along the Gulf of Mexico, and Brig. Gen. George Crook, Sheridan's former roommate, commanded the Army of West Virginia. Crook, in particular, proved to be a real asset to Little Phil. He was a fine tactician and possessed a first-rate mind. Sheridan would owe much of his success in the Valley to his oldest and closest friend.

After consulting with Grant at Monocacy on August 6, Sheridan moved to Harpers Ferry and took command. Grant issued explicit orders. "In pushing up the Shenandoah Valley, as it is expected you will have to go, first or last, it is desirable that nothing should be left to invite the enemy to return. Take all provisions, forage, and stock wanted for the use of your command; such as cannot be consumed, destroy," wrote the lieutenant general. "It is not desirable that the buildings should be destroyed; they should rather be protected; but the people should be informed that so long as an army can subsist among them recurrences of these raids must be expected, and we are determined to stop them at all hazards. Bear in mind the object is to drive the enemy south, and to do this you want to keep him always in sight. Be guided in your course by the course he takes." He concluded with decisive and important instructions: "Give the enemy no rest, and if it is possible to follow to the Virginia Central Railroad, follow that far. Do all the damage to railroads and crops you can. Carry off stock of all descriptions, and negroes, so as to prevent further planting. If the war is to last another year, we want the Shenandoah Valley to remain a barren waste."[6]

Sheridan had his work cut out for him. "My object was to destroy, to the best of my ability, that which was truly the Confederacy—its armies . . . every officer and man was made to understand that when a victory was gained," noted Sheridan in his report of the campaign, "it was not more than their duty, nor less than their country expected from her gallant sons."[7] His consolidated force of nearly forty-five thousand men was dubbed the Army of the Shenandoah and was responsible for the defense of the Middle Military Division, consisting of Maryland and the Shenandoah Valley region. Grant also gave Sheridan authority to choose his own cavalry commander. As senior division commander, Brig. Gen. William Woods Averell was entitled to the command.[8] Averell's force, which had been an independent command, merged with the veteran units from the Army of the Potomac. However, Sheridan exercised the discretion granted him by Grant and appointed Torbert chief of cavalry for the newly formed army. Merritt took command of the First Division, Averell commanded the Second Division, and Wilson the Third Division. In all, Sheridan's Army of the Shenandoah would generally outnumber Early's little army by about three to one as the campaign wore on.[9]

Sheridan took a few days to consolidate his new army and put his infrastructure into place. He knew that Early was camped near Little North Mountain, northwest of Winchester, about twelve miles from Harpers Ferry. He planned an advance that would flank Early out of his strong positions, place his army to the south of Early's army, as Grant had ordered and which would induce the Confederate commander to come out and fight. On August 10, Sheridan began his advance down the Valley. The Northern army moved to Berryville by way of Charles Town. As expected, Early retreated toward Winchester, and for two days the armies moved down the Valley. However, Grant had heard rumors that Longstreet's infantry corps was also on its way to the Valley to join Early. Early had in fact received Maj. Gen. Joseph Kershaw's division from Longstreet's Corps, but not the entire corps. Realizing that Sheridan's force was not strong enough to defeat two corps, Grant instructed Sheridan to go on the defensive, which he did promptly. Sheridan consulted the maps to find a suitable defensive position and then withdrew past Winchester to Halltown and, with the exception of cavalry missions, declined to give battle for nearly a month.

A skirmish took place on August 25, near Shepherdstown. Custer's Wolverines were taken by surprise and were chased across the Potomac River by gray-clad cavalrymen. Custer turned the tables on the Rebels, sending the Sixth Michigan Cavalry forward in a mounted saber charge. James H. Kidd acerbically noted, "That [the Michigan Brigade] escaped no thanks were due to General Torbert."[10]

Little Phil had not had an encouraging start. On August 26, correspondent James E. Taylor noted, "After an auspicious opening, in which he had penetrated to the upper valley within 20 days, he was back and bottled up in the works he left, which he honestly expected he would not again reoccupy while an armed grayback was in the valley. . . . That the general felt keenly this humiliating termination of his first essay in his new field, goes for the saying, and that it was looked upon with alarm by the Federal authorities in Washington cannot be questioned. Was history about to repeat itself in the valley, and was another military grave being dug?"[11] A few days later, Col. Rutherford B. Hayes, future president and commander of one of Crook's brigades, noted in a letter, "General Sheridan's splendid cavalry do a great share of the work; we look on and rest."[12]

Sheridan did not impress the Confederates. "When we move up the enemy fall back, and when they come in force we edge off to toll them up the valley," noted Brig. Gen. Bryan Grimes of North Carolina. "So far Genl Early has been very Successful indeed in all his Maneuvers."[13] Another of Early's soldiers echoed a similar theme. "About the prospect of a fight I cannot speak with much certainty," reported a Southerner on September 7. "It seems to be Genl. Sheridan's policy to avoid [one]."[14]

In mid-September, Grant cautioned Sheridan not to take the offensive "with the advantage against you."[15] A couple of days later, Sheridan pointed out that the Opequon Creek, which separated the two enemies, was a formidable barrier, and indicated that he intended to remain on the defensive, waiting to see what Early would do.[16] As a result of Sheridan's inactivity, Early returned a portion of his command, troops from the Army of Northern Virginia's First Corps, to Lee at Petersburg. On September 15, Kershaw's Division moved out for Petersburg, weakening the Army of the Valley.

Halleck and Stanton had instructed Sheridan to be cautious in his dealings with Early, and Sheridan had taken those instructions to heart. However, Grant worried about Sheridan's lack of activity and grew frustrated with his subordinate's complacency in the face of Early's army. "My purpose was to have him attack Early," Grant recalled, "or drive him out of the valley and destroy that

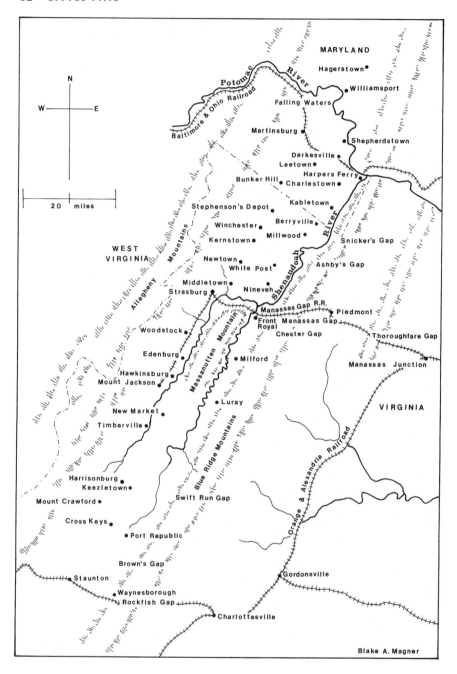

The Shenandoah Valley

source of supplies for Lee's army. I knew it was impossible for me to get orders through Washington to Sheridan to make a move, because they would be stopped there and such orders as Halleck's caution (and that of the Secretary of War) would suggest would be given instead, and would, no doubt, be contradictory to mine."[17] As a consequence, on September 16, Grant traveled to the Valley to confer with his subordinate, as he now believed that the time had come to drive the Confederates from the Valley. The two officers met at Charles Town. After reviewing the situation, Sheridan assured Grant that he could whip Early's army, and that he was preparing to do so. Grant, who had taken the liberty to draw up plans for the campaign, elected not to use them, and instead inquired whether Sheridan could advance within four days. When Sheridan assured the lieutenant general that he could move in the allotted time, Grant said simply, "Go in."[18] Sheridan spent the next few days finalizing his plans. He got help from Early, who sent a brigade of his cavalry and two infantry divisions off on an expedition toward Martinsburg to destroy the B&O railroad there, further reducing the strength of his little army.

On September 19, Sheridan attacked Early's position at Winchester. Cavalry Corps chief Torbert's instructions to his subordinates were clear and simple: "the move means fight."[19] These instructions proved prophetic. The gigantic Federal mounted force vastly outnumbered Early's horsemen, and this numeric disparity would tip the balance in the fight at Winchester. Wilson's horse soldiers kicked off the attack, splashing across the Opequon Creek at sunrise, followed by the Sixth Corps. An officer of Custer's Michigan Brigade commented, "Nothing was said, but every one knew that the army was in motion and that great things were in store for us."[20]

Sheridan had developed a battle plan that required speed, stealth, and coordination that his command could not execute. Further, Early had learned that Grant was in Charles Town, and had fallen back as a result. The Nineteenth Corps infantry, which was to support the Sixth Corps, did not kick off its attack as planned, ruining Sheridan's schedule for the day. Early launched a counterattack that turned the right flank of the Sixth Corps and drove one of the Federal divisions into the Berryville canyon. Early, an able tactician, had properly assessed Sheridan's plan, and had pulled off a stunning reversal of fortune with his successful counterattack. "By noon the battle was rather against [us]," reported Col. Hayes. "The Rebels were jubilant and in Winchester were cheering and rejoicing over the victory."[21]

One of Sheridan's division commanders, Brig. Gen. David Russell, fell mortally wounded while leading a counterattack. Recognizing that his plan was not working, Sheridan rode his lines, thundering profanity in an effort to rally his panicked troops. "Then it was that he, Sheridan, himself seeing the danger dashed up and for the first time in his history in the Valley, treated the infantry-men to a taste of the sweetest swearing that they had ever heard," recounted an observer. "The only time that he was heard to swear in such fearfully profane style was when the troops were breaking as in this instance, and the line in dan-ger, then he seemed to be beside himself. Ordering up a reserve brigade, he threw himself among [Brig. Gen. Cuvier] Grover's fugitives and fairly cursed them back into the lines, raving in such a fearful manner that they feared him more than the enemy."[22] Sheridan had tried to implement an unduly complicated battle plan that nearly led to the destruction of his army. Early's army had fought hard, and its execution was nearly flawless. Only hard fighting by Sheridan's larger force saved his infantry from being destroyed.

Years later, when he penned his memoirs, Sheridan remained defensive about his conduct of the battle. "The battle was not fought out on the plan in accor-dance with which marching orders were issued to my troops," he claimed. "I then hoped to take Early in detail, and with Crook's force cut off his retreat. I adhered to this purpose during the early part of the contest, but was obliged to abandon the idea because of unavoidable delays by which I was prevented from getting the Sixth and Nineteenth corps through the narrow defile and into position early enough to destroy Ramseur while still isolated." Blaming the delays and the change in plans on Wright, Sheridan claimed, "although the ultimate results did, in a measure, vindicate the change, yet I have always thought that by ad-hering to the original plan we might have captured the bulk of Early's army."[23] Crook's determined attack finally succeeded in turning Early's flank, and the stage was set for one of the most dramatic events of the Civil War.

As the infantry fight raged, the blue-clad cavalry looked for an opportunity to contribute. Breckinridge's division and a small force of cavalry blocked Mer-ritt's division, and two brigades of Confederate cavalry blocked Wilson's division on the left. Col. Kidd remembered, "During the long hours of morning the dismounted troopers reclined on the ground in front of their horses, gaily chat-ting and smoking, or cooking coffee, giving little heed to the ever-increasing roar of artillery and rattle of musketry, which, though it could not intimidate, too plainly indicated the desperate nature of the conflict. The sun had reached the meridian, and still the din of battle did not recede." The blue-clad troopers remained stymied from sunup until almost one-thirty that afternoon.[24]

About two-forty-five, Crook's men launched a counterattack that turned Early's left flank and pinned down the Confederate forces. As a result, Early pre-pared to break off the engagement and withdraw. When the Union cavalry finally broke through and dispersed the gray-clad horsemen, Torbert ordered a

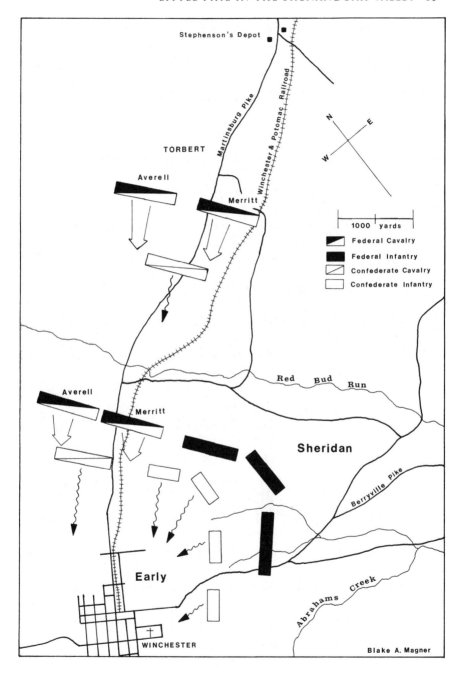

Third Winchester, September 19, 1864

massed mounted charge along a five-brigade front. The Yankee troopers started forward, first at a walk, then at a trot, and finally at a gallop. One Ohio foot soldier recalled that it was "the most gallant and exciting cavalry charge I ever saw." One member of the 5th Michigan Cavalry proudly remembered, "ten thousand troopers went forward on a charge with sabres gleaming in the sun and with a cheer that would enthuse a dead man. The scene was grand beyond description."[25] A Vermonter noted, "It was like a thunder-clap out of a clear sky, and the bolt struck home." One Wolverine recalled that the charge had to be the "grandest sight I saw during my army life." A New Yorker wrote, "Every man's saber was waving above his head, and with a savage yell, we swept down upon the trembling wretches like a besom of destruction."[26]

"The bands playing national airs, presented in the sunlight one moving mass of glittering sabers," Custer recounted colorfully. "This, combined with the various and bright-colored banners and battle-flags, intermingled here and there with the plain blue uniforms of the troops, furnished one of the most inspiring as well as imposing scenes of martial grandeur ever witnessed on a battle-field. No encouragement was needed to inspirit either man or horse."[27] Kidd also described the spectacle, recounting, "The Michigan brigade was on the left of the turnpike; to its left, the brigades of Devin and Lowell; on the right, Averell's division of two brigades—five brigades in all—each brigade in line of squadron columns, double ranks. This made a front of more than half a mile, three lines deep, of mounted men. That is to say, it was more than half a mile from Averell's right to Merritt's left." He added, "At almost the same moment of time, the entire line emerged from the woods into the sunlight. A more enlivening and imposing spectacle never was seen. Guidons fluttered and sabers glistened. Officers vied with their men in gallantry and in zeal. Even the horses seemed to catch the inspiration of the scene and emulated the martial ardor of their riders."[28] As the bugles called the charge, the vast mounted blue juggernaut quickly swept away the gray-clad resistance blocking its path. The road to Winchester lay open. The stage was set. Wesley Merritt later observed, "The field was open for cavalry operations such as the war had not seen."[29]

Dropping like a bombshell, the massed cavalry charge hit Early's lines as his withdrawal commenced. Kidd recalled, "I marvel exceedingly that then and there no effort was made to resist the charge by forming the hollow square, with its wall of bayonets; nor do I remember that it was resorted to under similar circumstances, during the war, although every regiment in either army was drilled in the evolution."[30] With the Wolverines in the van of the charge, the overwhelming blue wave tipped the scale of the battle. Carried away by the success of the charge, Custer told Maj. Charles Deane, of the 6th Michigan

Cavalry, "Major, this is the bulliest day since Christ was born."[31] One of Sheridan's staff officers claimed that the charge "sent the enemy whirling through Winchester."[32]

Only a stubborn stand by Confederate cavalry south of Winchester saved Early's army from total destruction. Maj. Gen. Robert Rodes, one of Early's division commanders, was killed in action. It was a great victory for Sheridan, bought by the hard fighting of his infantry and an improvised but successful attack by Crook that turned Early's flank and opened the door to victory. Sheridan's army suffered forty-five hundred casualties in the day's fighting. Sheridan failed to follow up on his victory by pursuing the Confederate army, to bring it to bay. In spite of the poor battle plan, Sheridan received a promotion to brigadier general in the Regular Army as a reward for the victory.[33] Early later wrote, "The enemy's very great superiority in cavalry and the comparative inefficiency of ours turned the scale against us."[34] Trooper John N. Opie, of the 6th Virginia Cavalry, observed, "What was left of our army now lost all confidence in General Early as a leader, and they were therefore much demoralized."[35]

The good news soon reached the Army of the Potomac. Col. Charles Wainwright scrawled in his diary, "At times I cannot help thinking that these victories are the beginning of the end, the death-blows to the rebellion. Certain it is that either Sheridan has an overwhelming majority of numbers, or the life has gone out of the rebels, for his best troops are from the Army of the Potomac, which has never been able to gain such complete victories as these."[36]

With Crook's men in pursuit as far as Milltown, Early formed a line of battle at Newtown, inviting Sheridan to give battle, an invitation declined by the Federal commander. Crook finally gave up the chase when a strong force of Confederate cavalry blocked his pursuit. Early then fell back to Fisher's Hill, south of Strasburg. Taking up a strong position atop the eminence of Fisher's Hill, Early's battered army licked its wounds and waited for Sheridan's inevitable pursuit. On September 21, the Army of the Valley moved on Fisher's Hill. Grant's chief engineer, Col. Cyrus B. Comstock, who inspected the position a few weeks later, observed, "The position was a strong one and could only have been carried as it was by a flank attack."[37] Crook developed a plan for his divisions, supported by Averell's cavalry, to flank Early's army out of its strong position on Fisher's Hill. Sheridan adopted the plan, and it went like clockwork.

Crook concealed his men in heavy timber north of Cedar Creek on the night of September 20, and they spent the next day hiding in the woods. On the afternoon of September 22, he crossed Cedar Creek and marched to Fisher's Hill under cover of ravines and heavy woods to the base of Little North Mountain. Taking position on Early's far left, Crook deployed his men into two columns, and at about four o'clock, the West Virginians unleashed a vicious flanking attack that crashed into the end of the Southern line.[38] They emerged with "triumphant shouts" and swept Lomax's dismounted cavalrymen from their rifle pits, "whom they sent, like startled rabbits, flying before him."[39] When he heard the sounds of Crook's flank attack, Little Phil cried, "By God, Crook is driving them!" Sheridan then unleashed a fierce frontal attack by the Sixth Corps, sweeping Early's little army off Fisher's Hill. He trailed the Sixth Corps infantrymen up the slope of Fisher's Hill, bellowing, "Run boys, run! Don't wait to form! Don't let them stop!" When a flatfoot called back that he was tired, Sheridan responded, "If you can't run, holler!"[40] Crook's well-laid plan worked. Emory's Nineteenth Corps detachment briefly pursued the fleeing butternuts up the Valley before Early's infantry blocked the pursuit at Tom's Brook on the Valley Pike, ending the chase and permitting Early's beaten army to escape intact.

That night, a triumphant Sheridan reported the victory to Grant: "I have the honor to report that I achieved a most signal victory over the army of General Early at Fisher's Hill to-day." After recounting the day's action, Sheridan claimed, "only darkness has saved the whole of Early's army from total destruction."[41] He intended to follow up his victory by sending two divisions of horse soldiers after Early's beaten ranks.

That same day, as Sheridan prepared to assault Fisher's Hill, Torbert, with almost two full divisions, led the Union cavalry on an expedition up the Valley toward Luray. In a running fight, Wilson's troopers encountered Thomas T. Munford's Rebel cavalry strongly positioned on high ground. Calling off the attack, and unsure of the results of the fight at Fisher's Hill, Torbert balked. He justified his decision in his report to Sheridan: "Not knowing that the army had made an attack at Fisher's Hill, and thinking that the sacrifice would be too great to attack without that knowledge, I concluded to withdraw to a point opposite McCoy's Ferry."[42] Sheridan never forgave Torbert for the failure to press the advantage gained by the victory at Fisher's Hill. "Had General Torbert driven this cavalry or turned the defile and reached New Market," complained Little Phil in his official report of the Campaign, "I have no doubt that we would have captured the entire rebel army."[43] Years later, when he wrote his memoirs, Little Phil was far more straightforward in his criticism of his cavalry chief. He accused Torbert of making only a feeble effort and stated that "to this day, I have been unable to account satisfactorily for Torbert's failure."[44]

Late on September 23 Sheridan relieved Averell; the next day, he placed Col. William H. Powell in command of Averell's division. Custer briefly commanded this division from September 27 until October 1, when he assumed command of Wilson's Third Division.[45] This move was very unpopular with the men of

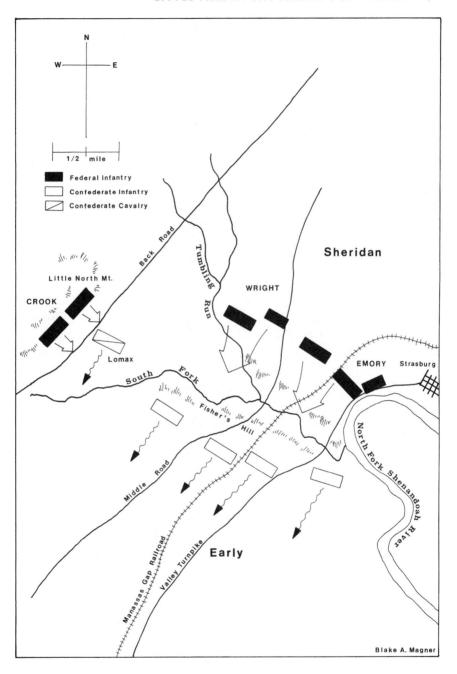

Fisher's Hill, September 22, 1864

the Michigan Brigade; more than four hundred Wolverines signed petitions asking that their brigade be transferred to the Third Division, a request that Sheridan denied.[46] Sheridan advanced to Harrisonburg, where he remained for two weeks.

On October 5, Early received reinforcements, including the return of Kershaw's division of infantry, and the small cavalry brigade of Maj. Gen. Thomas L. Rosser, Custer's West Point classmate and close friend. Rosser assumed command of a division of cavalry on October 5, including a veteran brigade drawn from the Shenandoah Valley. The locals proclaimed Rosser "Savior of the Valley," a moniker that haunted him in the coming weeks. Rosser's men knew what to expect. Gunner George M. Neese of Chew's Battery of horse artillery noted in his diary on October 4, "General Sheridan is in command of the Yankee army in the Valley of the Shenandoah, and if he has the men that he had at Trevilian Station, there will be some tough work on the boards yet this fall, for his cavalry is made out of first-class fighting stuff."[47]

During the first week of October, Sheridan ordered the Valley destroyed, taking the war to the civilian population. He wrote, "The destruction of the grain and forage from here to Staunton will be a terrible blow to [the Confederates]."[48] Known as "The Burning," the devastation of civilian farms and farm stocks enraged the locals. In November, an ugly episode of mutual hangings took place, with several of the Wolverines hanged in retaliation for the hanging of several of Lt. Col. John Singleton Mosby's men in Front Royal on September 23 upon Merritt's orders.[49] Mosby's guerrillas had also killed Lt. John R. Meigs, son of the Union quartermaster general, Maj. Gen. Montgomery Meigs, and Sheridan was in a rage.

One Rebel horse soldier, out on picket duty, recorded in his diary on October 6, "about 9 o'clock our cavalry began to advance + we were ordered to join our regiment, which we did near a place called Dayton. . . . All along our route were burning barns houses etc. The beautiful + fertile Valley of Virginia is in one vast cloud of smoke, + the very air is impregnated with the smell of burning property. I found a plank left by the Yankees, on which was written 'Remember Chambersburg.'"[50] Another observer commented, "The fire demon reigned supreme."[51] An officer of the Michigan Brigade noted that he did not relish the task of destroying the beautiful valley, later commenting, "What I saw there is burned into my memory."[52] A year after the war, he wrote, "the Valley of the Shenandoah . . . before the rebellion was the 'Eden of America,' but at the war's termination, was a desolate mass, with scarcely a barn, storehouse, mill, or fence, to relieve the monotony of the scene."[53] As Torbert's inferno spread northward, Rosser's troopers constantly annoyed the Federal flanks with probing attacks, as the Southern horse soldiers tried to protect their homes from the Yankee horde.[54]

"I rode down the Valley with the advance after Sheridan's retreating cavalry beneath great columns of smoke which almost shut out the sun by day, and in the red glare of bonfires," recounted Maj. Henry Kyd Douglas, a Confederate staff officer, "which all across the Valley poured out flames and sparks heavenward and crackled mockingly in the night air; and I saw mothers and maidens tearing their hair and shrieking to Heaven in their fright and despair, and little children, voiceless and tearless in their pitiable terror."[55] Sheridan later reported that more than two thousand barns filled with grain and implements, and more than seventy mills laden with wheat and flour, had been destroyed. In addition, more than seven thousand head of livestock were either confiscated or killed. He proudly noted, "This destruction embraces the Luray Valley and Little Fort Valley as well as the main valley . . . when this is completed, the Valley from Winchester up to Staunton, ninety-two miles, will have little in it for man or beast."[56]

In response, Early ordered his cavalry "to pursue the enemy, to harass him and to ascertain his purposes."[57] On October 8, Rosser moved to intercept the cavalry forces destroying the Valley. They collided at Tom's Brook, south of Strasburg. "Mad clear through" with Rosser's harassment, Sheridan instructed Torbert to "start out at daylight and whip the rebel cavalry or get whipped yourself," and ordered his cavalry chief to "finish this 'Savior of the Valley.'"[58]

On the morning of October 9, a massed attack by the Federal cavalry at Tom's Brook near Woodstock caught the Confederates in both the front and the flank. Custer's Third Division attacked on the Union right, while the First Division assaulted the left and center of Rosser's line. Torbert's horsemen drove the Rebel cavalrymen off the field in a wild rout, with their Yankee foes following for twenty miles before finally giving up the pursuit. Merritt, commanding the First Division, wrote, "The success of the day was now merely a question of the endurance of horseflesh. Each time our troopers came into view, they would rush on the discomfited rebels with their sabers, and send them howling in every direction." The pursuit only ended when the fleeing Rebels reached Early's infantry lines nearly twenty-six miles away. The defeat was total and was quickly dubbed "The Woodstock Races"; Merritt later reported taking forty-two wagons, three ambulances, four cannons, four caissons, five forges, twenty-five sets of harnesses, sixty-eight horses and mules, fifty-two prisoners, a wagon loaded with Enfield rifles, and the battle flag of the 34th Battalion of Virginia Cavalry.[59] A Michigan trooper crowed in his diary that Tom's Brook "was one of the worst whipens [sic] that the Reb cav ever got."[60] Lt. Robert C. Wallace of the 5th Michigan Cavalry gloated, "This cavalry fight was the most complete clean-up that had yet occurred and taught the enemy that the Yankee Cavalry was to be reckoned with and was no longer the joke it had been in the early part of the war."[61]

Custer captured Rosser's personal baggage and gleefully wore his old friend's dress uniform coat, even sending Rosser a taunting note asking the Texan "if he would have his tailor make the coattails of his next uniform somewhat shorter so it would fit better when [Sheridan] captured it."[62] Sheridan lost only nine killed and forty-eight wounded in achieving a victory "beyond my power to describe."[63] "After this catastrophe, Early reported to General Lee that his cavalry was so badly demoralized that it should be dismounted," Little Phil later recounted in his memoirs, "and the citizens of the valley, intensely disgusted with the boasting and swaggering that had characterized the arrival of the 'Laurel Brigade' in that section, baptized the action (known to us as Tom's Brook) the 'Woodstock Races,' and never tired of poking fun at General Rosser about his precipitate and inglorious flight."[64]

In fact, Early complained, "God knows I have done all in my power to avert the disasters which have befallen this command; but the fact is that the enemy's cavalry is so much superior to ours, both in numbers and equipment, and the country is so favorable to the operations of cavalry, that it is impossible for ours to compete with his." He concluded, "It would be better if they could all be put into the infantry; but if that were tried I am afraid they would all run off."[65] "I had hoped that when Gen. Rosser came up here that he would inaugurate a change—but he also appears to have come demoralized—that must be something contagious in this atmosphere or in the Valley Cavalry for they cause everything to stampede that comes in association with them," Confederate Brig. Gen. Bryan Grimes reported to his wife. "If I had a dictum in this matter at least one hundred of them would have been suspended on gibbets this morning as a warning to others . . . perhaps they would then rather risk their chances in battle than to be hung."[66] After the great victory at Tom's Brook, the Army of the Shenandoah encamped near Cedar Creek, blissfully unaware that Early was planning to unleash a massed attack on its camps.

After Fisher's Creek, Grant had suggested that Sheridan cross the Blue Ridge, advance on Charlottesville and the Virginia Central Railroad, and destroy Lee's lines of supply before marching east to join Meade's army at Petersburg. Claiming that it would be exceedingly difficult for his army to cross the Blue Ridge, Sheridan had steadfastly refused to do so. Instead of the aggressive action advocated by Grant, Sheridan turned cautious. He claimed that there were insufficient supplies available to provision his army, and suggested that the campaign end with the burning of crops and not with an aggressive movement east. Sheridan convinced Grant that his plan was the proper course of action, and a sterling opportunity to win the war slipped away.

"In a day or day and a half of good marching, the Union infantry and artillery could have been in Charlottesville," observed Wert. "Early, if he contested the

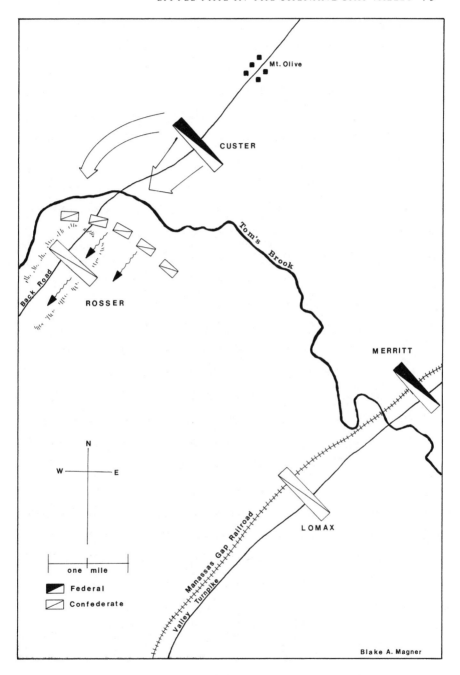

Tom's Brook, October 9, 1864

advance, would have had to do it at Waynesborough, with his outnumbered army with its back against the mountain and its escape route through one narrow gap. Sheridan had the chance to strike a mortal blow to the Confederacy, most likely shortening the war in the East by months." Instead, Sheridan responded by being passive and offering a barrage of excuses.[67]

Early ordered a reconnaissance in force on the morning of October 13. His men set out from their camps and soon encountered Federal infantry near Hupp's Hill, not far from Strasburg. Early's first shells caught the Yankees by surprise, but they quickly rallied and started fighting back. A brisk fight developed, with one of Sheridan's brigade commanders, Col. George Wells, mortally wounded in combat. Early's men repulsed a Federal attack and drove the Yankee troops back across Cedar Creek. As night fell, Early broke off the engagement, which had raged for several hours. Between them, the two sides suffered more than four hundred casualties in the stubborn fight. Early then pulled back to his old position atop Fisher's Hill, retaking the very trenches Sheridan had driven him from just three weeks earlier. In the meantime, Little Phil had sent the Sixth Corps off to Alexandria, to rejoin the Army of the Potomac. However, on October 13, Sheridan countermanded that order and instructed the Sixth Corps to rejoin the Army of the Valley. It seemed nothing had changed.[68]

Sheridan received instructions to come to Washington as soon as possible to meet with Secretary of War Stanton and Halleck; Maj. Gen. Horatio G. Wright, the senior corps commander, would run the Army of the Shenandoah in his absence.

The army had selected a good defensive position straddling the Valley Pike and along the banks of Cedar Creek. The position had been intended to be a brief layover on the army's way up the Valley. Only part of the force entrenched and prepared rifle pits while the commanding general was gone. In addition, Col. William H. Powell's division (formerly Averell's command) did not position itself correctly to cover the army's left flank, leaving a hole in the Federal left. Torbert, the chief of cavalry, probably deserves the blame for these poor dispositions. Early's Confederates would exploit that hole.

Wright, commanding the army in Sheridan's absence, actually ordered a reconnaissance in force for the morning of October 19, intending to send three brigades of infantry and a cavalry brigade out to find the Confederates. He never got the opportunity. That morning, with Sheridan at Winchester on his way back from the strategy meetings in Washington, Early stole a march on the Yankee army and launched a massive surprise attack on the Army of the Shenandoah. One day earlier, Capt. Jedediah Hotchkiss, Stonewall Jackson's superb engineer, and Maj. Gen. John B. Gordon, one of Early's division commanders, climbed to the top of Massanutten Mountain to survey the disposition of the Union camps. From this vantage point, Gordon and Hotchkiss determined that the Army of the Shenandoah's flank was in the air and that it was ripe for an attack.

"When I left my command on the 16th," claimed Sheridan in his memoirs, "little did I anticipate that anything like this would happen. Indeed, I felt satisfied that Early was, of himself, too weak to take the offensive." He continued, "Still the surprise of the morning might have befallen me as well as the general on whom it did descend."[69]

"My plan was to dismount our cavalry and attack Sheridan's Cavalry when dismounted, and keep them from moving," recalled Gordon. "I knew if we could do this, we would gain a great victory."[70]

The area south of Cedar Creek was difficult ground for offensive operations. Adopting Hotchkiss and Gordon's recommendations, Early devised a complex, five-pronged attack that required a great deal of coordination. His force was greatly outnumbered, but Early counted on the element of surprise to even the odds. It was a brilliant plan, worthy of Stonewall Jackson's Valley veterans. Catching the blue-clad soldiers in their camps in a heavy fog, Early's massed flank attack met with initial success, driving Maj. Gen. William H. Emory's routed Union solders several miles west until they fell back to Wright's position near Middletown before they rallied and stiffened their resistance. Stubborn resistance by the Sixth Corps forced Early to pause to consolidate and realign his lines, giving the Federals sufficient time to rally and reform their lines.

In the meantime, Sheridan rode more than ten miles straight to the battlefield. He mounted about nine in the morning, and spent the next hour and a half riding hard to the sound of the guns. "I felt," he claimed, "that I ought to try now to restore their broken ranks, or, failing in that, to share their fate because of what they had done hitherto."[71] Several miles from the battlefield, he encountered panicked Yankee soldiers, fleeing to the rear. "Boys, if you don't want to fight yourselves," he thundered, "come back at others fighting. We will whip them out of their boots before 4 o'clock."[72] As he neared the front, he spotted demoralized Federals skulking by the side of the road. "Boys, turn back," bellowed Sheridan, "face the other way! I am going to sleep in that camp to-night or hell!"[73] Sheridan arrived on the battlefield about ten-thirty, where he found his demoralized corps commanders. Torbert was the first to greet him, saying, "My God! I'm glad you have come!"[74]

Sheridan rode out to check on his army's dispositions. Approaching the Sixth Corps' Vermont Brigade, a colonel sang out, "General, we're glad to see you!" Sheridan responded, "Well, by God, I'm glad to be here!" After spotting the army commander's return, the men "sprang to their feet and cheered as only

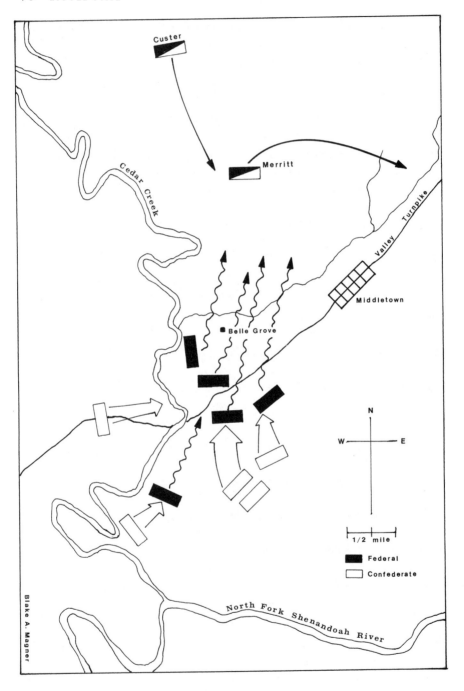

Custer

Merritt

Cedar Creek

Valley Turnpike

Middletown

Belle Grove

N

W — E

1/2 mile

Federal

Confederate

North Fork Shenandoah River

Blake A. Magner

Cedar Creek, October 19, 1864

men under such circumstances can. . . . Hope and confidence returned at a bound. No longer did we merely hope that the worst was over, that we could hold our ground until night," wrote a Northern infantryman, "or, at worst, make good an orderly retreat to Winchester. Now we all burned to attack the enemy, to drive him back, to retrieve our honor and sleep in our old camp that night."[75]

Sheridan rode back to consult with Wright and Emory. A tired, demoralized, and bleeding Wright said, "Well, we've done the best we could." In fact, Wright, whose face had been creased by a bullet, had rallied his men and halted their retreat. While the crisis had passed, the situation remained dangerous, and the ultimate outcome of the fight remained in doubt. Emory suggested that once his corps was reorganized, his troops could cover the retreat to Winchester. "Retreat, hell," harrumphed Sheridan, "we'll be back in our camps tonight."[76] Wright had already rallied the troops, who were fighting back, tenaciously holding their ground. The tide of the battle had already turned by the time that Sheridan arrived, but his sheer force of will and personality would help to convert the morning's losses to a Northern victory.

In the meantime, the opposing cavalry forces had engaged. Rosser was ordered to "occupy the enemy's cavalry" while the infantry attack stepped off, and his skirmishers pinned down the Wolverines along the banks of Cedar Creek.[77] Rosser's troopers engaged Col. William Wells's brigade near the bank road about the time that Early's main assault kicked off. Rosser's Confederates stalemated Wells's horsemen until nearly two o'clock that afternoon, effectively removing them from the fight.

While Wells struggled against Rosser, Torbert deployed his cavalry, who brushed Rosser out of their way and marched across the farm fields, drawing artillery fire the whole way. Col. Alexander C. M. Pennington's brigade went to cover the Sixth Corps and then moved to the Valley Pike. Col. Charles R. Lowell's Reserve Brigade drew the task of supporting Emory's dawn reconnaissance in force while Merritt's troopers rounded up stragglers. The Michigan Cavalry Brigade moved east along the Old Forge Road and took up a position to the east of the Valley Road. The Wolverines remained mounted, ready to go into combat at a moment's notice. There, they had a vista of the fight unfolding in front of them.

About three-thirty, the Yankee infantry received orders to advance. Emory's infantrymen turned Gordon's flank and shoved Early's infantry back. As he prepared to commence the all-out counterattack, Sheridan ordered Merritt to charge a Rebel battery. Merritt sent three brigades forward across the farm fields, chasing away the battery and clearing the way for the infantry attack. Kidd commented, "Heavens, what a din! All along the Confederate line the cannon volleyed and thundered . . . the Union artillery replied, the roll of musketry became incessant."[78] However, the charge succeeded at the cost of the life of Col. Charles Russell Lowell, commander of Merritt's Reserve Brigade.

Merritt later wrote, "The [Michigan Brigade], in column of regiments in line, moved forward like an immense wave, slowly at first, but gathering strength and speed as it progressed, overwhelmed a battery and its supports amidst a desolating shower of canister and a deadly fire of musketry at short range." He crowed, "Never has the mettle of the division been put to a severer test than at this time, and never did it stand the test better."[79]

Sheridan's counterattack, now unimpeded by the battery, pitched into the Confederates, who made a stand for nearly an hour before one of Early's division commanders, Maj. Gen. Stephen Dodson Ramseur, fell mortally wounded. After Ramseur fell, the demoralized Confederates broke and ran. An enraged Early watched his broken ranks streaming back all the way to Fisher's Hill, bellowing, "Run, run, God damn you, they will get you!"[80] Torbert proudly wrote, "The service of the cavalry on this day to the army and the country can never be appreciated."[81] What began as a major disaster for Sheridan turned into a great victory, with Early's army once again scattered and demoralized. The Army of the Shenandoah had won again, but the toll had been severe—Little Phil's army suffered six thousand casualties that day, at least in part as a result of Sheridan's haphazard dispositions.[82] A Federal officer correctly observed of Early, "His prestige was gone, his army destroyed and, from that moment, for the Confederacy to continue this hopeless struggle was criminal folly."[83]

Col. Thomas C. Devin's cavalry brigade battled Brig. Gen. John Pegram's division until Pegram crossed Cedar Creek and broke. Devin followed Early's trains to Strasburg and captured twenty-two of Early's guns. Sheridan made no other attempt to pursue, meaning that Early's army escaped intact once again. Instead, the Army of the Shenandoah went back into camp near Cedar Creek. Rosser wryly commented, "There was no effort made by Sheridan to pursue us and really he did not appear to realize the completeness of his victory. If he had pursued vigorously on the morning of the 20th, he could have galloped over every obstruction we could have thrown in his path and could have captured Early and his army."[84] This would have denied Robert E. Lee the return of Early and his army to the siege lines at Petersburg and might have shortened the war by a few weeks. Thus, Sheridan squandered a great opportunity by not pursuing the ragged and beaten Army of the Valley with more vigor.

In spite of the defeat at Cedar Creek, the Southerners remained full of fight. "If they give us time to reorganize," said an optimistic North Carolinian, "we may still give Sheridan a lively time."[85] On November 12, Early advanced his forces north of Cedar Creek toward Middletown, and his cavalry deployed across the Valley, screening the advance. In response, Sheridan sortied Col. William Powell's cavalry division and Col. Alexander C. M. Pennington's Third Division cavalry brigade toward Nineveh Church. Pennington's men encountered Rosser's cavalry on the Back and Middle Roads, about ten miles west of Ninevah Church, and drove them back a few miles until Rosser could rally and reunite his scattered command. Reinforced by Lomax's division, the Confederates counterattacked and routed Pennington's troopers. A series of lively skirmishes broke out, particularly at Nineveh Church. There a Federal mounted charge dispersed the plucky Southern horse soldiers. Early then retreated to New Market. His foray "proved the last demonstration by the Confederates in the Lower Valley during the war."[86] On November 16, the infantry of the Army of the Valley began pulling out of the lines and moving back to return to the Army of Northern Virginia's lines at Petersburg.[87]

Despite his failure to follow up on his great victory on October 19, Sheridan later claimed that Cedar Creek "practically ended the campaign in the Shenandoah Valley. When it opened we found our enemy boastful and confident, unwilling to acknowledge that the soldiers of the Union were their equal in courage and manliness; when it closed with Cedar Creek this impression had been removed from his mind, and gave place to good sense and a strong desire to quit fighting."[88] This version belies the truth. In October 1864, Sheridan was still "scared like hell" of Early, and retired to Kernstown just as soon as the presidential ballots were cast on November 8, 1864. Nevertheless, as a reward for his great victory, Sheridan received a personal letter of congratulations from President Lincoln and a second promotion, this time to major general in the Regular Army.[89] Its assigned task evidently completed successfully, Sheridan's grand army started disbanding, as its elements returned to their original commands. The cavalry remained, for some hard work was unfinished.

For the entire campaign, Lt. Col. John Singleton Mosby's guerrillas continuously plagued Sheridan, who was unable to stop them.[90] Mosby, a thirty-year-old lawyer described by one correspondent as "the Panther of the Valley," led his 43rd Battalion of Virginia Cavalry on repeated, daring raids intended to harass the Federals. "There was a great stake to be won," wrote Mosby, "and I resolved to play a bold game to win it."[91] And play a bold game he did. In August, some of Mosby's men caught nearly thirty members of the 5th Michigan Cavalry burning houses at Berryville and killed twenty-nine of them, setting off a great hue and cry among the Federals. Later, when some of Mosby's men killed Lt. Charles McMaster of the 2nd U.S. Cavalry, the Federals retaliated by hanging a number of the Rangers on September 23. Mosby responded by executing several of the Wolverines on November 6, leaving a note on one of the corpses that read, "These men have been hung in retaliation for an equal number of Colonel Mosby's men hung by order of General Custer, at Front Royal, Measure for Measure."[92] On November 11, Mosby sent a note through the lines to Sheridan. "Hereafter any prisoner falling into my hands will be treated with the kindness due their condition, unless some new act of barbarity shall compel me reluctantly to adopt a course of policy repulsive to humanity."[93]

While there were no more reported executions, Sheridan had to devote significant resources to chasing Mosby, a fruitless effort. One Federal later wrote that Mosby's men "caused perhaps more loss than any single body of men in the enemy's service."[94] Sheridan had to dedicate a significant portion of his command to eradicate Mosby's force. Still, Sheridan still failed miserably. Despite Little Phil's best efforts, only the end of the war brought about the dissolution of Mosby's Battalion.

At the end of November, and perhaps in retaliation for the hanging of the Wolverines, Merritt led the First Cavalry Division on an expedition into the Loudoun Valley (also known as Mosby's Confederacy), looking for Mosby's Rangers. Mosby's men had killed Sheridan's chief quartermaster and medical inspector in October, and Little Phil was furious. Perhaps this raid resulted from Sheridan's embarrassment and frustration—every previous tactic had failed, from small unit actions to the destruction of homes to the hanging of Mosby's men. So Sheridan next chose brute force. "I will soon commence work on Mosby," he bragged to Grant. "Heretofore I have made no attempt to break him up, as I would have employed ten men to his one, and for the reason that I have made a scapegoat of him for the destruction of private rights. Now there is going to be an intense hatred of him in that portion of the valley which is nearly a desert." With great bluster, Sheridan proclaimed, "I will soon commence on Loudoun County, and let them know there is a God in Israel. Mosby has annoyed me considerably, but the people are beginning to see that he does not injure me a great deal, but causes a loss to them of all they have spent their lives in accumulating." He concluded, "Those people who live in the vicinity of Harper's Ferry are the most villainous in the valley, and have not yet been hurt much."[95]

Sheridan informed Brig. Gen. Jonathan D. Stevenson, the commander of the Federal garrison at Harpers Ferry, of the impending expedition. "Should any complaints come in from the citizens of Loudoun County," proclaimed Little Phil, "tell them that they have furnished too many meals to guerrillas to expect much sympathy."[96] High expectations hung over Merritt's expedition.

The First Division set off to punish Mosby. After four days of destruction, Merritt completed his mission. "In all these movements the orders from army headquarters were most fully carried out; the country on every side of the general line of march was in every instance swept over by flankers from the columns, and in this way the entire valley was gone over. The guerrillas were exceedingly careful to avoid any encounter with any of the parties, even the smallest, that were out on this duty," he reported. "Efforts were made to run them down or capture them by stratagem, but these in most instances failed. The sides of the mountain bordering the Loudoun Valley are practicable throughout their entire extent for horsemen, and the guerrillas, being few in numbers, mounted on fleet horses and thoroughly conversant with the country, had every advantage of my men."[97]

On December 21, Torbert took the First and Second Divisions on a fruitless raid up the Valley toward Gordonsville. Leaving Winchester, Torbert led the cavalry across the Blue Ridge and up the Valley. A member of the 5th Michigan Cavalry complained, "we started on an expedition up the Valley, reaching within two miles of Gordonsville, returning by way of Madison, Culpeper, Fauquier, Rappahannock, and Loudoun Counties, covering 160 miles going and returning, if in a straight line, and occupying 10 days in the worst weather of the year."[98] Custer's Third Division clashed with Rosser at Lacey Spring on December 21. Torbert pushed on toward Gordonsville, and met a repulse near the town. Frustrated, he withdrew and returned to Winchester, drawing Sheridan's ire. Failure cost Torbert his job the following spring.[99] The remaining elements of the Army of the Shenandoah went into their winter encampment. Sheridan's Valley Campaign was over. The Valley lay in shambles.

Although Phil Sheridan ultimately conquered Jubal Early and his tenacious band, does his conduct of the Valley Campaign justify the praise heaped on his performance by history? A careful review of the facts demonstrates that it was not deserved.

Initially, Sheridan utterly failed to control or stop Mosby's partisan rangers. Mosby's men proved to be a constant thorn in the side of the Yankee commander, who devoted a tremendous amount of resources to try to corral the Gray Ghost. After the war, Mosby wrote, "the main object of my campaign against Sheridan was to vex and embarrass Sheridan and, if possible, to prevent his advance into the interior of the State."[100] Mosby succeeded, perhaps beyond his wildest dreams. One Northern officer observed that "a more harassing enemy could not well be imagined."

In 1911, Mosby pointed out that Sheridan had made him "the greatest general in history, not even excepting Caesar, Hannibal, or General Grant himself," based on Sheridan's statements that even though Sheridan had "an army of 94,000 men effective for service, and Early but 15,000, that when these generals met, Sheridan's force was no larger than Early's because of the detachments out of action which had to guard attacks and skirmishes from behind." In other words, and applying Sheridan's analysis, Mosby's three hundred men neutralized nearly eighty thousand Yankee soldiers.[101] While this appears to be an exaggeration, Mosby's tiny force tied up a disproportionate amount of Federal resources and frustrated Sheridan to no end.

In spite of Sheridan's vigorous efforts, the Union did not suppress Mosby's Rangers. "From first to last," noted historian Bruce Catton, "the Northerners never really found an effective answer, not even when they had ruthless operators like Grant and Sheridan on the scene."[102] Perhaps no commander could have suppressed Mosby. However, Sheridan certainly failed. Mosby's most recent biographer, James A. Ramage, noted, "The only way Sheridan could have defeated Mosby would have been to capture or kill him or remove his sanctuary of civilian support, and [this] was politically impossible. Like American forces in Vietnam, Sheridan fought a limited war against Mosby, a fight with one hand tied behind his back . . . at the end of the war, travelers going south from Washington into Virginia saw a symbol of Mosby's victory. In the last eleven months of the conflict the Union cavalry on the early-warning screen had been on the defensive, pinned down by Mosby's men in a thirteen-mile line of stockades, two or three miles apart."[103]

Sheridan was promoted to the fourth ranking general in the U.S. Army, behind only Grant, Sherman, and Meade, for his performance in the Valley Campaign. There is no doubt that his Army of the Shenandoah prevailed, and that it vanquished Early's Army of the Valley. How brilliant was Sheridan's generalship? First, Sheridan had an overwhelming numerical advantage during the Valley campaign. For almost the entire effort, Sheridan enjoyed at least a nominal three-to-one advantage over his tenacious foe. Nearly two thousand years before the American Civil War, Sun Tzu wrote, "the art of using troops is this . . . when five times his strength, attack him."[104] Civil War doctrine dictated that a ratio of at least two to one was necessary for an aggressor to prevail. By the dictates of warfare, Sheridan had the capability to defeat Early. But did Sheridan have the leadership and tactical skills to do so?

Ironically, Sheridan recognized this himself. His oldest and closest friend, George Crook, recorded Little Phil's words, spoken while he basked in the light of his victory at Cedar Creek. That night, Sheridan and his generals sat around a roaring fire, rehashing the day's events. With uncharacteristic candor, Sheridan turned to Crook and said, "Crook, I am going to get much more credit for this than I deserve, for, had I been here in the morning the same thing would have taken place, and had I not returned today, the same thing would have taken place." Crook later noted that "this statement was full of meat, but made little impression on me at the time."[105] While Sheridan gets credit for brilliant generalship, even he might have recognized that his role in the campaign would be overstated by history.

Jubal Early demonstrated superior generalship throughout most of the campaign. Sheridan employed unimaginative and often flawed tactics. His plan for Third Winchester nearly caused his own defeat when he tried to implement it. In spite of his numeric inferiority, Early nearly inflicted a catastrophic defeat upon the Army of the Shenandoah. Only Crook's successful flank attack carried the day. "A skillful and energetic commander of the enemy's forces would have crushed Ramseur before any assistance could have reached him, and thus ensured the destruction of my whole force," Early wrote years after the war, "and later in the day, when the battle had turned against us, with the immense superiority in cavalry which Sheridan had, and the advantage of the open country would have destroyed my whole force and captured everything I had." Acidly, the Confederate commander concluded, "As it was, considering the immense disparity in numbers and equipment, the enemy had very little to boast of. . . . When I look back to this battle, I can but attribute my escape from utter annihilation to the incapacity of my opponent."[106]

In addition to Crook, Sheridan had good subordinates to carry out his wishes. Competent men such as Wright, Emory, Merritt, and Devin made Sheridan's successes in the Valley possible. These quality subordinates compensated for Sheridan's tactics and overcame many of the errors that he committed in the field. William Swinton, who chronicled the campaigns of the Army of the Potomac, commented about Cedar Creek, "General Wright had already brought order out of confusion and made dispositions for attack." He continued, "The dramatic incidents attending the arrival of Sheridan have perhaps caused General Wright to receive less credit than he really deserves. The disaster was already over by the time Sheridan arrived; a compact line of battle was formed, and Wright was on the point of opening the offensive. Wright certainly had not the style of doing things possessed by Sheridan, but no one who knows the steady qualities of that officer's mind can doubt that he would have himself retrieved whatever his troops had lost of honor."[107] To be fair, Sheridan's arrival energized the army, and the army's subsequent counterattack carried the day.

Torbert, Sheridan's chief of cavalry, did not perform well during the Valley Campaign. On almost every occasion, Torbert did not meet his commander's expectations, and on each occasion, Sheridan permitted him to remain in command of the Cavalry Corps. Little Phil failed to remove Torbert until after the November Loudoun Valley raid, and an incompetent officer remained in an important command position far longer than he should have. In hindsight, it is obvious that Torbert possessed neither the vision nor the ability to command an entire corps of horse soldiers. Perhaps a more competent chief of cavalry might have brought a faster and more successful end to the campaign, and Sheridan must be faulted for keeping Torbert in place for as long as he did. By contrast, Sheridan abruptly and unjustly relieved Averell, when Averell probably would have made a fine chief of cavalry. He was an effective organizer and administrator and probably would have thrived in corps command.

The one time Sheridan aggressively took the fight to the Confederates on his own initiative, at Fisher's Hill, he implemented a battle plan developed by his able subordinate, Crook. Crook devised the strategy and tactics for the flank move that drove the Confederates from Fisher's Hill, but never got the credit he deserved. One of the Northern artillerists recorded, "It was fully understood by everyone at Corps Headquarters . . . that Crook had suggested this movement."[108] Predictably, Sheridan claimed the credit for the plan.[109]

Likewise, Early's audacious and effective plan for Cedar Creek nearly succeeded. His unexpected attack fell upon the Federal flank. Only fortune's intervention kept disaster from shattering the Army of the Shenandoah on the day Col. William Powell's division left the Federal's flank in the air. "A combination of factors," historian Jeffry D. Wert notes, ". . . contributed to the initial success of the Confederate offensive: the belief that the campaign had concluded, which fostered a lack of vigilance; the terrain and the faulty arrangement of Union infantry units; and the misplacements of the cavalry which left the army's vulnerable left flank improperly guarded. For these errors, Sheridan remains primarily accountable."[110]

"This was a case of a glorious victory given up by my own troops after they had won it," observed Early. "It is to be accounted for on the ground of the partial demoralization caused by the plunder of the enemy's camps, and from the fact that the men undertook to judge for themselves when it was proper to retire. Had they but waited, the mischief on the left would have been remedied."[111] Early's army as much lost the fight at Cedar Creek as Sheridan won it. While Sheridan deserves a great deal of credit for motivating his men by his dramatic ride, the tide of the battle had already turned by the time that he arrived on the battlefield at Cedar Creek. The fierce fighting spirit of the men of the Sixth Corps turned that tide.

Sheridan was not aggressive at all in this campaign, in spite of Grant's express orders that he get south of Early's army. The combination of Early's hard fighting and Sheridan's lack of aggressiveness meant that the campaign dragged on much longer than it should have, and that it cost many more lives than was necessary. Sheridan should have shown some initiative in August, when the Army of the Shenandoah first took the field. The odds were very much in his favor, but Grant's orders to go on the defensive quickly ended Sheridan's advance. Sheridan's lack of initiative, however, "had satisfied me that the commander opposed to me was without enterprise, and possessed an excessive caution which amounted to timidity," observed Early. "If it was his policy to produce the impression that his force was too weak to fight me, he did not succeed, but if it was to convince me that he was not an energetic commander, his strategy was a complete success, and subsequent events have not changed my opinion."[112]

Once he took the field, Little Phil did not demonstrate a killer instinct. His single-minded determination, combined with the dogged aggressiveness that brought him to Grant's attention in the first place, had gotten him command of the Army of the Shenandoah. Ironically, once he assumed command of the army, those traits evidently abandoned him, perhaps because Grant had instructed him to be cautious in August. Instead of pushing on mercilessly, as Grant expected, Little Phil failed to press the advantages gained by his men, allowing Early's army to slip away, largely unmolested. The failure to pursue Early after Winchester "granted us two days to sleep and rest and pull ourselves together for the struggle of September 22," claimed Gen. Gordon.[113] Two days after the victory at Fisher's Hill, Grant made his wishes known. "Keep on, and you will cause the fall of Richmond," he cajoled.[114]

On three separate occasions, including at Fisher's Hill, Sheridan defeated Early in battle, and on three separate occasions, he failed to follow up on those victories by vigorously pursuing the vanquished enemy. In particular, he let Early's beaten army escape, largely intact, after Cedar Creek. Each time, the Army of the Valley lived to fight another day. Only after Lee ordered Kershaw's division and the rest of Early's corps to join the Army of Northern Virginia at Petersburg did Early's threat to the Shenandoah Valley end. Then, in March 1865, Grant recalled Sheridan and the campaign ended indecisively, without military victory by Sheridan. "When I say that [Sheridan's] twenty-six days of apparent indecision, of feeble pursuit, of discursive and disjointed fighting after his two crushing victories, are to me a military mystery," observed Gordon, "why did he halt or hesitate, why turn to the torch in the hope of starving the enemy, instead of beating him in resolute battle? Would Grant have thus hesitated for a month or a day under such conditions—with a broken army in his front, and his own greatly superior in numbers and inspired by victory? How long would it require any intelligent soldier who fought under Grant, or against him, to answer that question?"[115] Napoleon wrote, "The strength of an army, like the power in mechanics, is estimated by multiplying the mass by the rapidity; a rapid march augments the *morale* of an army, and increases its means of victory. Press on!"[116] Sheridan repeatedly failed to follow this fundamental maxim of war. "Sheridan had the opportunity before him not only to finish off Early's army once and for all, but possibly to end the war in Virginia that fall by moving against Richmond from the west," observed historian Theodore C. Mahr, in reviewing Sheridan's conduct of the Battle of Cedar Creek. "If Early can be criticized for his lack of initiative in pressing his advantage in the morning's battle, then Sheridan must be equally criticized for his failure to reap the fruits of his victory in the evening." Mahr concluded, "In reference to Grant's suggestion that Sheridan was a 'great' general . . . at Cedar Creek 'a Sherman, or a Grant—not to speak of a Hannibal or a Napoleon—would have done more' to make the victory complete."[117]

Another historian correctly reported, "it is remarkable that a campaign so completely victorious in the field should be so barren of decisive results, and thus can be accounted for only on the supposition of very faulty strategy."[118] Ironically, Sheridan's failure during the Trevilian Raid triggered Early's Valley Campaign in the first place. When Grant selected Sheridan to command the Middle Military District, he fully expected Sheridan to wage a vigorous campaign against Early's dogged little band. Instead, Little Phil's complacency, his willingness just to savor his victories, needlessly prolonged the war. A truly great general, one with the killer instinct, would have pressed on to destroy his foe. In doing so, Sheridan would have brought the war to a faster conclusion. When he failed, Little Phil doomed the war in the east to drag on for an additional six frustrating months. Many more good men lost their lives as a result.

Thomas Rosser states:

> Sheridan's success in the Valley against Early was not due to his skill as a general so much as to the fact that Early misunderstood his true character. Early handled his army as infantry against cavalry, while Sheridan handled both his cavalry and infantry as *infantry*...As an infantry officer, Sheridan possessed fair ability; as a cavalry officer, he was the most absolute failure of all the many failures, which one after another was laid aside by Mr. Lincoln as the war developed them.[119]

NOTES

1. Jeffry D. Wert, *From Winchester to Cedar Creek: The Shenandoah Campaign of 1864* (Carlisle, Pa.: South Mountain Press, 1987), 7.
2. O.R., vol. 37, part 2, 558.
3. Wesley Merritt, "Sheridan in the Shenandoah Valley," in *B&L*, 4:501.
4. Grant, *Personal Memoirs*, 2:321.
5. Quoted in A. Wilson Greene, "Union Generalship in the 1864 Valley Campaign," in *Struggle for the Shenandoah: Essays on the 1864 Valley Campaign*, ed. Gary W. Gallagher (Kent, Ohio: Kent State University Press, 1991), 43.
6. O.R., vol. 43, part 1, 697–98.

7. Ibid., 54.

8. Sheridan noted in his memoirs, "The transfer of Torbert to the position of chief of cavalry left Merritt . . . in command of the First Cavalry Division. He had been tried in the place before, and from the day he was selected as one of a number of young men to be appointed general officers, with the object of giving life to the Cavalry Corps, he filled the measure of expectation." Sheridan, *Memoirs,* 1:474.

9. In fact, the disproportion in strength will be analyzed later in this chapter, when Sheridan's generalship in the Valley is assessed.

10. Sheridan, *Memoirs,* 1:380–81.

11. Taylor, *Sketchbook,* 259.

12. Charles Richard Williams, ed., *The Diary and Letters of Rutherford B. Hayes, Nineteenth President of the United States,* 5 vols. (Columbus: Ohio Historical Society, 1922), 2:500.

13. Bryan Grimes to his wife, September 10, 1864, Bryan Grimes Papers, Southern Historical Collections, University of North Carolina, Chapel Hill.

14. Power, *Lee's Miserables,* 146.

15. O.R., vol. 43, part 2, 49.

16. Ibid., 69.

17. Grant, *Personal Memoirs,* 2:327.

18. Ibid., 2:327–28; Wert, *From Winchester to Cedar Creek,* 43.

19. O.R., vol. 43, part 2, 104.

20. Kidd, *Personal Recollections,* 385.

21. Williams, *Rutherford B. Hayes,* 2:508–9.

22. Frederick Whittaker, *A Complete Life of Gen. George A. Custer, Major-General of Volunteers, Brevet Major-General U.S. Army, and Lieutenant-Colonel Seventh U.S. Cavalry* (New York: Sheldon & Co., 1876), 235.

23. Sheridan, *Personal Memoirs,* 2:30–32.

24. *Ionia* (Michigan) *Sentinel,* June 5, 1866.

25. Robert C. Wallace, *A Few Memories of a Long Life* (Fairfield, Wash.: Ye Galleon Press, 1988), 49.

26. Wert, *From Winchester to Cedar Creek,* 95; William O. Lee, comp., *Personal and Historical Sketches and Facial History of and by Members of the Seventh Regiment Michigan Volunteer Cavalry, 1862–1865* (Detroit: Ralston Co., 1901), 168.

27. O.R., vol. 43, part 1, 498.

28. Kidd, *Personal Recollections,* 390–1.

29. O.R., vol. 43, part 1, 444.

30. *Ionia Sentinel,* June 5, 1866.

31. Jeffry D. Wert, *Custer: The Controversial Life of George Armstrong Custer* (New York: Simon & Schuster, 1996), 183.

32. O.R., vol. 43, part 1, 54.

33. Sheridan, *Personal Memoirs,* 2:29.

34. O.R., vol. 43, part 1, 458.

35. John N. Opie, *A Rebel Cavalryman with Lee, Stuart, and Jackson* (Chicago: W. B. Conkey Co., 1899), 252.

36. Nevins, *A Diary of Battle,* 465.

37. Merlin E. Sumner, comp., *The Diary of Cyrus B. Comstock* (Dayton, Ohio: Morningside House, 1987), 294–95.

38. O.R., vol. 43, part 1, 363–64.

39. Taylor, *Sketchbook,* 403.

40. Wert, *From Winchester to Cedar Creek,* 129.

41. O.R., vol. 43, part 1, 26–27.

42. Ibid., 428.

43. Ibid., 48.

44. Sheridan, *Personal Memoirs,* 2:40–42.

45. Averell's unjustified relief will be explored in detail in chapter 5.

46. Gregory J. W. Urwin, *Custer Victorious: The Civil War Battles of George Armstrong Custer* (East Brunswick, N.J.: Associated University Presses, 1983), 190.

47. George M. Neese, *Three Years in the Confederate Horse Artillery* (New York: Neale, 1911), 317.

48. Ibid., 210.

49. Wert, *From Winchester to Cedar Creek,* 147–56.

50. Beverly Whittle diary, entry for October 6, 1864, Alderman Library, University of Virginia, Charlottesville. Whittle refers to Early's burning of the town of Chambersburg, Pennsylvania, during his raid on the north in July 1864. The burning of Chambersburg caused howls of outrage to spread throughout the north.

51. John L. Heatwole, *The Burning: Sheridan in the Shenandoah Valley* (Charlottesville, Va.: Rockbridge Publishing, 1998), 34.

52. Kidd, *Personal Recollections,* 399.

53. *Ionia Sentinel,* June 5, 1866.

54. Heatwole, *The Burning,* 184. Most of Rosser's Laurel Brigade consisted of Valley residents. Rosser himself later wrote, "It was the homes of the men of my brigade that were being given to the flames by Sheridan, and the fierceness of their attack showed me the bitterness of their hatred of the wretches who were thus destroying their homes." Thomas L. Rosser, *Riding with Rosser,* ed. S. Roger Keller (Chambersburg, Pa.: Burd Street Press, 1998), 46.

55. Henry Kyd Douglas, *I Rode with Stonewall* (Chapel Hill: University of North Carolina Press, 1940), 302.

56. O.R., vol. 43, part 1, 30–31.

57. Ibid., 442.

58. Ibid., part 2, 327.

59. Ibid., part 1, 447.

60. J. W. Monaghan diary typescript, Bentley Historical Library, University of Michigan, Ann Arbor, 10.

61. Wallace, *A Few Memories,* 53.

62. Theodore C. Mahr, *The Battle of Cedar Creek: Showdown in the Shenandoah, October 1–30, 1864* (Lynchburg, Va.: H. E. Howard Co., 1992), 55.

63. O.R., vol. 43, part 1, 339.
64. Sheridan, *Personal Memoirs,* 2:59.
65. O.R., vol. 43, part 1, 559.
66. Power, *Lee's Miserables,* 166.
67. Wert, *From Winchester to Cedar Creek,* 143.
68. Mahr, *The Battle of Cedar Creek,* 65–69.
69. Sheridan, *Personal Memoirs,* 2:95–96.
70. Taylor, *Sketchbook,* 485.
71. Sheridan, *Personal Memoirs,* 2:79–80.
72. Wert, *From Winchester to Cedar Creek,* 222.
73. Ibid., 223.
74. Sheridan, *Personal Memoirs,* 2:82.
75. Hazard Stevens, "The Battle of Cedar Creek," *The Shenandoah Campaigns of 1864–1865, Personal Memoirs of the Military History Society of Massachusetts* 6 (Boston: Military History Society of Massachusetts, 1907), 124–25.
76. Hagemann, *Fighting Rebels and Redskins,* 291.
77. Kidd, *Personal Recollections,* 411.
78. Ibid., 421–23.
79. O.R., vol. 43, part 1, 450.
80. Wert, *From Winchester to Cedar Creek,* 236.
81. O.R., vol. 43, part 1, 435.
82. Ibid., 59.
83. Kidd, *Personal Recollections,* 424–25.
84. Rosser, *Riding with Rosser,* 52.
85. Power, *Lee's Miserables,* 175.
86. Taylor, *Sketchbook,* 557.
87. O.R., vol. 43, part 1, 35, 130, 437, 454–55, 533–34, 537.
88. O.R., vol. 43, part 1, 54.
89. Sheridan, *Personal Memoirs,* 2:92.
90. Taylor, *Sketchbook,* 285.
91. Dennis E. Frye, " 'I Resolved to Play a Bold Game': John S. Mosby as a Factor in the 1864 Valley Campaign," in *Struggle for the Shenandoah: Essays on the 1864 Valley Campaign,* ed. Gary W. Gallagher (Kent, Ohio: Kent State University Press, 1991), 126.
92. Wert, *From Winchester to Cedar Creek,* 155.
93. O.R., vol. 43, part 2, 420.
94. Hagemann, *Fighting Rebels and Redskins,* 261.
95. O.R., vol. 43, part 2, 675.
96. Ibid., 687.
97. Ibid., part 1, 672.
98. J. K. Lowden, "A Gallant Record: Michigan's 5th Cav. in the Latter Period of the War," *National Tribune,* July 30, 1896.
99. O.R., vol. 43, part 1, 677–79.
100. John S. Mosby, *The Memoirs of Colonel John S. Mosby* (New York: Little, Brown & Co., 1917), 284.

101. John S. Mosby, "Retaliation," *Southern Historical Society Papers* 27 (1899): 315.

102. See Bruce Catton, "Introduction," in Virgil Carrington Jones, *Gray Ghosts and Rebel Raiders* (New York: Henry Holt & Co., 1956), viii.

103. James A. Ramage, *Gray Ghost: The Life of Col. John Singleton Mosby* (Lexington: University of Kentucky Press, 1999), 242.

104. Sun Tzu, *The Art of War*, trans. Samuel B. Griffith (London: Oxford University Press, 1963), 79.

105. Martin F. Schmitt, ed., *General George Crook: His Autobiography* (Norman: University of Oklahoma Press, 1946), 134.

106. Jubal A. Early, *Autobiographical Sketch and Narrative of the War Between the States* (Philadelphia: J. B. Lippincott & Co., 1912), 427–28.

107. William Swinton, *Campaigns of the Army of the Potomac* (New York: Charles Scribner's Sons, 1882), 563.

108. Greene, "Union Generalship," 54.

109. See Sheridan, *Personal Memoirs*, 2:35. ("In consequence of the enemy's being so well protected from a direct assault, I resolved on the night of the 20th to use again a turning-column against his left, as had been done on the 19th at the Opequon. To this end I resolved to move Crook, unperceived if possible, over to the eastern face of Little North Mountain, whence he could strike the left and rear of the Confederate line, and as he broke it up, I could support him by a left half-wheel of my whole line of battle.") Sheridan's pettiness in claiming credit for the battle plan infuriated Crook, who complained about the shoddy treatment for years. For a more detailed discussion of this episode, see chapter 5.

110. Wert, *From Winchester to Cedar Creek,* 242.

111. Early, *Autobiographical Sketch,* 451.

112. Ibid., 415.

113. John B. Gordon, *Reminiscences of the Civil War* (New York. Charles Scribner's Sons, 1903), 326.

114. O.R., vol. 43, part 2, 152.

115. Gordon, *Reminiscences,* 328.

116. Napoleon Bonaparte, *Napoleon's Art of War,* trans. Lt. Gen. Sir G. C. D'Aguilar, Maxim IX (New York: Barnes & Noble, 1995), 19.

117. Mahr, *Cedar Creek,* 350, quoting Raoul S. Naroll, "Sheridan and Cedar Creek—A Reappraisal," *Military Analysis of the Civil War: An Anthology by the Editors of Military Affairs* (Millwood, N.Y.: KTO Press, 1977), 381.

118. L. W. V. Kennon, "The Valley Campaign of 1864: A Military Study," *The Shenandoah Campaigns of 1862 and 1864 and the Appomattox Campaign of 1865: Papers of the Military Historical Society of Massachusetts* 6 (Boston: The Military Historical Society of Massachusetts, 1907), 52–53.

119. Thomas L. Rosser, *Addresses of Gen'l T. L. Rosser at the Seventh Annual Reunion of the Association of the Maryland Line* (New York: L. A. Williams Printing Co., 1889).

CHAPTER 4

SHERIDAN'S DISOBEDIENCE
TO ORDERS

My duty is to obey orders." Those six simple words formed the cornerstone of Stonewall Jackson's life and military career.[1] These six simple words also provide the cornerstone for all military discipline and hierarchy. Without reasonable expectations that orders will be obeyed, a commander can have no confidence of success, or confidence that the discipline so essential to an army's ability to function will hold up under the stress of combat. In short, armies rely on their chain of command. Superior officers issue orders, and lower-ranking subordinates obey those orders. This is how it has always been, and this is how it always must be.

Philip Sheridan had a long and well-documented history of refusing to obey the direct orders of superior officers in the Civil War. While most instances of disobedience result in general courts-martial, Sheridan instead received promotions and commendations for his conduct. Ironically, he had no tolerance for disobedience by those serving under him, and at the drop of a hat would ruin a man's life and career if he felt that his orders were not carried out to the letter. This chapter juxtaposes Sheridan's actions with his exacting demands of his subordinates.

His first, and perhaps most telling, incident nearly got him expelled from West Point. As recounted in chapter 1, when Cadet Sgt. William R. Terrill of Virginia gave Cadet Pvt. Sheridan a direct order, Little Phil, instead of obeying the order, attacked Terrill with his bayonet, threatening to run him through. Fortunately, Sheridan regained control of himself before actually attacking Terrill, and pulled back. Nevertheless, the shocking breach of discipline and protocol left Terrill with no alternative but to put Sheridan on report, as the incident had happened in front of nearly the entire cadet corps. The next day, when his "ire was so inflamed by [Terrill's] action," Sheridan assaulted Terrill, and a fistfight ensued. Bystanders quickly broke up the altercation, but the damage had already been done. When the superintendent of the Military Academy asked for written explanations, Sheridan admitted that he had perpetrated the attack, but he also blamed Terrill for the episode. After reading both parties' explanations, the superintendent let Sheridan off the hook with a light punishment: a year's suspension.[2]

"At the time I thought, of course, my suspension a very unfair punishment," recounted Sheridan in his memoirs, "that my conduct was justifiable and the authorities of the Academy all wrong, but riper experience has led me to a different conclusion, and as I look back, though the mortification I then endured was deep and trying, I am convinced that it was hardly as much as I deserved for such an outrageous breach of discipline."[3] With the wisdom of age and maturity, Sheridan recognized that he had escaped lightly indeed. He was fortunate that he was not expelled from the Military Academy for such an egregious breach of order and discipline.

Maj. Gen. James H. Wilson, who was not one of Sheridan's admirers, had a keen observation about this incident. "In this incident the boy displayed the most marked characteristic of the man," noted Wilson, "and the one to which he was principally indebted for the high rank and great distinction which he reached in the war of the Rebellion."[4] Wilson's facetious remark about Sheridan's "most marked characteristic" refers to Sheridan's broad streak of stubborn disobedience, a streak that ran through his conduct on numerous occasions throughout the Civil War. As Wilson correctly observed, this unflattering characteristic reared its ugly head early in Sheridan's military career, and he never escaped it. If anything, the patronage of such superiors as Grant and Rosecrans only reinforced this unflattering trait.

That was only the first episode of Sheridan's disregard for the orders of superior officers and the chain of command; it would not be the last. The next episode doomed the Army of the Potomac to slug it out with Robert E. Lee's Army of Northern Virginia for two long, bloody, brutal weeks.

This second incident occurred on May 8, 1864, after the defeat at Todd's Tavern. By way of review, both Meade and Sheridan had issued conflicting orders to David Gregg, confusing the division commander and causing the cavalry to fail to take and hold Todd's Tavern. That failure meant that the Confederates beat the Army of the Potomac to Spotsylvania Court House, and the two armies ended up fighting it out there for nearly two ghastly weeks. Had Meade not acted, he would have violated his own orders from Grant, who had written, "Make all preparations during the day for *a night march to take position at Spotsylvania C. H. with one corps,* at Todd's Tavern with one, and another near the intersection of the Piney Branch and Spotsylvania road with the road from Alsop's to Old Court House."[5] Earlier that evening, Sheridan had reported that the road to Spotsylvania Court House was open. At one o'clock in the morning, Meade learned that Sheridan had not issued orders to either Merritt or Gregg, and he grew concerned.

Accordingly, relying upon Sheridan's earlier report that the road to Spotsylvania Court House was clear, the army commander issued the orders himself, instructing Gregg: "Move with your command *at 5 A.M.,* on the Catharpin Road, crossing at Corbin's Bridge, and taking position at Shady Grove Church. *General Merritt will follow you,* and at Shady Grove Church will take the left hand, or Block House Road, moving forward and taking up position at that point. Immediately after he has passed, you will move forward with your division, *on the same road,* to the crossing of Po River, where you will take up position *supporting* General Merritt. General Wilson with his division will march from Alsop's by way of Spotsylvania Court House and the Gate to Snell's Bridge, where he will take up position. . . . *The infantry march to Spotsylvania tonight.*"[6] Meade also gave instructions to Merritt. "It is of the utmost importance that not the slightest delay occur in your opening the Brock Road," he ordered, "as an infantry corps is on its way to occupy that place."[7]

Having made the dispositions for the cavalry, the army commander focused his attention on his cavalry chief. "I find Generals Gregg and [Merritt] without orders. They are in the way of the infantry," wrote Meade, "and there is no time to refer to you. I have given them the enclosed orders, which you can modify after the infantry corps are in position."[8] By giving orders directly to Gregg, and not through Sheridan, Meade infuriated Sheridan, who believed that Meade had superseded the chain of command and countermanded his orders. The waspish tone of Meade's note probably added fuel to the fire already burning in Little Phil's belly. However, Sheridan's orders, also issued about one o'clock, did not reach Gregg until well after Meade's. In them, Sheridan ordered the cavalry to use roads then occupied by heavy columns of Confederate infantry, also racing for possession of Spotsylvania Court House.[9]

When he wrote his memoirs, Sheridan defended his conduct. "Had Gregg and Merritt been permitted to proceed as they were originally instructed, it is doubtful whether the battles fought at Spotsylvania would have occurred," he claimed outrageously, "for these two divisions would have encountered the enemy at the Po River, and so delayed his march as to enable our infantry to reach Spotsylvania first, and thus force Lee to take up a line behind the Po." Not surprisingly, Sheridan laid all of the blame on Meade. Meade's "disjointed and irregular instructions" rendered the Cavalry Corps "practically ineffective."[10]

The attempt to take Spotsylvania proved a disaster. With the Fifth Corps and Custer's Michigan Brigade clogging the roads between Todd's Tavern and Spotsylvania, Lee won the race for the crucial crossroads.[11] This failure infuriated an already frustrated George Meade.

Relations between Meade and Little Phil were not good. They had fundamentally disagreed about the proper role of the Cavalry Corps when Sheridan had first assumed command of it. The two officers had argued about the role of the horse soldiers during the spring, and Sheridan had been unhappy about the tasks assigned his men during the Battle of the Wilderness. On May 5, as the fighting raged, Meade instructed Sheridan to call in his cavalry to protect the army's wagon trains. An unhappy Sheridan complained to Meade, "I cannot do anything with the cavalry except to act on the defensive. Why cannot infantry be sent to guard the trains and let me take the offensive?"[12] Although Meade tempered the orders by granting his cavalry commander some latitude to act, relations between the two officers had grown strained, setting the stage for the ugly confrontation that followed.

Meade, who possessed an "excitable temper which under irritating circumstances became almost ungovernable," summoned Sheridan to his headquarters. Meade "was unfortunately of a temper that would get beyond his control, at times," observed Grant of his subordinate, "and make him speak to officers of high rank in the most offensive manner."[13] The army commander, known to his aide Col. Lyman as the "Great Peppery," had worked himself "into a towering passion regarding the delays encountered in the forward movement."[14]

There, "a very acrimonious dispute took place between the two generals." Meade sharply told Sheridan "that his cavalry was in his way, though he had sent him orders to leave the road clear."[15] A staff officer who witnessed the exchange recalled that Meade "went at him hammer and tongs, accusing him of blunders, and charging him with not making a proper disposition of his troops, and letting the cavalry block the advance of the infantry." Unable to restrain his own temper, Sheridan "was equally fiery, and, smarting under the belief that he was unjustly treated, all the hotspur in his nature was aroused." Responding with a barrage of expletives, the angry cavalry chief "insisted that Meade had created the trouble by countermanding his orders, and that it was this act which had resulted in mixing up his troops with the infantry."[16]

When Little Phil indicated that he had not received the orders, Meade apologized, but the damage had already been done. Theodore Lyman, one of the army commander's staff officers, noted, "Sheridan was plainly full of suppressed anger, and Meade too was in ill temper."[17] Sheridan reported later that Meade "had broken up my combinations, exposed Wilson's division and kept Gregg unnecessarily idle, and . . . such disjointed operations as he had been requiring of the cavalry . . . would render the corps inefficient and useless."[18] Sheridan blamed the disgraceful behavior of the infantry, and especially of Maj. Gen. Gouverneur K. Warren's Fifth Corps, for the failure, not the cavalry. Lyman astutely noted, "Maybe this was the beginning of [Sheridan's] dislike of Warren and ill-feeling against Meade."[19]

The discussion took on a loud and ominous tone. As the two tense generals traded barbs, Little Phil suggested to Meade "that I could whip Stuart if he would only let me." Then Sheridan crossed the line of appropriate conduct. "Since he insisted on giving the cavalry directions without consulting or even notifying me," he claimed, Meade "could thenceforth command the Cavalry Corps himself—that I would not give it another order."[20] Trying to make peace, Meade placed his hand on Sheridan's shoulder and said, "No, I don't mean that," but it was too late. The furious Cavalry Corps chief then stomped out of the army commander's tent.[21]

An enraged Meade undoubtedly wanted to remove the insubordinate little Irishman of command, and marched straight to Grant's tent and recounted what had occurred to the commanding general. When Grant heard Sheridan's remarks about whipping Stuart, he responded, "Did Sheridan say that? Well, he generally knows what he is talking about. Let him start right out and do it."[22] Instead of sanctioning the Cavalry Corps commander for his insubordination, Grant rewarded the conduct by giving Sheridan an independent command. That afternoon, Sheridan received orders to "immediately concentrate [his] available mounted force, and with [his] ammunition trains and such supply trains as are filled proceed against the enemy's cavalry."[23] Little Phil got his dearest wish—independent command.

Some evaluation of these events is warranted. First, Meade acted properly in issuing orders directly to David Gregg. He did so only after he could not locate Sheridan. Meade then learned that both Gregg and Merritt lacked any orders, and that they needed some direction in order to coordinate the arrival of the Fifth Corps on the scene. He waited until after midnight to issue those instructions, waiting to see whether Sheridan would accept the responsibility for directing the actions of his subordinates. Thus, Meade acted to assure the orderly passage of his army to Todd's Tavern, and not to usurp Sheridan's authority over the Cavalry Corps, although Meade undoubtedly was unhappy with his subordinate's failure to make the necessary arrangements.

Richard O'Connor, a stout defender of Sheridan's conduct, keenly observed that the clash between Meade and Sheridan was inevitable. "It was a collision of high tempers from which neither party fully recovered and which neither was ever to forget or forgive, a scene that was recorded with sorrow and embarrassment," observed O'Connor. O'Connor thought the conflict stemmed, at least in part, from the class differences between these two men. Meade was a brainy Philadelphia aristocrat while Sheridan was a rough Irish immigrant from the frontier of Ohio. Meade was a careful engineer "who relied on well-laid plans, Sheridan the cavalryman who placed just as much faith in dash, intuition and taking advantage of opportunities as they suddenly presented themselves in battle."[24] There is probably some merit to this analysis, but class differences do not justify Sheridan's conduct. Grant extended his protective umbrella over Sheridan, meaning that Sheridan's conduct was acceptable to the general in chief. In short, Meade's authority as army commander was undermined. O'Connor correctly noted, "If Meade hoped that Sheridan would be relieved . . . he was quickly disenchanted."[25]

Defending indefensible conduct, Sheridan's most recent biographer justified Little Phil's reaction. Roy Morris Jr. noted, "Sheridan was never one to admit failure, or to return a soft answer in the face of wrath." Not even Sheridan's apologists could avoid the fact that he had been disobedient and disrespectful to a superior officer. "Once again, as at Perryville," observed Morris, quite correctly, "bluster and blarney had overshadowed command mistakes, and Sheridan had successfully avoided censure for his actions."[26]

Bvt. Lt. Col. Carswell McClellan, a first cousin of the former commander of the Army of the Potomac, Maj. Gen. George B. McClellan, served on the staff of the Cavalry Corps.[27] After the publication of Sheridan's posthumous memoirs, McClellan wrote a scathing rebuttal to many of Sheridan's contentions. In addressing the question of Meade's orders, McClellan observed that Meade "did not countermand or modify the order of General Sheridan, for that officer's orders reached the troops after those of General Meade had been issued." He also noted, "That General Meade's orders could not have prevented the success of General Sheridan's plans and combinations, is abundantly shown by the fact that, at, and from the time when General Sheridan's orders were written, the roads upon which he ordered his troops to operate from Todd's Tavern were held in force by the moving columns of the enemy."[28]

McClellan also commented on the meeting between Sheridan and Meade. "It is difficult, and by no means pleasant, to any true American, to understand how a General commanding the Army of the United States could have written General Sheridan's account of his interview with General Meade a little before noon on May 8th, 1864," he commented. "Doubtless, General Meade did display some traces of 'peppery temper' on that occasion. There can be found on record few military saints who, in the presence of the enemy, could, or would, quietly submit to being charged with imbecility in their command, and defied in their authority, by a subaltern. Officers have forfeited life, as well as honor, for less than General Sheridan claims," concluded McClellan.[29]

McClellan saved his harshest words for Sheridan's disobedience. "General Sheridan, if the language of his Memoirs has weight in evidence," he commented, "neglected the orders and rebelled against the authority of his superior and commanding officer, and Lieutenant-General Grant ordered him to the separate command that he coveted." McClellan found Sheridan's bragging about the episode disgusting. "It remained, however, for the last General of the U.S. Army to *boast* of the fact to the country that had elevated him, and to leave the, at least questionable precedent as a legacy to the Army for whose *esprit* and discipline he was thought to have been intelligently responsible."[30] The point was well taken. In most armies, officers were court-martialed and cashiered from the service for far less significant acts of disobedience. In some armies, where absolute discipline reigned, the only response to such acts of disobedience was a quick firing squad. Instead, Grant rewarded Sheridan by giving him an independent command. As McClellan correctly observed, Grant's endorsement of this conduct did not set a good precedent.

Finally, this incident soured the relationship between Sheridan and Meade. The two officers had clashed several times already, beginning with Sheridan's arrogant pronouncements about changing the focus of the Cavalry Corps' mission. They then disagreed vociferously over the proper role of the horsemen in the Battle of the Wilderness. With a tense relationship, these two strong personalities never worked together effectively. This incident sealed their mutual animosity. Meade resented Sheridan's appointment to command in the Shenandoah Valley, and became very bitter when Sheridan received a promotion to major general in the Regular Army before he did, even though Meade outranked Little Phil and had commanded an army for more than a year longer. The two men never got along again, and the episode on May 7 probably served as the catalyst for their mutual dislike.[31]

The third episode occurred during the winter of 1865. As Grant planned the spring offensive, he knew that the end of the war was in sight. The Confederacy's resources had been stretched to the limits, and desertions plagued Lee's army. One good, coordinated push from the Federal forces in the field would bring the war to an end. Almost since Sheridan took command of the Middle Military District, Grant had wanted Sheridan to cross the Blue Ridge and bring his army to bear on the siege lines at Petersburg. For months, Sheridan had found excuse after excuse to ignore or disobey Grant's wishes.

Finally, Grant grew weary of Sheridan's persistence in disregarding his suggestions. "On the 8th of February I ordered Sheridan, who was in the Valley of Virginia, to push forward as soon as the weather would permit and strike the canal west of Richmond at or about Lynchburg," wrote Grant.[32] Little Phil delayed his departure, claiming that the weather prevented him from carrying out the lieutenant general's orders. "The weather here still continues very bad," he wrote on February 12. "The deep snow is still on the ground and very cold. It is utterly impossible to do anything here in such weather."[33] Sheridan was playing for time, hoping for an opportunity for a creative application of Grant's instructions.

A few days later, on February 20, Grant clarified his wishes. As soon as the weather permitted, Sheridan was to take his cavalry and move on the important railroad junction town of Lynchburg and cut the rail lines there. From there, he was to destroy the railroads and canals in all directions, and then "strike south, heading the streams in Virginia to the westward of Danville, and push on and join Sherman." If Sheridan could not make his way to Sherman, he was to return to Winchester. Nothing in Grant's unambiguous orders gave Sheridan authority to march to join the Army of the Potomac. Grant wanted Little Phil to act quickly, because coordinated assaults were being launched on all fronts, and "Sherman with a large army eating out the vitals of South Carolina—is all that will be wanted to leave nothing for the rebellion to stand upon."[34]

On February 25, a displeased Sheridan wrote to Grant, looking for further information about Sherman's whereabouts. For months, Sheridan had been agitating about leading the Army of the Shenandoah's cavalry to Petersburg in order to rejoin the Army of the Potomac. For months, those pleas had fallen on deaf ears. Grant wanted Sheridan to remain in the Shenandoah Valley, guarding the Army of the Potomac's flank. The lieutenant general informed Little Phil that he expected Sherman's army to be in the vicinity of Fayetteville, on his way to Goldsboro. Grant then provided Sheridan with a loophole that allowed him to disobey yet another direct order. "If you reach Lynchburg you will have to be guided in your movements by the information you obtain," Grant wrote.[35]

These orders made Sheridan very unhappy. He realized that the end was at hand. When he wrote his memoirs, Little Phil admitted that he had decided "that it was useless to adhere to my alternate instructions to return to Winchester. I now decided to destroy more thoroughly the James River Canal and the Virginia

Central Railroad, and then join General Grant in front of Petersburg." He also admitted that because he was "feeling that the war was nearing its end, I desired my cavalry to be in at the death."[36] Sheridan had no intention of tramping about the Carolinas searching for Johnston's army. Instead, he was determined to join Grant to be in at the kill. "He had gotten into the habit of interpreting Grant's orders liberally, and he was about to do so again," biographer Morris observed.[37]

Sheridan moved out. A division of cavalry under George Custer pounced on the ragtag remnants of Early's once-proud army at Waynesborough on March 2, scattering it and effectively clearing the Valley of remaining Confederate forces. Little Phil then captured Charlottesville and destroyed the locks along the James River Canal in the vicinity of Lynchburg. His men turned their attention to the Virginia Central and Richmond, Fredericksburg, and Petersburg railroads, destroying tracks and bridges. Little Phil then liberally applied Grant's orders and decided not to join Sherman in North Carolina. Instead, he announced, "After finishing the Fredericksburg road I will join you, unless otherwise directed."[38] Phil Sheridan was not about to miss the war's dénouement in the trenches around Petersburg. "No one thought to accuse him of insubordination, of course," noted historian Richard O'Connor, "but it would seem that Sheridan made things work out his own way, without undue deference to Grant's plans."[39]

Brig. Gen. Henry E. Davies, one of Sheridan's division commanders, participated in the expedition. "The impossibility of crossing prevented the execution of that part of the plan of movement that related to effecting a junction with the army of General Sherman, and as no enemy remained in the Shenandoah Valley and a return to Winchester would effect no useful purpose and would only serve to remove the troops to a greater distance than they now were from the scene of future active operations about Richmond and Petersburg," Davies wrote, in justification of Sheridan's disobedience. "General Sheridan decided to destroy more thoroughly the canal and railroad and then make his way to the east and join General Grant in front of Petersburg."[40]

On March 14, Grant acquiesced to the inevitable. "I am disposed now to bring your cavalry over here and unite it with what we have," instructed the lieutenant general. "When you start I want no halt made until you make the intended raid, unless rest is necessary; in that case take it before crossing the James."[41] These words were music to Sheridan's ears. He moved as quickly as possible, arriving near Petersburg on March 26, just in time for the breakout that led to the war's final campaign. "The reunited corps was to enter upon the campaign as a separate army, I reporting directly to General Grant," commented Sheridan in his memoirs, "the intention being to reward me for foregoing, of my own choice, my position as a department commander by joining the armies at Petersburg."[42] Given the simmering animosity between Meade and Sheridan, Grant probably felt that he had no choice but to retain Little Phil in an independent command.

When he arrived at City Point on March 26, Grant had already planned his next move. Two days later, he summoned Little Phil to his headquarters for a face-to-face meeting and delivered written orders to him. Worried that Lee's army might escape and link up with Gen. Joseph E. Johnston's army in North Carolina, Grant wanted the cavalry to pass near or through Dinwiddie, but not to attack the enemy there. Instead, Grant wanted Sheridan to draw the Confederates out to attack him. If the Southerners wouldn't respond, Sheridan was to destroy the railroads converging on Petersburg, and then either return to the army, or go to North Carolina to join Sherman. Had Sheridan done so, he would have blocked the escape route of Confederate President Jefferson Davis, and also would have been positioned to attack Johnston's rear.[43]

After reading the orders, Sheridan made his displeasure with the new assignment abundantly known to Grant. "I saw that after Sheridan had read his instructions, he seemed somewhat disappointed at the idea, possibly, of having to cut loose again from the Army of the Potomac, and place himself between the two main armies of the enemy," recorded Grant. Grant followed his unhappy subordinate out of the tent and reassured Little Phil that his real intention was to capture Five Forks, driving the Confederates from Petersburg and Richmond. Reassured, Sheridan responded, "I am glad to hear it, and we can do it." However, Grant specifically ordered Sheridan not to make his movement against Five Forks until receiving further instructions from the commanding general. Those orders came a couple of days later.[44] Once again, Grant coddled Sheridan and rewarded his disobedience, instead of penalizing his insubordination. Sheridan's refusal to do as ordered left Davis's escape route open, and probably extended the war because it prevented Sherman from bringing the power of the Cavalry Corps to bear against Johnston.

Sheridan also wrote that when he reported to Grant at City Point, the lieutenant general concluded the interview by saying, "that it was rare a department commander voluntarily deprived himself of independence, and added that I should not suffer for it."[45] Of course, Sheridan glossed over the fact that had he obeyed Grant's original orders, he never would have been in a position to deprive himself voluntarily of independence. On March 27, Grant summoned Sheridan to City Point for a meeting with Sherman.[46] The subject of Sheridan's joining the Army of the Tennessee arose again during that meeting, much to Little Phil's great consternation. "I made no comments of the projects for moving his own (General Sherman's) troops, but as soon as opportunity offered, dissented emphatically from the proposition to have me join the Army of the Tennessee, repeating in substance what I had previously expressed to General Grant," recounted Sheridan in his memoirs. "My uneasiness made me somewhat too earnest, I fear, but General Grant soon mollified me, and smoothed matters over . . . so I pursued the subject no [further]."[47]

Having gotten his way, and having had his insubordination rewarded once again with an independent command, Sheridan received yet another honor, one that garnered him undying fame: Grant made him a wing commander. Fronting Grant's left wing, Sheridan led the Union army's pursuit of the Army of Northern Virginia across the Old Dominion. As time passed, the war's last two weeks became known as "eminently General Sheridan's campaign," and it was, undoubtedly, his finest moment of the war and the crowning achievement of his career.[48]

Why Grant tolerated Sheridan's penchant for creatively interpreting his orders has never been explained, and the lieutenant general left no clues to the answer. While the sort of disrespect demonstrated by Phil Sheridan's conduct has often cost men their careers and even their lives in some instances, his career thrived because of it. After each episode of disobedience, superior officers rewarded him with promotions and higher levels of command. However, Sheridan lived by a double standard: He had a hair trigger for relieving good men from command for perceived episodes of disobedience, and remained intransigent about his actions, even when the evidence proved that he was wrong.

On at least two occasions, Sheridan relieved officers of command—and ruined their careers: He relieved Brig. Gen. William W. Averell of command of his cavalry division in the days just after the Battle of Fisher's Hill, citing Averell's failure to pursue Early as the justification. Then, on April 1, 1865, after the overwhelming Union success at the Battle of Five Forks, Sheridan removed Maj. Gen. Gouverneur K. Warren from command of the Army of the Potomac's Fifth Corps. Sheridan claimed that Warren had failed to obey his orders for the conduct of the battle at Five Forks, eight days before the end of the war. He also accused Warren of not being with his troops—just the conduct that had caused Meade to issue direct orders to Sheridan's subordinates in 1864. The irony is striking. While history ultimately exonerated Warren, Sheridan categorically refused to back down from his claims and never changed his story. The episodes involving Averell and Warren will be explored in detail in chapter 5.

Col. McClellan correctly assessed the nature of Little Phil's conduct in the episodes with Meade in May 1864, and in disobeying Grant's orders in March 1865. "It remains, therefore, that General Grant rewarded the insubordination of General Sheridan at Spotsylvania Court House by detaching him from the command of General Meade," observed McClellan, "that he again rewarded him, by changing for his benefit the Cavalry Corps of the Army of the Potomac into the independent command entitled 'the army of the Shenandoah,' after he (General Sheridan) had decided for himself that it was useless to adhere to the instructions under which he had been operating in the Shenandoah Valley, and had—*in defiance of rules and articles of war*—withdrawn his command from the department to which he had been assigned without any more urgent necessity than that, 'feeling that the war was nearing its end, he [I] desired his [my] cavalry to be in at the death.'"[49]

Saving his most scathing words for Sheridan's treatment of Warren, McClellan wrote "that finally, he 'mollified' the same officer's emphatic discontent and objection to the duties to which his command might possibly be assigned, by concessions in his favor. *While General Sheridan boasts, and General Grant admits, such facts, one can scarcely credit with much of dignity the efforts of the last Generals of the U.S. Army to justify the arbitrary removal of General Warren from the command he graced, and from participation in the final triumph of the cause to which he had devoted the best years of his unselfish, earnest life.*"[50]

Considering that a soldier's chief duty is to obey the lawful orders of a superior officer, Phil Sheridan repeatedly failed in that duty. In the strictest sense, his persistent disobedience meant that Sheridan was not a good soldier, even though the results of his defiance seemingly justified the conduct. Still, almost any other officer would have suffered the consequences, and only Grant's protection saved Sheridan from his fate. Whether Sheridan realized it, or whether he appreciated his patron's help and protection, remains an open question. The fact remains, however, that Sheridan could not have achieved his exalted position in history without Grant's willingness to overlook his disregard of orders and the chain of command. Considering that Grant despised liars, his faithful support of Sheridan is all the more remarkable.[51]

Sylvanus Cadwallader, a newspaper correspondent who traveled with Grant's headquarters, had many opportunities to observe the interplay between Grant and Sheridan, and offered a logical explanation for Grant's tolerance of Sheridan's insubordination. "It is well-known to Gen. Grant's intimates, that he considered Sheridan incomparably the greatest general our civil war produced," wrote the newspaperman. "Other generals might be equally good under ordinary circumstances, under the eyes of an able superior commander, and up to the point of a given or limited number of men. Sheridan he believed could be more safely trusted with an independent army than any of them; and he often said in private confidential conversation, that no army would ever be raised on this continent so large that Sheridan could not competently command it." Cadwallader concluded, "In this last respect, Grant had unbounded confidence in, and admiration for Sheridan."[52]

While Sheridan had many good qualities as a soldier, his tendencies toward disobedience and inconsistency in his treatment of the men who served under him did not speak well. Neither did his cruelty and pettiness toward his brother officers.

NOTES

1. Peter G. Tsouras, ed., *Military Quotations from the Civil War* (New York: Sterling Publishing, 1998), 171.
2. Sheridan, *Personal Memoirs,* 1:11–12.
3. Ibid., 1:12.
4. Quoted in McClellan, *Notes,* 24.
5. O.R., vol. 36, part 3, 481; emphasis added.
6. Ibid., 552; emphasis added.
7. Ibid., 552.
8. Ibid., 551.
9. Humphreys, *The Virginia Campaign,* 1:60–72.
10. Sheridan, *Personal Memoirs,* 1:366–67.
11. Gordon C. Rhea, *The Battles for Spotsylvania Court House and the Road to Yellow Tavern, May 7–12* (Baton Rouge: Louisiana State University Press, 1997), 45.
12. O.R., vol. 36, part 2, 513.
13. Grant, *Personal Memoirs,* 770.
14. Porter, *Campaigning with Grant,* 84.
15. Agassiz, *Meade's Headquarters,* 105. See also Porter, *Campaigning with Grant,* 83–84.
16. Porter, *Campaigning with Grant,* 84.
17. Agassiz, *Meade's Headquarters,* 106.
18. Sheridan, *Personal Memoirs,* 1:368.
19. Agassiz, *Meade's Headquarters,* 106.
20. Sheridan, *Personal Memoirs,* 1:368–69. Sheridan grew to despise Warren. Those feelings undoubtedly brought about the ugly incident at Five Forks in April 1865, set forth in chapter 5.
21. Rodenbough, "Sheridan's Richmond Raid," 189.
22. Porter, *Campaigning with Grant,* 84.
23. O.R., vol. 36, part 3, 552.
24. O'Connor, *Sheridan the Inevitable,* 160.
25. Ibid., 161.
26. Morris, *Sheridan,* 164.
27. As was his more famous cousin, Carswell McClellan was a Philadelphian. Interestingly, his brother, Maj. Henry B. McClellan, served as assistant adjutant general to the great Confederate cavalry commander, Jeb Stuart.
28. McClellan, *Notes,* 16–17.

29. Ibid., 21.
30. Ibid., 23.
31. Meade, *Life and Letters of General George Gordon Meade,* 2:246–47. Meade complained bitterly that Sheridan had been promoted over his head, and it took Grant's intervention for Meade to obtain a concomitant promotion, backdated to rank Sheridan's, to calm the army commander's hot temper.
32. Grant, *Personal Memoirs,* 676.
33. O.R., vol. 46, part 2, 545.
34. Ibid., 606.
35. Ibid., 701.
36. Sheridan, *Personal Memoirs,* 2:119.
37. Morris, *Sheridan,* 237.
38. O.R., vol. 46, part 2, 918.
39. O'Connor, *Sheridan the Inevitable,* 238.
40. Davies, *General Sheridan,* 211.
41. O.R., vol. 46, part 2, 980.
42. Sheridan, *Personal Memoirs,* 2:124.
43. O.R., vol. 46, part 3, 234.
44. Grant, *Personal Memoirs,* 695–96.
45. Sheridan, *Personal Memoirs,* 2:127.
46. O.R., vol. 46, part 3, 215.
47. Sheridan, *Personal Memoirs,* 2:132–33.
48. Edward P. Tobie, "Personal Recollections of General Sheridan," *Personal Narratives of Events in the War of the Rebellion, Being Papers Read before the Rhode Island Soldiers and Sailors Historical Society* 6 (Providence, R.I.: Published by the Society, 1889), 201.
49. Ibid., 201; emphasis in original.
50. Ibid., 201; emphasis in original.
51. Sheridan's rampant mendacity will be the subject of chapter 6.
52. Cadwallader, *Three Years with Grant,* 306.

CHAPTER 5

LITTLE PHIL'S
CAVALIER DESTRUCTION OF
LIVES AND CAREERS

Philip H. Sheridan's propensity toward disobedience to the lawful orders of his superior officers, and his own unwillingness to accept that kind of conduct from his subordinates, was closely tied to his disregard for how his actions had an impact on the lives and careers of those men who incurred his wrath. In one instance, Sheridan's pettiness destroyed a lifelong friendship. In two other instances, the military careers of two good men were destroyed by Sheridan's intransigence in dealing with officers whose conduct displeased him.

CROOK: NO CREDIT GIVEN

George Crook was born on a farm near Dayton, Ohio, on September 8, 1828, one of ten children. His large family lived a comfortable life, marked by hard work and plentiful food. George was a bright lad, and his father had marked the boy as the heir apparent of the farm. Only the intervention of the local congressman led to Crook's appointment to West Point in 1848. Because the boy came from an area of limited educational resources, he did not do well in his first year at West Point, finishing near the bottom of his class. He graduated thirty-eighth in a class of forty-three, far from a stellar academic performance. However, he possessed a good mind for battlefield tactics. Crook and Sheridan were roommates at West Point, and the earliest known photograph of Sheridan shows Little Phil's arm draped across the shoulder of his fellow Buckeye.[1]

Crook had a "stalwart frame and rugged features," but was not an especially handsome man. He wore a white braided, rimmed soft felt hat and an ordinary private's uniform blouse, marked only by the two stars on the shoulders. "Such was the make-up of this Ohio boy without pretense of show," wrote correspondent James E. Taylor, "whom the regulation cut caused little concern. He had left his vanities, if such he ever had, at the Point, along with his apprenticeship."[2] One of Sheridan's staff officers recalled that Crook was "easy going and kindly," and that he had "done more good service than has been blown to his credit through 'the trumpet that speaks of fame.'"[3] An artillerist who served under Crook remembered Crook as "genial, patient, slow-speaking, and inclined to reticence"—in short, he was the antithesis of Phil Sheridan.[4] Because he was so easy going, Crook allowed Sheridan to take advantage of him, and that eventually soured their relationship.

The two men shared a forty-year friendship, and Crook was probably the closest friend Little Phil ever had. They served together in the Army of the Cumberland, sharing Rosecrans's patronage. In 1864, Crook came east and assumed command of the First Division of the Army of West Virginia. When Maj. Gen. David Hunter declined to take overall command of the Middle Military Division, Crook became the corps commander. He was the final commander of the Army of the Potomac's Cavalry Corps in the last days of the war. He became the most successful of all of the Regular Army's Indian fighters in the years following the Civil War. William T. Sherman eventually described Crook as the greatest Indian fighter and manager the U.S. Army ever had.[5] When Sheridan took command of the Middle Military District in August 1864, Crook's corps came under his command. Perhaps as a result of their close and enduring friendship, Crook quickly became Sheridan's principal lieutenant. His keen tactical mind repeatedly paid dividends for Sheridan that bloody fall.

These two men were radically different. "Crook was a notably keen and clear-headed man, whose equanimity was rarely, if ever disturbed, even under the most trying of circumstances." Sheridan, on the other hand, "was naturally eager and impulsive, which characteristics, as we have seen, seem to have fully accounted for his abrupt change of plan at the battle of Winchester on the 19th of September."[6] The contrast in their personalities usually made them a more effective team. However, even a man as easy-going as George Crook had a breaking point. Sheridan eventually caused Crook to reach his.

Crook had proposed the flank attack that helped carry the day at Third Winchester. "Crook's skill and his men turned the Rebel left, making victory possible, and the cavalry saved it when it was in danger of being lost," wrote Col. Rutherford B. Hayes, a future U.S. president.[7] Crook had also designed the crushing flank attack that sent Early's army flying off Fisher's Hill. He followed along behind his men as they attacked, carrying an armful of rocks to fling at any man inclined to turn back.[8]

However, after the Union victory, Sheridan claimed credit for the attacks, although the men knew Crook had provided the intellect and tactical expertise behind Sheridan's success. A Yankee soldier recorded, "It was fully understood by everyone at Corps Headquarters . . . that Crook had suggested this movement."[9] Col. Hayes, who commanded troops at Fisher's Hill, wrote in a letter, "At Fisher's Hill the turning of the Rebel left was planned and executed by Crook against the opinions of the other corps generals. . . . General Sheridan is a whole-souled, brave man, and believes in Crook, his old class and roommate at West Point." Hayes summed things up quite nicely when he said, "Intellectually [Sheridan] is not Crook's equal, so that, as I said, General Crook is the brains of this army."[10]

The public never knew or understood that Crook had been the architect of Sheridan's success in the Shenandoah Valley. Historically, commanding generals receive the glory, not their subordinates. Thus, it fell upon Sheridan to make certain that the public knew the roles played by his subordinates. As we shall see, Sheridan's relentless pursuit of his own agenda meant that Crook did not get the credit that he so richly deserved for his contributions to the campaign's successes. In 1866, when he wrote his report of the campaign, Sheridan claimed credit for conceiving the turning movement at Third Winchester, instead of giving it to Crook. Sheridan also credited this success to his horse soldiers, denying it once again to his former roommate.[11]

In addressing Fisher's Hill, Sheridan said he developed the flanking movement. All Sheridan ever said about Crook's role was, "At Fisher's Hill it was again the good fortune of General Crook's command to start the enemy."[12] Sheridan never changed his tune. "General Crook has nobody to write him or his command up," complained Hayes.[13] "In consequence of the enemy's being so well protected from a direct assault, I resolved on the night of the 20th to use again a turning-column against his left, as had been done on the 19th at the Opequon," claimed Sheridan in his memoirs. "To this end I resolved to move Crook, unperceived if possible, over to the eastern face of Little North Mountain, whence he could strike the left and rear of the Confederate line, and as he broke it up, I could support him by a left half-wheel of my whole line of battle."[14]

Crook deeply resented his treatment at the hands of his old friend. In writing of Sheridan's account of the attack at Third Winchester, Crook noted, "I complained of this to Gen. Sheridan, who asked me to say nothing of it in my report, but that he saw the whole affair, and would give me credit for it. But instead of that he didn't write his report until after the war was over, and then instead of giving me the credit I deserved, he treated the subject something in this wise: that I was placed in a fortunate position where I could turn the enemy's flank, giving the impression that my turning the enemy's flank was part of his plan, whereas so far as I know the idea of turning the enemy's flank never occurred to him, but I took the responsibility on my own shoulders."[15]

It did not end there. Crook also addressed the question of the flanking attack at Fisher's Hill. "Gen. Sheridan's first idea was for me to turn the enemy's right flank," noted Crook, "but after discussion saw the folly of such an undertaking, and finally let me go to the right, their left."[16] In finishing the Civil War section of his memoirs, Crook sniped at his former friend. "I regret that I learned too late that it was not what a person did," he sneered, "but it was what he got the credit of doing that gave him a reputation, and at the close of the war gave him position."[17] Sheridan had ridden the wave of his successes and wore the twin stars of a major general in the Regular Army. Crook, however, reverted to lieutenant colonel and watched two of his subordinates get promoted to colonel ahead of him. No wonder he was bitter. Sheridan apparently did nothing to help his friend get the rank and recognition he so clearly deserved.

Years after the end of the Civil War, when their relationship had deteriorated, Crook vented his anger. In December 1889, Crook visited the Cedar Creek battlefield for the first time since the end of the war. Little Phil had died a few months earlier. "After examining the grounds and the position of the troops after twenty five years which have elapsed and in the light of subsequent events, it renders Gen. Sheridan's claims and his subsequent actions in allowing the general public to remain under the impressions regarding his part in these battles, when he knew they were fiction, all the more contemptible," Crook scrawled in his diary. "The adulations heaped on him by a grateful nation for his supposed genius turned his head, which, added to his natural disposition, caused him to bloat his little carcass with debauchery and dissipation, which carried him off prematurely."[18]

Nevertheless, history has bestowed a proud title on George Crook as the most effective Indian fighter in the history of the U. S. Army. He ended up wearing the twin stars of a major general of Regulars, and he enjoyed a thirty-eight-year career in the military. Crook's skill, coupled with his innate talent for diplomacy, made him very effective in dealing with the Plains Indians, a terribly frustrating task in even the best of circumstances. The climax of his career came when Crook successfully persuaded Geronimo's band of renegade Apaches to submit to the authority of the U.S. government with minimal bloodshed involved. Not long after, Crook refused to disarm a band of Indians, preferring to use them as his scouts. Sheridan promptly relieved his old friend of command for familiar reasons—insubordination, ending their long-term friendship on a sour note.[19]

In the end, Sheridan's greed and zeal for self-advancement at all costs did not destroy his old friend's career. It only destroyed an old friendship. Unfortunately, neither William Woods Averell nor Gouverneur K. Warren could say that. They crossed Sheridan's path, felt his wrath, and their careers were forever destroyed as a result.

AVERELL: A MILITARY CAREER DESTROYED

William Woods Averell was born in Cameron, New York, on November 5, 1832. He came from a hearty stock—his father had been one of the first settlers of the area, and his grandfather had fought in the Revolutionary War. More importantly, his great-grandfather, Josiah Bartlett, had been the first constitutional governor of New Hampshire and had signed the Declaration of Independence.[20] Young William spent his youth in school and worked as a drug store clerk. He was nominated to West Point in 1851, and graduated in the bottom portion of the class of 1855. Averell was a superb horseman and a natural for the cavalry. He was commissioned as a lieutenant in the Regiment of Mounted Rifles, later the 3rd U.S. Cavalry. While at the Military Academy, Averell became close friends with classmate Fitzhugh Lee, a nephew of the Academy's commandant, Lt. Col. Robert E. Lee. Fitz Lee also wanted to serve in the cavalry, and the two became as close as brothers.[21]

Not long after being commissioned, Averell went to the Cavalry School at the Carlisle Barracks, Pennsylvania, and spent a tour of duty as the adjutant to the commanding officer. In 1857, he was transferred to a post in New Mexico, where he fought Indians and received a serious leg wound that nearly forced him to leave the service. He spent two years on recuperative leave. Averell went to Washington with the coming of war in April 1861. After a stint as a staff officer that placed him on the battlefield at First Bull Run in July 1861, Averell was commissioned colonel of the 3rd Pennsylvania Cavalry.

Although an ambitious man, Averell was not an aggressive commander. Rather, he was cautious and treated a battlefield like a chessboard, subject to complex tactical maneuvers. He believed that troops needed extensive training and did not want to take troops into the field if he did not believe them to be ready. As a result of his efforts, the 3rd Pennsylvania soon gained the reputation of being one of the best trained and best disciplined volunteer cavalry regiments assigned to the Army of the Potomac. "He was an excellent drillmaster, with proper views of what constituted proper discipline," recalled an admiring trooper. "Instruction in a systematic manner, with a view of preparing these men for the service expected of them, was commenced and persistently followed in the most industrious and painstaking manner."[22]

Averell's personality mirrored that of the army's commander, Maj. Gen. George B. McClellan, a trait that cost him dearly. "McClellan and Averell would take time to reorganize, reequip and retrain their forces even if it meant stopping the momentum of battle. Lack of a visceral desire to aim for the jugular of a defeated enemy eventually would cost both men their commands."[23]

Averell was a Democrat, as was his hero, McClellan. Averell did not trust politicians, and he certainly did not trust the Republican administration, whose bungling he blamed for the war. He also did not believe that amateur soldiers and politicians had any role in the army, believing that only professional soldiers like him should command large bodies of troops in the field. These traits would not sit well with the mercurial Sheridan.

Under McClellan's leadership, Averell commanded a brigade of cavalry during the 1862 Peninsula Campaign. He fell victim to a malarial fever in the aftermath of the campaign, requiring five weeks of recuperation. A relapse of the fever forced him to miss the Antietam Campaign in the fall of 1862. In spite of the illness, Averell assumed command of a division later that fall.[24]

On March 17, 1863, Averell and his horsemen splashed across the Rappahannock River at Kelly's Ford and engaged his old friend Fitz Lee in a daylong fight. Although Averell outnumbered Lee's brigade, he nevertheless fought a defensive battle and withdrew across Kelly's Ford as the dim winter sun began to set. The battle was a tactical draw, although Lee held the battlefield at the end of the day. Not decisive in any sense, the Battle of Kelly's Ford is often called the Union cavalry's first victory of the war.

In the spring of 1863, Maj. Gen. Joseph Hooker, then commanding the Army of the Potomac, conceived a daring cavalry raid designed to disrupt communications in the Confederate rear while his army stole a march of Robert E. Lee. Unleashing a raid deep into the enemy heartland, Cavalry Corps commander Maj. Gen. George Stoneman led twelve thousand horsemen into action at the end of April 1863. Averell's division waded the Rappahannock at Kelly's Ford and quickly ran into strong Confederate resistance. After forcing his way through, Averell learned that a very strong enemy cavalry force lay waiting at nearby Brandy Station, under personal command of Jeb Stuart. Averell decided not to take on Stuart's entire division, and instead marched to Culpeper, sacked the town, and then established a camp at Rapidan Station. Several days later, a furious Hooker recalled Averell's division and summarily relieved him of command at the raid's conclusion. A critical Hooker noted, "If he disregarded all instruction, it was his duty to do something. If the enemy did not come to him, he should have gone to the enemy."[25]

A disappointed Averell was sent to take command of the poorly organized cavalry forces attached to the Department of West Virginia. He took a ragtag force, trained it, and made it an effective command. His men conducted three long raids, including a daring, successful, and perilous winter foray to Salem, Virginia, that helped break the Confederate siege of Knoxville.[26] Then, when Sheridan assumed command of the Army of West Virginia, Averell, the senior cavalry officer associated with the newly formed army, was entitled to command of Sheridan's Cavalry Corps. However, in his orders to Sheridan, Grant wrote, "Do not hesitate to give commands to officers in whom you repose confidence, without regard to claims of others on account of rank. If you deem Torbert the best man to command the cavalry, place him in command and give Averell some other command, or relieve him from the expedition, and order him to report to General Hunter." The lieutenant general concluded, "What we want is prompt and active movements after the enemy, in accordance with instructions you already have."[27] These orders would create great problems as the campaign developed.

By the fall of 1864, Brig. Gen. William Woods Averell had commanded a division of cavalry for almost the entire war. Still, Sheridan chose Torbert. Years later, instead of admitting that he had selected Torbert, Sheridan blamed Grant. Little Phil claimed, "When I was assigned to the command of the 'Middle Military Division' I had determined in my own mind to make General Averell my Chief of Cavalry. I knew him to be a thorough Soldier, and his success in the valley had won for him the position as the leading cavalry officer in the service, and with his knowledge of the country, he was in my judgment well qualified for this position." He continued, "In consulting with General Grant in relation to my new field, he specially requested me to assign General Torbert to that position."[28] Sheridan's *ex post facto* rationalization of his conduct does not hold up under scrutiny, particularly because it directly contradicts the express language of Grant's orders.

Sheridan later asserted that Averell had refused to serve under Torbert, and that Averell had suggested that Sheridan relieve him of command. "This I refused to do, and said to General Averell that all his orders would be given direct to him," claimed Sheridan, "and I would not ask him to serve under Torbert."[29] Again, these contentions do not bear up to scrutiny. Such a system would have been unwieldy and impractical. Instead, Averell's division joined the Army of the Shenandoah's Cavalry Corps and fought under the direct command of Alfred Torbert.

In truth, Sheridan probably was biased from the start. Crook did not like Averell and blamed the New Yorker for his defeat at Second Kernstown in July 1864. He had accused Averell of being drunk during the fight. "Our cavalry was of little or no assistance," claimed Crook. He blamed Averell's horse soldiers for stampeding, adding to the magnitude of the debacle.[30] Considering the warm, close relationship between Little Phil and Crook, Crook probably stated these feelings to his old roommate, poisoning Sheridan's perceptions and influencing Sheridan's handling of Averell's situation.

"Major General Sheridan illegally assumed the prerogative of the President of the United States," complained Averell, "and ordered me to report to a junior officer on the 23rd of August without any just cause."[31] These complaints certainly did not endear him to Little Phil, who began looking for reasons to relieve Averell of command. As the campaign developed, Sheridan grew unhappy with Averell's lack of aggression, even though Averell's troopers had performed admirably at Third Winchester.

Averell's horse soldiers participated in the successful assault on Fisher's Hill, coordinating and cooperating with Crook's flank attack. They did not follow up on the attack with a vigorous pursuit because they really had nowhere to go. When Averell arrived at Sheridan's headquarters the next day, the army commander erupted. "We had some hot words," recounted Sheridan in his memoirs.[32] Sheridan demanded to know where Averell had been and asked why he had not pursued Early's beaten army during the night. Averell informed Sheridan that he had received neither orders nor information from headquarters. Sheridan exploded, exclaiming that he had been unable to locate him. Averell testily responded by asking if Sheridan had even tried to find him. Livid, Sheridan described Early's army as "a perfect mob" that would disintegrate in the face of a vigorous pursuit. James Bowen, the chaplain of the 19th New York Cavalry, witnessed this exchange. "It can be stated from positive knowledge that while Averell maintained a calm and civil demeanor, Sheridan manifested unreasonable anger, refusing to listen to any explanations," Bowen recounted.[33] "The tone, manner, and words of the major-general commanding," sniffed Averell in his report, "indicated and implied dissatisfaction. I did not entertain the opinion that the rebel army was a mob." Nevertheless, Sheridan instructed Averell to join Devin's brigade in pursuing the beaten Confederates.[34]

Just to make sure that the point had been driven home, Sheridan dispatched written instructions to Averell on September 23. "I do not want you to let the enemy bluff you or your command," warned Sheridan, "and I want you to distinctly understand this note. I do not advise recklessness, but I do desire resolution and actual fighting with necessary casualties, before you retire. There must now be no backing or filling by you without a superior force of the enemy engaging you."[35] Sheridan's warning could not have been more unambiguous.

Averell's men, joined by Devin's brigade, made a perfunctory attack, but Averell's cautious nature held them back. Instead of vigorously assaulting the beaten Confederates, Averell decided that the enemy position was too strong to take on. Devin and Averell instead deployed their men along the Confederate front and suspended action for the day. Furious, Little Phil removed Averell from command two days later. "I have relieved Averell from his command," raged Sheridan. "Instead of following the enemy when he was broken at Fisher's Hill (so there was not a cavalry organization left), he went into camp and let me pursue the enemy for a distance of fifteen miles with infantry, during the night."[36] Sheridan claimed that Averell's "indifferent attack" was not worthy of "the excellent soldiers he commanded." Later, Sheridan wrote in his memoirs, "The removal of Averell was but the culmination of a series of events extending back to the time I assumed command of the Middle Military Division. . . . I therefore thought that the interest of the service would be subserved by removing one whose growing indifference might render the best-laid plans inoperative."[37]

That night, Sheridan's assistant adjutant general delivered an order to Averell. "Bvt. Maj. Gen. W. W. Averell, commanding Second Cavalry Division, Department of West Virginia, is relieved from duty with that command and will at once proceed to Wheeling, W. Va.," Sheridan had written. Averell was "there to await orders from these headquarters or higher authority." Sheridan permitted Averell to take only his personal staff with him, and a colonel took command of his division.[38] The flabbergasted Averell rightly believed the removal to be unjustified.

The dismayed Averell "called the officers together and addressed them, enjoining upon them to continue as energetic and attentive in the future as they had been in the past, and to yield the same obedience to his successor as they had to him." The men of his division were very fond of Averell, and his relief "caused a universal feeling of amazement in [the] army, and it is thought that some question of rank between General Averell and General Torbert is involved," reported a correspondent of the *New York Herald*. As the downtrodden general took leave of his command, his "division officers and men exhibited their devotion to him by the most marked demonstrations. The officers, who seemed to love him as an elder brother, shed tears at his departure, and as the general rode along the lines for the last time the men greeted him with the most enthusiastic cheers and many expressions of affection."[39]

James E. Taylor, another correspondent, watched Averell's departure from Sheridan's camps. The "sight of a big blond general on horseback" caught Taylor's eye, and he watched Averell in "earnest conversation with a dismounted officer." Taylor had never seen Averell before, and the sight intrigued him. "It was with feelings of melancholy interest I observed him," commented the correspondent, "while speculating on the uncertainties of a military career, for his, up to a fortnight back, was full of promise. Now he clasps his friend's hand and rides away."[40] Sheridan had sent Averell to Wheeling to await further orders that never came. William Woods Averell never commanded troops in the field again.

When he wrote his report of the campaign, Averell was understandably bitter. He suggested that Sheridan had deliberately refused to acknowledge his contributions to the Union victories at Third Winchester and Fisher's Hill. Also, he believed that Sheridan's order relieving him of command tramped upon . . . [my] record and upon all military courtesy and justice." The unhappy general continued, "An officer who has served the Government nine years, who has suffered from wounds in battle, cannot without any assigned cause or pretext be suddenly relieved from the command of a division whose record tells of nothing but success and victories without having his sensibilities outraged and his reputation jeopardized." He wrote, "I have evidence that it was determined to relieve me in order to make Brigadier-General Torbert chief of cavalry before Major-General Sheridan assumed command of the Middle Military Division."[41]

Averell would never forgive or forget the injustice done him by Sheridan. As a McClellan Democrat in the days just before the 1864 presidential election, Averell believed that his relief was politically motivated. Averell carried a grudge against Sheridan for spoiling an otherwise distinguished military record. Five years after the war ended, the two men had a chance encounter at a social event. Although social graces prevented Averell from showing his contempt in public, he nevertheless gave Little Phil a piece of his mind. "I was the victim of a grievous wrong or great mistake and I cannot permit you to entertain the impression from our exchange of civilities this morning that I am willing to resume friendly intercourse with you until some explanation from you of your actions on the occasion I have referred to has been received by me," he growled in a subsequent letter to Little Phil.[42]

The removal devastated Averell and completely destroyed his military career. "Sheridan's action shattered Averell in a way that physical damage incurred by bullets or fever during the war had not," claimed the editors of Averell's memoirs. "For the rest of his life he would try to refute this action and gather evidence to substantiate his belief that the removal was politically rather than militarily motivated."[43] This episode caused Averell so much pain that he did not address it when he wrote his memoirs long after the end of the Civil War. He spent years trying to get a satisfactory explanation but never did. However,

Averell got some satisfaction in the years after the war. Several people reported to him that Sheridan regretted his actions in relieving Averell and that he had come to view his actions as a mistake.

Once again, though, Sheridan's justifications do not hold up under scrutiny. Claiming that the awkward command structure of having Averell report directly to him had created problems of command, control, and coordination, Sheridan alleged, "I found it impossible to successfully direct the movements of my army without a Chief of Cavalry. I was compelled to relieve General Averell against my judgment, and personal preference." Astonishingly, Sheridan boldly claimed, "I regarded Averell as a superior officer over Torbert. I have always regretted my action on General Averell's account and also for the reason that General Torbert failed to come up to the standard, and I was finally compelled to assign General Merritt to this position."[44] This postwar spin directly contradicts Sheridan's contemporary words and suggests that he was merely trying to mollify Averell. Sheridan never apologized to Averell, and he never did anything to right the wrong he had perpetrated by relieving him of command.

Were Sheridan's actions justified? An analysis of the historical records suggests that they were not. In spite of his relief from command, Averell received a brevet to major general of volunteers at the end of the war. While Sheridan may not have appreciated Averell's skills, the government did recognize them, as well as Averell's contributions to the Union victory in the Civil War. Averell's principal attributes—discipline and caution—caused him to run afoul of Sheridan. The editors of Averell's memoirs noted, "William Averell was not a failure during the Civil War; he was a victim of change. He had been just what the army needed early in the conflict—disciplined, capable and cautious. He took untrained horsemen and molded them into a cavalry force of which any commander could be proud." Even though his career had ended in disgrace like his mentor McClellan's, Averell, like McClellan, remained popular with the men who had served under him. Those horse soldiers carried a fondness for him for the rest of their lives.[45]

Averell's "greatest flaw might have been that he was an outsider, an officer not associated with the Cavalry Corps of the Army of the Potomac," observed historian Jeffry D. Wert.[46] By contrast, Torbert, who was closely associated with the Army of the Potomac's Cavalry Corps, had been guilty of the same sin that cost Averell his command. Torbert had failed to make a vigorous pursuit of the beaten Confederates and had halted in front of New Market instead of assaulting a strong defensive position held by Col. Thomas T. Munford's Confederate cavalry brigade. When he wrote his report of the campaign in 1866, Sheridan publicly complained about Torbert's performance. "Had General Torbert driven this cavalry or turned the defile and reached New Market, I have no doubt but that we would have captured the entire rebel army," groused Sheridan, "I feel certain that its rout from Fisher's Hill was such that there was scarcely a company organization held together."[47]

In his memoirs, Sheridan accused Torbert of making "only a feeble effort." While admitting that Munford held a formidable defensive position, Sheridan believed that "Torbert ought to have made a fight." In Sheridan's eyes, not even the strong defensive position excused the lack of aggressiveness by his chief of cavalry. "To this day," he wrote years later, "I have been unable to account satisfactorily for Torbert's failure."[48] In spite of the same failures that had led to Averell's punishment, Sheridan did not censure his corps commander. Instead, Torbert remained in command of the Army of the Shenandoah's Cavalry Corps until the end of February 1865.

On reflection, it appears that Averell was justified in choosing not to attack on September 23. As his division took position that day, Averell could plainly see Early's camps bristling on the plateau above. Early dispatched an infantry division to meet the threat posed by Averell's horsemen and supported it with five pieces of artillery. Further, the Confederates had dug extensive rifle pits to strengthen their position. "The enemy was fully on the alert and perfectly able to hold the position against five times my force," recounted Averell, "and a signal officer reported to me that the enemy was moving a brigade or division around my right." Unlike the enemy, Averell did not have a good defensive position for his outnumbered division. His left rested on a river, and he had an "almost impassable creek" in his rear. Facing a much larger force, supported by artillery, with a poor position, Averell's decision not to attack seems perfectly reasonable.[49]

Considering that Torbert's failure was worse, that Torbert received unequal treatment at Sheridan's hands, and that Averell's decision not to attack appears to have been a prudent and well-reasoned one, the harsh penalty meted out by Sheridan was unwarranted and unjust. Fortunately, Averell had a successful career after the Civil War, and several inventions made him a very wealthy man, somewhat ameliorating the sting of Sheridan's actions.

Gouverneur K. Warren, on the other hand, did not have the same luxury. Instead, Sheridan's precipitous actions ruined his life and career.

WARREN: A LIFETIME TRYING TO CLEAR HIS NAME

Gouverneur Kemble Warren was also a New Yorker. He was born in Cold Spring, on the Hudson River across from West Point, on January 8, 1830. The young man received an appointment to the Military Academy in 1846, and graduated second in the class of 1850. His class ranking led to an appointment in the topographical engineers, including service as chief engineer in Brig. Gen. William S. Harney's expedition into Nebraska to punish the Brule Sioux in 1856. Warren also taught mathematics at West Point.

With the coming of war, the young officer accepted an appointment as lieutenant colonel of the 5th New York Infantry on May 14, 1861. He participated in the war's first battle, Big Bethel, on June 10. In August, he received a promotion to colonel, and was wounded in combat while leading a brigade of the Fifth Corps at the Battle of Gaines's Mill during McClellan's Peninsula Campaign. In August 1862, his brigade made a brief but heroic stand in the face of an overwhelming Confederate attack during the Battle of Second Manassas. He led its survivors at Antietam on September 17, 1862, and received a promotion to brigadier general of volunteers less than two weeks later.

With a keen eye for terrain, Warren became the Army of the Potomac's chief engineer the following spring. On his own initiative, during the second day of the Battle of Gettysburg, he rode up the important hill called Little Round Top, where he spotted an imminent, massed Confederate attack. Accepting responsibility for his actions, Warren ordered a brigade of the Fifth Corps to hold the hill at all costs, and he received well-deserved acclaim as the savior of Little Round Top. On August 8, he was promoted to major general of volunteers and assumed temporary command of the Second Corps while the regular corps commander, Maj. Gen. Winfield S. Hancock, recovered from his Gettysburg wound. During the Mine Run Campaign that fall, Warren, exercising caution and deliberation, spotted a trap laid for the Union army by Robert E. Lee and refused to attack. Although Meade was angry at Warren for not attacking, he quickly realized that Warren had been right.

When Hancock returned to duty in the spring of 1864, Warren took command of the Fifth Corps, drawing Sheridan's anger for blocking the roads to Todd's Tavern in the aftermath of the Wilderness. Both Grant and Meade found him difficult to deal with, and, his engineer's natural caution made him less aggressive than either general might have liked.[50] By the spring of 1865, when Sheridan returned to the Army of the Potomac, Grant had largely run out of patience with Warren's personality; he believed Warren to be disobedient and timid. The situation was a recipe for disaster, and Phil Sheridan became the catalyst for that disaster.

The Army of the Potomac fought a successful action along the Boydton Plank Road on March 29, 1865, extending Lee's lines around Petersburg to the breaking point. Warren's infantry made first contact and bore the brunt of a savage fight. On March 31, Warren moved toward an important road intersection along the White Oak Road. His men had an indecisive fight with Confederate

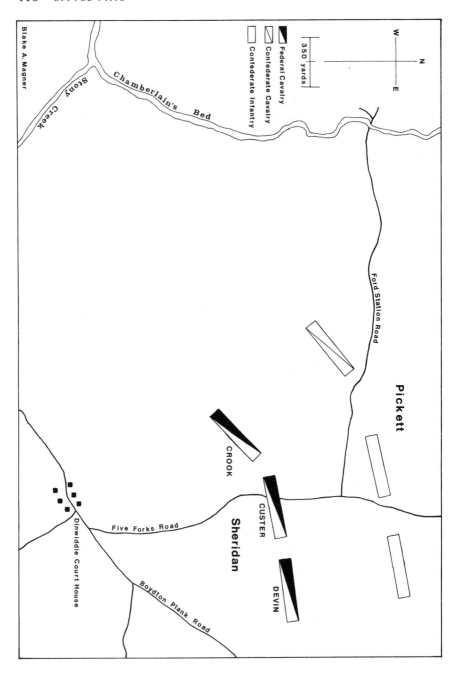

Dinwiddie Court House, March 29, 1865

infantry. In the interim, Sheridan's troopers had a prolonged fight with Maj. Gen. George E. Pickett's gray-clad infantry at Dinwiddie Court House, where his dismounted horse soldiers successfully held off a desperate attack by Pickett's Division. However, the dogged fight by Pickett's men had prevented Sheridan from fulfilling his mission, and the Federal cavalry had nearly been dealt a decisive defeat.[51] That night, Sheridan reported to Meade that the enemy's infantry was now isolated and ripe for the picking. Meade then suggested to Grant that the Fifth Corps be sent to Sheridan "to smash up the force in front" of the cavalry. Grant promptly approved the request and placed the Fifth Corps under Sheridan's direct command for an assault on the crucial road junction at Five Forks.[52]

Sheridan had not wanted either Warren or the Fifth Corps. Instead, he wanted his old familiar Sixth Corps, with which he felt very comfortable. Sheridan rode to headquarters to register his complaints. "His plea was that the Sixth Corps had been with the cavalry in the Shenandoah Campaign; officers and men knew and trusted each other; that the Fifth Corps were strangers; and when hard pressed, said he had no confidence in Warren, under such circumstances. He would not like to be subordinated to [Sheridan] and he expected nothing but trouble." Grant heard out his subordinate's complaints, but made it clear that Warren and the Fifth Corps, and not Wright and the Sixth Corps, would be sent to Sheridan.[53]

Grant, looking to mollify his unhappy subordinate and concerned about Warren's caution himself, "notified General Sheridan that he was authorized to relieve General Warren, if, in his judgment, it was for the best interests of the service to do so; that I was afraid he would fail him in a critical moment."[54] While Grant respected the corps commander's many good qualities, the lieutenant general believed that Warren had "a defect which was beyond his control, that was very prejudicial to his usefulness in emergencies like the one just before us. He could see every danger at a glance before he had encountered it. He would not only make preparations to meet the danger which might occur, but he would inform his commanding officer what others should do while he was executing his move."[55]

Sheridan eagerly awaited his chance to pitch into the fray. On the night of March 31, Sheridan grew increasingly anxious and excited. As he discussed his plans for the coming fight with Col. Horace Porter, one of Grant's staff officers, Little Phil became very animated. When Porter inquired about fodder and supplies, Sheridan gave a characteristic response. "Forage?" he asked. "I'll get all the forage I want. I'll haul it out if I have to set every man in the command to corduroying roads, and corduroy every mile of them from the railroad to Dinwiddie. I tell you, I'm ready to strike out tomorrow and go to smashing things."

Porter observed that the pacing Sheridan "chafed like a hound in the leash."[56] Sheridan's anxiety only grew. His nervous energy created the problem that cost Gouverneur K. Warren his career.

An anxious Sheridan prepared orders for Warren. "I am holding in front of Dinwiddie Courthouse on the road leading to Five Forks, for three-quarters of a mile, with General Custer's division. The enemy are in his immediate front, lying so as to cover the road just this side of A. Adams's house, which leads out across Chamberlain's bed or run," he wrote. "I understand you have a division at J. Boisseau's; if so, you are in the rear of the enemy's line and almost on his flanks. I will hold on here. Possibly they may attack at daylight; if so attack instantly and in full force. Attack at daylight anyhow, and I will make an effort to get the road this side of Adams's house, and if I do you can capture the whole of them."[57]

The next morning, April 1, 1865, Sheridan planned to march on Five Forks with his cavalry, under Merritt and Crook. At three o'clock in the morning, Sheridan gave Warren his marching orders for the day. In addition to what he had written, Sheridan instructed, "Any force moving down the White Oak Road, will be in the enemy's rear, and in all probability get any force that may escape you by a flank movement. Do not fear my leaving here. If the enemy remains, I shall fight at daylight."[58] Warren's infantry would support the attack.

Little Phil's battle blood was up that day. The cavalry pitched into Pickett's infantry that morning, and Sheridan waited impatiently for the Fifth Corps to come up and join the attack. About one o'clock that afternoon, Sheridan ordered Warren to bring up the Fifth Corps and join the fighting around Five Forks. Warren joined Sheridan at the front. Sheridan laid out his plan for winning the battle, "telling Warren how the enemy was posted, explaining with considerable detail, and concluding by stating that I wished his troops to be formed on the Gravelly Church Road, with two divisions to the front, aligned obliquely to the White Oak Road, and one in reserve, opposite the centre of these two." Sheridan later claimed that "General Warren seemed to understand me clearly, and then left to join his command."[59]

In spite of his clear understanding, Warren did not move quickly enough to satisfy Sheridan. It did not appear to Sheridan that Warren was making any effort to hurry his troops into battle, and Sheridan's "disappointment grew into disgust." Sheridan spurred over to Warren's location and "expressed my fears that the cavalry might expend their ammunition before the attack could be made, that the sun would go down before the battle could be begun, or that troops from Lee's right, which, be it remembered, was less than three miles away from my right, might, by striking my rear, or even by threatening it, prevent the attack on Pickett."[60] Sheridan believed that Warren was apathetic, and his limited patience had about run out.

Brig. Gen. Joshua L. Chamberlain, himself a hero of the fight for Little Round Top, commanded a brigade in the Fifth Corps. He knew Warren well and was very familiar with the corps commander's personality and style. "Those who knew Warren best saw no indifference," wrote Chamberlain. "He was not in his usual spirits,—and we cannot wonder at it,—but he was intense rather than expressive. He knew what was depending, and what was called for, and put his energies into the case more mentally than muscularly. His subordinates understood his earnestness."[61]

After thoroughly examining the ground, Warren opened the attack at four o'clock. When his foot soldiers went in, Sheridan was not happy with their dispositions and tried to recall them. Warren was not at the head of his column, where Little Phil expected him to be. Instead, the corps commander was off looking for one of his division commanders, Brig. Gen. Samuel W. Crawford, whose troops had wandered off course. Warren's absence from the front proved to be the last straw for Sheridan. "Crawford's division had moved off in a northerly direction, marching away from Ayres, and leaving a gap between the two divisions. Sheridan became exceedingly annoyed at this circumstance, complained that Warren was not giving adequate personal supervision to the infantry, and sent nearly all his staff-officers to the Fifth Corps to see that the mistakes made were corrected."[62]

So annoyed was he, in fact, that Sheridan committed a shocking breach of protocol by expressing his dissatisfaction with Warren to his staff. Lt. Col. Frederic C. Newhall, Sheridan's assistant adjutant general, recounted that "we remarked to each other that there would be a deuce of a row if the V Corps was not ready to move out soon. He evidently considered that General Warren was throwing cold water on the proposed assault; and if he arrived at this conclusion, doubtless General Warren helped him to it by something more than an indifferent manner."[63] Nevertheless, Warren's men carried the day, shattering the Confederate line and driving the panicked Southerners from the field in a wild rout. The corps commander's horse was shot out from under him in the final assault on the enemy line. Although he had not moved as quickly as Sheridan might have liked, the Fifth Corps provided the impetus for a decisive victory at Five Forks.

Pacing like a caged tiger, the anxious Sheridan searched for Warren. Unable to locate the corps commander, Sheridan grabbed the first general officer to happen by, Brig. Gen. Romeyn B. Ayres, who commanded a division in the Fifth Corps. "Where's Warren?" growled Little Phil to Ayres. Ayres informed

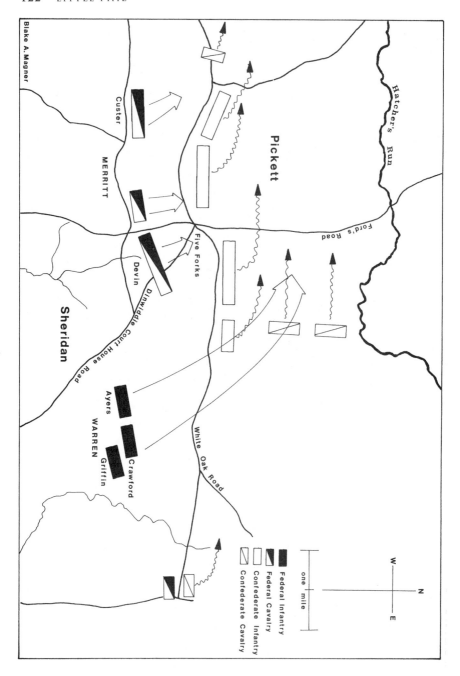

Blake A. Magner

Five Forks, April 1, 1865

Sheridan that Warren was back at the rear, prompting Sheridan to snap, "That's where I expected to find him."[64] Still unable to find Warren, Sheridan rode out to position troops himself. Watching Chamberlain directing his troops to fill a breach in the Union line, Sheridan roared, "By God, that's what I want to see: general officers at the front!" With Sheridan in their lead, Chamberlain's foot soldiers shattered the Confederate line, beginning the rout that forced Lee to abandon Petersburg and Richmond.[65]

Sheridan then sent his adjutant, Newhall, to find Warren's senior division commander, Maj. Gen. Charles Griffin. Sheridan instructed Griffin to take command of the Fifth Corps. In the meantime, Warren sent one of his staff officers, Col. Frederick Locke, to Sheridan with news of the breakthrough and to await further orders. An enraged Sheridan raised a fist. "Tell General Warren," he snarled, "I say, by God, he was not at the front. That's all I've got to say to him!" One of Sheridan's staff officers hastily scribbled an order, and it was done.[66]

When Warren returned from his successful assaults on the enemy lines, the staff officer greeted him and handed him the order: "Major-General Warren, commanding Fifth Army Corps, is relieved from duty, and will report at once to Lieutenant-General Grant, commanding armies of the United States."[67] When he learned of his relief, Warren rushed to Sheridan's headquarters to ask Sheridan to reconsider his decision. "Reconsider?" thundered Little Phil. "Hell! I don't reconsider my determination. Obey the order!" "With almost the agony of death upon his face," the heartbroken Warren rode off. "With bowed head and without a word, he turns from the spectral groups of friend and foe mingled in the dark, forbidding cloud of night, to report to the one man on earth who held power over what to him was dearer than life, and takes his lonely way over that eventful field, along that fateful White Oak Road, which for him had no end on earth."[68]

Sheridan had grown unhappy with Warren's conduct of a segment of the successful assault. "During this attack, I again became dissatisfied with General Warren," he claimed. "During the engagement portions of his line gave way when not exposed to a heavy fire, and simply from want of confidence on the part of the troops, which Warren did not exert himself to inspire. I therefore relieved him from the command of the Fifth Corps, authority for this action having been sent to me before the battle, unsolicited."[69] When he wrote his report of the war's final campaign in 1866, Sheridan justified his actions: "General Warren did not exert himself to get up his corps as rapidly as he might have done, and his manner gave me the impression that he wished the sun to go down before dispositions for the attack could be completed."[70] The great irony of this, of course, is that Warren had been sent to rescue Sheridan. His men had, in fact, carried the day at Five Forks, and Warren was ignominiously removed from command as a result. Perhaps Sheridan did not want to share the limelight, or perhaps he was unwilling to share the glory for the great victory at Five Forks. Nevertheless, Warren lost his command a week before the war ended, all for no good reason.

Warren never got an adequate explanation of the reasons for his relief. His men had carried the burden of the fighting at Five Forks, and they had shattered Pickett's Division. Some of his supporters contended that Sheridan had relieved Warren of command in order to insure that he, and not Warren, received the credit for the victory at Five Forks.[71] "Greatly to my astonishment, just at dark, after the fighting was all over," Warren wrote to his wife, "General Sheridan ordered me to report to General Grant. This I did at once, and reached him about 10 P.M. He then told me that he had designed to relieve me from the command of the Fifth Corps and assign me to other duty. He spoke very kindly of my past services and efforts, but thought I was too self-reliant in executing my duties, and did not strictly obey orders and cooperate in his general plans close enough." Shocked, Warren noted, "I was quite astonished again at hearing this, as I had been entrusted with so much and so often."[72]

So were a number of observers. Sylvanus Cadwallader, a correspondent with the *New York Herald* and no supporter of the embattled corps commander, recounted, "The most unexpected event of the day (April 1st), or of the season, was the removal from command, in the presence of the enemy, by General Sheridan, of Major-General Warren, so long commanding the Fifth army corps. His corps was turned over to General Griffin, as the ranking officer." Cadwallader also was no supporter of the embattled corps commander. "But little has transpired as to the immediate provocation, or justification, but it is understood to have been because of General Warren's tardiness or refusal to obey orders, by charging the rebel lines," he reported. "From a tolerably thorough acquaintance with General Warren's usual behavior in somewhat similar circumstances, I have not a particle of doubt that his removal was right and proper."[73] Not surprisingly, this statement stirred up controversy that raged for years.

Sheridan's many supporters loudly and roundly criticized Warren in order to justify the relief of the corps commander. Sheridan "sincerely believed that [Warren] was not in a proper frame of mind to conduct vigorous operations; that he overestimated the ability and strength of the enemy; that he hesitated to strike boldly, and impaired the efficiency of his corps by his own apathy," claimed Newhall, "that . . . he was a millstone hanging around the necks of 15,000 men, and a clog in their final steps toward victory."[74] Others echoed similar notes.

Meade tried to help. Even though the two officers had clashed a number of times, Meade nevertheless recognized the injustice of Sheridan's actions. On April 18, after Lee's surrender at Appomattox, Meade wrote to Grant, "Your attention is called to the necessity of a permanent commander being assigned to the 5th Corps. My views on this point have been made known to you. Should you be disposed to reassign Major General Warren, I shall make no objection thereto." Grant ignored the request. "Your dispatch, calling attention to the necessity of a permanent commander for the Fifth Corps, is received. You will please continue it in the temporary command of General Griffin for the present. Orders will be sent to General Warren in a few days."[75] Nothing came of it, although Grant later claimed in his memoirs that "I was very sorry that it had been done, and regretted still more that I had not long before taken occasion to assign him to another field of duty."[76] In other words, had Grant acted promptly, the entire fiasco could have been avoided. If the lieutenant general was displeased with Warren's performance, he should have done something about it sooner, instead of creating a volatile situation.

Warren's career was in shambles. He immediately demanded a court of inquiry to clear his name, a request stonewalled by Grant until after Grant had left the White House. He never gave up trying to clear his name. When he penned his report of Five Forks, Warren complained, "In this battle I claim to have done my duty myself, and I believe a perusal of this report and of those of my subordinates will show that the opinion of General Sheridan—that I did not exert myself as I should—must have arisen from some misapprehension or misconception of my efforts. His implied charge of neglect in stating that I failed to reach Dinwiddie Court House before midnight, as expected, the Lieutenant General must know now is unjust, for it was impossible for my troops to get there before daybreak." Warren concluded by pleading for his name to be cleared. "I trust, therefore, that I may yet receive some unequivocal acknowledgment of my faithful services at the Battle of Five Forks, that will forever free me from opprobrium."[77] Maj. Gen. Andrew A. Humphreys, commander of the Second Corps, noted, "These are very grave accusations or imputations, and of such serious character that no officer could rest under them. Any officer against whom they were made would be entitled, whatever his rank might be, to an investigation of them before a proper court."[78]

Capt. Charles H. Porter, an officer of the Fifth Corps, summed up Warren's plight quite well. "Thus, on the field of battle, after the most successful day's work that he had ever taken part in, was Warren deprived of the command of the corps which had commanded since March, 1864," Porter wrote, "and a position he earned by the right of soldierly courage and brilliant operations on many fields. Beginning at . . . Big Bethel, his name is associated with every field upon which the Army of the Potomac was engaged."[79]

Sheridan steadfastly refused to consider any alternative other than his own version of events. The night of April 1, Sheridan rode over to the subordinate commanders of the Fifth Corps. To their great surprise, Sheridan apologized for his conduct that day. "Gentlemen, I have come over to see you," he said. "I may have spoken harshly to some of you today; but I would not have it hurt you. You know how it is: we had to carry this place, and I was fretted all day till it was done. You must forgive me. I know it is hard for the men, too; but we must push. There is more for us to do together. I appreciate and thank you all."[80] However, Sheridan never found it within himself to apologize to Warren, a man to whom he owed an apology.

Within a couple of days of the relief of Warren, a newspaper correspondent asked Sheridan directly why he had removed Warren from command of the Fifth Corps. "He said there was no alternative left to him. He was obliged to remove Warren." The same reporter claimed that "Sheridan always spoke of the matter in a subdued sorrowful tone of voice in the many conversations I had with him in relation to it."[81] Sheridan never budged from this belief, even in the wake of the court of inquiry's findings years later. In his memoirs, Sheridan stuck to his version of events. "The occasion was not an ordinary one, and as I thought that Warren had not risen to its demand in the battle," he wrote, "I deemed it injudicious and unsafe under the critical conditions existing to retain him longer. That I was justified in this is plain to all who are disposed to be fair-minded."[82] It is clear that, even though he denied it in his memoirs, Sheridan was predisposed to find fault with an officer that he had never wanted to have assigned to him, and it is clear that Warren suffered as a result.

In spite of his acknowledged brilliance and his years of loyal service, Warren only achieved the rank of lieutenant colonel in the Regular Army years after the injustice done him by Sheridan. Once again, Grant protected Sheridan, shielding him from criticism by repeatedly finding excuses to deny Warren the long-requested court of inquiry. Warren understood what was going on immediately. The day after his removal, Warren informed his wife, "Ever since General Grant came here, every chance and favor has been given to the western generals, and they have shown a spirit that is extremely sectional. Coldness in their ordinary intercourse, and remarks behind our backs, have made this only too apparent."[83] Thus, Warren missed the end of the war and did not lead his victorious and beloved Fifth Corps down Pennsylvania Avenue during the Grand Review in May 1865.

In protest, Warren resigned his commission as major general of volunteers in May 1865. "The treatment I have received for the past is not encouraging to my spirits for the future," he wrote to his wife, "and convinces me that, if a complication should arise, the greatest use those who employ me would think me capable of, would be to sacrifice my reputation to try and shield their own."[84] Warren spent the rest of his distinguished career in the Corps of Engineers, where he built railroads. He also spent the rest of his life trying to clear his name, but found his efforts stonewalled at every step.

Finally, in 1879, after Grant had left the White House, President Rutherford B. Hayes ordered that Warren receive a court of inquiry to determine whether Sheridan had acted correctly in relieving Warren of command. Although he later claimed otherwise, this act enraged Sheridan, who was powerless to prevent the panel from convening. Perhaps he knew that his actions would not be upheld, or perhaps he genuinely believed that his actions were above reproach. Irrespective of Sheridan's displeasure, a panel of three career Regulars, including two of the Army of the Potomac's former corps commanders, heard the evidence. At the time, Sheridan was a lieutenant general, the army's second highest-ranking officer after General in Chief William T. Sherman. These three officers took their careers in their own hands in sitting on the panel.

After a lengthy hearing where Sheridan and Grant both testified, the court of inquiry cleared Warren, finding that his relief had been unjustified. Sheridan admitted that he had gotten "angry and frustrated" and that he had not taken steps to find Warren or to hear Warren's side of the story. He insisted that Warren had been insubordinate and that only the emergency on the battlefield led to the relief. "And if that condition had not existed I probably would not have relieved General Warren," he claimed. "I hate to punish a man as much as anybody in the world. I did not relieve him to punish him. I relieved him in order to meet the new emergency."[85]

After more than one hundred days of testimony from dozens of witnesses, the court found that:

a) Warren had fully committed his corps to the fight at White Oak Road on March 31, 1865, and not only a portion of it, as charged by Sheridan;

b) Warren had not been responsible for the escape of the enemy's infantry after Dinwiddie Court House;

c) Warren had not tarried in bringing the Fifth Corps to the fight at Five Forks, and that he had acted reasonably in his conduct of the march; and

d) Warren was not indifferent in his handling of the troops under his command that day.

The panel also criticized Sheridan's handling of the relief, finding that Warren had been doing precisely what a corps commander should have been doing, by correcting the disposition of his troops.[86]

General in Chief Sherman added his own dissenting opinion to the court's findings. "General Sheridan, then using the authority vested in him, relieved General Warren of his command, and devolved it on the next in rank, General Griffin. He had full authority for so doing; was sustained at the time by his immediate superior, Lieutenant-General Grant, and his action was never questioned by President Lincoln, or his immediate successor, Johnson. There the matter ought to have ended." Sherman censured Warren for his years of trying to clear his name and then concluded on a critical note. "No one has questioned the patriotism, integrity, and great intelligence of General Warren. These are attested by a long record of most excellent service, but in a clash of arms at and near Five Forks, March 31 and April 1, 1865, his personal activity fell short of the standard fixed by General Sheridan, on whom alone rested the great responsibility for that and succeeding days," Sherman wrote. "My conclusion is that General Sheridan was perfectly justified in his action in this case, and he must be fully and entirely sustained if the United States expects great victories by her armies in the future."[87] Once again, Sheridan's patrons circled the wagons around him and protected him.

When the court announced its findings, an indignant Phil Sheridan fired off a letter to Secretary of War Robert Todd Lincoln, son of the martyred president. "They are more in the nature of apologies than annunciation of the facts as shown in the evidence," he claimed. "The General of the Army clearly sees this in his review, and has raised the case to a higher plain where it properly belongs, than that on which the court works, as shown by the apologies and insignificant technical excuses submitted by the court. It is only fair to me," Little Phil continued, "and it is perfectly proper to embrace General Sherman's review in the promulgation of the proceedings to the Army, especially since the reports industriously circulated in the newspapers as to the cause of the death of General Warren."[88] These pleas fell on deaf ears, and the findings of the court of inquiry were disseminated with Sherman's dissent appended.

The court stopped short of actively criticizing Sheridan; it would have been career suicide for these three officers to do that. It had taken courage for them to find in Warren's favor, but it was too much to expect them to snipe publicly at Sheridan. Joshua Chamberlain later noted, "The traditions of the whole War Department were for sustaining military authority. We would not expect a Court to bring in a verdict of censure of General Sheridan or anything that would amount to that. We can only wonder at the courage of all who gave Warren any favorable endorsement or explanation."[89]

Chamberlain was clearly sympathetic to Warren's plight. "I am by no means sure but that injustice must be taken by a military officer as a necessary part of his risks, of the conditions and chances of his service, to be suffered in the same way as wounds and sicknesses, in patience and humility," he wrote. "But when one feels that his honor and the truth itself are impugned, then that larger personality is concerned wherein one belongs to others and his worth is somehow theirs. Then he does not satisfy himself with regret,—that strange complex feeling that something is right which is now impossible,—and even the truth made known becomes a consolation."[90]

Warren never knew this consolation and, sadly, did not see his name cleared. Shattered by these events, the former officer died in August 1882, before the lengthy hearing concluded. "Broken was the soldier's heart by the strain of his long and lonely battle for the right," wrote Warren's biographer. "Too long had he been required to stand at his post; too heavy were the blows dealt him by bureaucracy's delays; sapped at the last was his soldier's faith in the honor of his superiors; vain the support and encouragement brought him by his friends." The old soldier's last words were, "The flag! The flag!" However, as he was laid to rest, he wore civilian clothes, not the blue uniform of a Civil War hero.[91]

Chamberlain, a general from Maine, observed that the personalities of Sheridan and Warren differed widely. Sheridan was an emotional sort, prone to making snap decisions and unduly critical of those serving under him. "As a rule, our corps and army commanders were men of brains rather than of magnetism. Warren was one of these," he wrote. "He was well capable of organizing an entire plan of battle on a great field. The broad ground of reason—and a valid one if substantiated by fact—for dissatisfaction with General Warren's conduct in the battle, and for his removal from command in consequence, would be that he was not in proper position during the battle to command his whole corps, and did not effectually command it." He concluded, "That at a sharp and critical point he was not present where General Sheridan wanted him is another matter, which does not in itself support the former conclusion."[92]

"Like Averell and Torbert before him," observed Sheridan's recent biographer Roy Morris Jr., "Warren had failed Sheridan where it counted most, on the battlefield. Sheridan could forgive the occasional blunder by youngsters such as Custer—Armstrong fought like hell when the time came. But slowness, timidity, or caution—these Sheridan could not excuse."[93] It did not matter whether Warren had actually been slow, timid, or cautious to Sheridan; the perception that he had been slow destroyed a good man's life for no good reason.

Bvt. Lt. Col. Carswell McClellan offered an insightful analysis into the circumstances of Warren's removal. In discussing Sheridan's contention that Warren's supposed tardiness in moving frustrated his plan for the battle, McClellan suggested that when Warren moved Ayres' division and also overtook the wayward division of Crawford, Warren "performed with it the very movement General Sheridan has put such stress upon." With great irony, McClellan continued, "It is unnecessary to comment upon General Sheridan's issuing instructions to a division commander of the Fifth Corps when the corps commander was present and actively engaged in his duties, further than to again recall how bitterly he himself resented the fact that his commanding officer, General Meade, issued orders to two divisions of the Cavalry Corps of the Army of the Potomac when the commander of that corps was absent from duty on the night of May 7, 1864."[94] Once again, the hypocrisy of Sheridan's conduct glares.

McClellan also pointed out that an 1829 general order still in effect in 1865 governed this situation. This order provided in pertinent part, "An officer entrusted with the command of a post, detachment, guard, or separate command, will not surrender it to another, unless regularly relieved from the duty assigned him, except in case of sickness or inability to perform his duty, when the officer next in rank, present and on duty with such command, will succeed as a matter of course." Accordingly, Warren should have demanded to see the written authority under which Sheridan relieved him of command, lest Warren violate the 1829 regulations by improperly abandoning his command. Sheridan also should have placed General Crawford, who was the senior division commander, in command of the corps, instead of Griffin. "The supposition that any emergency called for such an exercise of illegal power cannot be maintained. Legitimate means were available, and ample for all necessities," McClellan wrote. "If General Sheridan was satisfied that General Warren had in any way failed in his duty on April 1, 1865, he had it rightfully in his power, as commanding officer to report in arrest to his army commander, General Meade." McClellan concluded, "In that event, however, General Warren could not have been denied an immediate hearing before a tribunal of his peers."[95] As McClellan pointed out, Grant protected Sheridan and permitted him to remove Warren from command in violation of settled army policy.

McClellan correctly concluded that Grant had rewarded Sheridan's insubordination by giving him an independent command in May 1864, and also by giving him command of a wing in 1865. At the same time, "While General Sheridan boasts, and General Grant admits, such facts, one can scarcely credit with much of dignity the efforts of the last Generals of the U.S. Army to justify the arbitrary removal of General Warren from the command he graced, and from participation in the final triumph of the cause to which he had devoted the best years of his unselfish, earnest life."[96] McClellan's impassioned argument illustrates the steps that Grant took to protect his protégé from the consequences of his own actions, irrespective of whether those actions were justified.

These three examples show that Sheridan was inflexible and incapable of admitting that he was wrong, even if subsequent facts plainly demonstrated that his actions were unjustified. They also demonstrate that he had little concern for the well-being of the officers and men who served under his command, even where his actions destroyed the lives of men who crossed his path. A great commander cares about the men who serve under him and does not treat them with disregard. Sheridan, whose pettiness, hypocrisy, and inflexibility ruled his actions, did not protect the lives and careers of the men who served under his command. Great commanders do not throw away the lives and careers of their subordinates, and they certainly do not make themselves look better at the expense of their oldest and closest friends. Sheridan did, repeatedly.

NOTES

1. Warner, *Generals in Blue,* 102–3.
2. Taylor, *Sketchbook,* 122.
3. Frederick C. Newhall, *With General Sheridan in Lee's Last Campaign* (Philadelphia: J. B. Lippincott, 1866), 229.
4. David R. Mayhew, "Sheridan and Crook: Anatomy of a Failed Friendship," *Civil War* 70 (October 1998): 35.
5. Schmitt, *General George Crook,* xiii.
6. Henry A. DuPont, *The Campaign of 1864 in the Valley of Virginia and the Expedition to Lynchburg* (New York: National Americana Society, 1925), 135.
7. Williams, *Rutherford B. Hayes,* 2:511.
8. Mayhew, "Sheridan and Crook," 22.
9. Greene, "Union Generalship," 54.
10. Williams, *Rutherford B. Hayes,* 2:514.
11. O.R., vol. 43, part 1, 47. ("I still would not order Crook in, but placed him directly in rear of the line of battle; as the reports, however, that the enemy were attempting to turn my right kept continually increasing, I was obliged to put him in on that flank, instead of on the left as was originally intended. He was directed to act as a turning column, to find the left of the enemy's line, strike it in flank or rear, break it up, and that I would order a left half-wheel of the line of battle to support him.")
12. Ibid., 48, 54.
13. Williams, *Rutherford B. Hayes,* 2:514.
14. Sheridan, *Personal Memoirs,* 2:35.
15. Schmitt, *General George Crook,* 127.
16. Ibid., 129.
17. Ibid., 141.
18. Ibid., 134.
19. For a good analysis of the breakdown of the friendship of Sheridan and Crook, see Mayhew, "Sheridan and Crook."

20. Francis Smith Reader, *History of the Fifth West Virginia Cavalry, Formerly the Second Virginia, and Battery G First West Virginia Light Artillery* (New Brighton, Pa.: Daily News, 1890), 197.
21. Ezra J. Warner, *Generals in Blue: The Lives of the Union Commanders* (Baton Rouge: Louisiana State University Press, 1964), 12–13.
22. Edward K. Eckert and Nicholas J. Amato, eds., *Ten Years in the Saddle: The Memoir of William Woods Averell, 1851–1862* (San Rafael, Calif.: Presidio Press, 1978), 388.
23. Eckert and Amato, *Ten Years in the Saddle*, 5.
24. Darrell L. Collins, *General William Averell's Salem Raid* (Shippensburg, Pa.: Burd Street Press, 1998), 9.
25. O.R., vol. 25, part 1, 1076–77. For more detail, see Ben F. Fordney, *Stoneman at Chancellorsville: The Coming of Age of the Union Cavalry* (Shippensburg, Pa.: White Mane, 1998).
26. For a detailed analysis of Averell's Salem Raid, see Collins, *General William Averell's Salem Raid.*
27. O.R., vol. 43, part 1, 719.
28. W. Blakely to T. R. Kerr, March 18, 1889, William Woods Averell Papers, New York State Library, Albany.
29. Blakely to Kerr, March 18, 1889.
30. Schmitt, *General George Crook*, 123.
31. O.R., vol. 43, part 1, 500–1.
32. Sheridan, *Personal Memoirs*, 2:43.
33. James R. Bowen, *Regimental History of the First New York Dragoons* (Battle Creek, Mich.: privately published, 1900), 240.
34. O.R., vol. 43, part 1, 500.
35. Ibid., 505.
36. Ibid., part 2, 171.
37. Sheridan, *Personal Memoirs*, 2:44–45.
38. O.R., vol. 43, part 1, 505.
39. *New York Herald*, September 27, 1864.
40. Taylor, *Sketchbook*, 458.
41. O.R., vol. 43, part 1, 500–1.
42. Eckert and Amato, *Ten Years in the Saddle*, 400.
43. Ibid., 401.
44. Blakely to Kerr, March 18, 1889. Several similar accounts also found their way back to Averell, but Sheridan never apologized to Averell for his actions.
45. Eckert and Amato, *Ten Years in the Saddle*, 403.
46. Wert, *From Winchester to Cedar Creek*, 133.
47. O.R., vol. 43, part 1, 48.
48. Sheridan, *Personal Memoirs*, 2:41–42.
49. O.R., vol. 43, part 1, 500.
50. Warner, *Generals in Blue*, 541–42.

51. For additional detail, see Chris Calkins, *The Appomattox Campaign, March 29–April 9, 1865* (Conshohocken, Pa.: Combined Publishing, 1999), 9–27.
52. O.R., vol. 46, part 2, 341–42.
53. Cadwallader, *Three Years with Grant*, 301.
54. Transcript of the Court of Inquiry of Gouverneur K. Warren, 2 vols., included in *Supplement to the Official Records of the Union and Confederate Armies*, 100 vols. (Wilmington, N.C.: Broadfoot Publishing, 1995), vol. 9, 1028.
55. Grant, *Personal Memoirs*, 702.
56. Horace Porter, "Five Forks and the Pursuit of Lee," in *B&L*, 4:710.
57. O.R., vol. 46, part 2, 419.
58. Ibid., 419–20.
59. Sheridan, *Personal Memoirs*, 2:160.
60. Ibid., 2:161.
61. Joshua L. Chamberlain, *The Passing of the Armies* (Dayton, Ohio: Morningside House, 1989), 168.
62. Porter, *Campaigning with Grant*, 440–41.
63. Newhall, *With General Sheridan*, 98–99.
64. Morris, *Sheridan*, 248.
65. Ibid., 250.
66. Emerson Gifford Taylor, *Gouverneur Kemble Warren: The Life and Letters of an American Soldier* (Boston: Houghton-Mifflin Co., 1932), 222.
67. O.R., vol. 46, part 2, 420.
68. Chamberlain, *The Passing of the Armies*, 151.
69. O.R., vol. 46, part 1, 1105.
70. Ibid.
71. Taylor, *Warren*, 230–32.
72. Ibid., 227.
73. Cadwallader, *Three Years with Grant*, 305.
74. Newhall, *With General Sheridan*, 117.
75. O.R., vol. 46, part 2, 822–23.
76. Grant, *Personal Memoirs*, 702.
77. O.R., vol. 46, part 1, 836–37.
78. Humphreys, *The Virginia Campaign*, 2:357.
79. Charles H. Porter, "Operations of the Fifth Corps on the Left, March 29 to Nightfall March 31, 1865; Gravelly Run," *Papers of the Military Historical Society of Massachusetts 6* (Boston: Military Historical Society of Massachusetts, 1907), 254.
80. Chamberlain, *The Passing of the Armies*, 152–53.
81. Cadwallader, *Three Years with Grant*, 303, 332.
82. Sheridan, *Personal Memoirs*, 2:169.
83. Taylor, *Warren*, 229.
84. Ibid., 237.
85. Transcript of the Warren Court of Inquiry, 101, 104.

86. Report of the Warren Court of Inquiry, 1545–1600.
87. Ibid., 1602.
88. Sheridan to Robert T. Lincoln, November 15, 1882, Philip H. Sheridan Papers, Box labeled "1882 Official," Manuscripts Division, Library of Congress, Washington, D.C.
89. Chamberlain, *Passing of the Armies,* 178–79.
90. Ibid., 179.
91. Taylor, *Warren,* 248.
92. Chamberlain, *Passing of the Armies,* 154, 168.
93. Morris, *Sheridan,* 251.
94. McClellan, *Notes,* 39.
95. Ibid., 61–63.
96. Ibid., 66.

Maj. Gen. Philip H. Sheridan. NATIONAL ARCHIVES

Lt. George Crook (left) and Cadet Phil Sheridan with an unidentified officer. Although they entered West Point in the same year, Little Phil is in a cadet uniform and Crook in an officer's jacket because of the delay occasioned by Sheridan's suspension from West Point for a year. U.S. MILITARY ACADEMY

Lt. Gen. Ulysses S. Grant, Sheridan's
principal patron. NATIONAL ARCHIVES

Below left:
Maj. Gen. William T. Sherman,
the first of Sheridan's patrons.
NATIONAL ARCHIVES

Below right, top:
Maj. Gen. Henry W. Halleck, another
of Sheridan's patrons. NATIONAL ARCHIVES

Below right, bottom:
Maj. Gen. William S. Rosecrans, who
was Sheridan's second major patron.
NATIONAL ARCHIVES

Sheridan with his former commanding officer, Maj. Gen. William S. Rosecrans (second from left), in this photo taken in September 1863. U.S. ARMY MILITARY HISTORY INSTITUTE

Maj. Gen. George H. Thomas, commander of the Army of the Cumberland during the Battle of Chattanooga. NATIONAL ARCHIVES

Maj. Gen. Don Carlos Buell. NATIONAL ARCHIVES

Top right:
Maj. Gen. Gordon
Granger. Sheridan
succeeded Granger in
command of the 2nd
Michigan Cavalry.
Granger was also
Sheridan's corps
commander at
Chickamauga and
Chattanooga.
NATIONAL ARCHIVES

Maj. Gen.
George Meade,
commander of the
Army of the Potomac.
Sheridan was grossly
insubordinate of
Meade and was
rewarded with an
independent
command.
NATIONAL ARCHIVES

Right:
Maj. Gen. Alfred
Pleasonton, whom
Sheridan succeeded
in command of the
Cavalry Corps.
LIBRARY OF CONGRESS

Maj. Gen. Gouverneur K. Warren, whose life was ruined by Sheridan. NATIONAL ARCHIVES

Bvt. Maj. Gen. Joshua L. Chamberlain of Little Round Top fame, who severely criticized Sheridan's relief of Warren. NATIONAL ARCHIVES

Top right:
Maj. Gen. Charles Griffin, who succeeded Warren in command of the Army of the Potomac's Fifth Corps. NATIONAL ARCHIVES

Right:
Maj. Gen. Winfield Scott Hancock. NATIONAL ARCHIVES

Brig. Gen. David M. Gregg of Pennsylvania, commander of the Army of the Potomac's Second Cavalry Division, and the only one of Sheridan's division commanders with significant experience commanding cavalry. LIBRARY OF CONGRESS

Brig. Gen. William W. Averell, unjustly fired by Sheridan on September 23, 1864.

NATIONAL ARCHIVES

Top left:
Maj. Gen. Alfred T. A. Torbert, commander of the Army of the Shenandoah's Cavalry Corps.

U.S. ARMY MILITARY HISTORY INSTITUTE

Right:
Bvt. Maj. Gen. Wesley Merritt, who became Sheridan's primary cavalry commander.

LIBRARY OF CONGRESS

Maj. Gen. James H. Wilson, one of Sheridan's harsher critics. NATIONAL ARCHIVES

Left:
Bvt. Maj. Gen. George A. Custer.
CATHY MARINACCI

Bvt. Maj. Gen. Thomas C. Devin.
NATIONAL ARCHIVES

Brig. Gen. Henry E. Davies.
LIBRARY OF CONGRESS

Maj. Gen. George Crook, Sheridan's West Point roommate and trusted subordinate. NATIONAL ARCHIVES

Maj. Gen. Horatio G. Wright, commander of the Sixth Corps. Wright was Sheridan's primary infantry commander in the Shenandoah Valley. NATIONAL ARCHIVES

Top left:
Maj. Gen. August V. Kautz, commander of the cavalry division assigned to the Army of the James. Sheridan's lack of vigor almost resulted in the destruction of Kautz's cavalry division in June 1864. NATIONAL ARCHIVES

Maj. Gen. William H. Emory, commander of the 19th Corps in the Valley. NATIONAL ARCHIVES

This group includes, from left to right: Merritt, D. M. Gregg, Sheridan, Davies, Wilson, and Torbert. Taken in the Shenandoah Valley in October 1864. NATIONAL ARCHIVES

Sheridan, Custer, Devin, Merritt, and Brig. Gen. James "Tony" Forsyth, Sheridan's chief of staff in early 1865, just before Sheridan returned to the Army of the Potomac.
NATIONAL ARCHIVES

Gen. **Robert E. Lee.** NATIONAL ARCHIVES

Right:
Lt. Gen. James Longstreet.
COOK COLLECTION, VALENTINE MUSEUM

Lt. Gen. John B. Gordon.
NATIONAL ARCHIVES

Below right:
Lt. Gen. Richard S. Ewell.
NATIONAL ARCHIVES

Lt. Gen. Jubal Early, commander of the Army of the Valley.
LIBRARY OF CONGRESS

Above left:
Lt. Gen. A. P. Hill.
NATIONAL ARCHIVES

Left:
Maj. Gen. George E. Pickett, the losing commander at the Battle of Five Forks. NATIONAL ARCHIVES

Maj. Gen. J. E. B. Stuart, the legendary Southern cavalry commander who was mortally wounded by one of Sheridan's troopers on May 11, 1864. NATIONAL ARCHIVES

Lt. Gen. Wade Hampton, the Confederate cavalry chieftain who bested Sheridan on every occasion where their horsemen clashed. NATIONAL ARCHIVES

Maj. Gen. Fitzhugh Lee.
U.S. ARMY MILITARY HISTORY INSTITUTE

Maj. Gen. Matthew C. Butler of South Carolina. LIBRARY OF CONGRESS

Maj. Gen. Thomas L. Rosser.
LIBRARY OF CONGRESS

Maj. Gen. Lunsford L. Lomax.
LIBRARY OF CONGRESS

Brig. Gen. Williams C. Wickham.
LIBRARY OF CONGRESS

Right:
Col. John Singleton Mosby, the legendary
partisan ranger who never surrendered to
Union forces, disbanding instead when the
war was over. NATIONAL ARCHIVES

Above:
Gutzon Borglum
statue depicting
Sheridan at Cedar
Creek that graces
Sheridan Circle on
Washington's
Embassy Row.
DAVID ARTHUR

Above right:
The Sheridan
monument in
Greenwich Village,
New York.
JAMES D. NOLAN

Right:
The Sheridan
monument located
on Sheridan Road
in Chicago.
MARSHALL D. KROLICK

Above right:
The Sheridan monument in front of the statehouse in Albany, New York, the city that Little Phil claimed was his hometown. DANIEL LORELLO

Above left:
The Sheridan monument at Fort Sheridan, Illinois, depicts Little Phil's ride to Cedar Creek atop Rienzi.
DAVID A. POWELL

Left:
Sheridan's birthplace in Killinkere, Ireland.
PAT CLARKE

The monument at Sheridan's birthplace. The inscription on the monument reads:

"The Birthplace of General Philip H. Sheridan
General in Chief of U.S. Army
Born 1836 Died 1888"

"He belongs to the very first rank
of captain, not only of our
army but of the world. I rank him
with Napoleon and Frederick and
the great commanders of
history. Ulysses S. Grant"

The small placard to the right says, "Erected by the Department of Ireland Veterans of
World War I of the U.S.A., Inc. 20-6-1969." PAT CLARKE

CHAPTER 6

SHERIDAN'S MENDACITY

Philip H. Sheridan's dishonesty was well known to all, including the enemy. "Sheridan was a great liar," wrote John Singleton Mosby years after the end of the Civil War.[1] A number of Sheridan's acts of perfidy have been addressed in prior chapters, and will not be repeated here. On close review of these incidents and others, it becomes clear that Philip Sheridan's ambitious drive for self-aggrandizement knew no bounds. Lying was just a part of his aggressive plan for advancing his own self-interests. He regularly lied to cover his mistakes at all costs. He seems to have been a congenital liar, and his perfidy often exposed him to public ridicule and criticism. Sheridan did not care. He lied anyway.

Maj. Gen. James H. Wilson, who commanded a cavalry division under Sheridan's command, knew Little Phil well. They served together through most of 1864, and in some ways they were rivals. Writing fifty years after the end of the war, Wilson keenly observed that Sheridan "never failed in a doubtful situation to contend to the utmost for victory, *nor to claim it strenuously whether he had won it clearly or not.*"[2] Sheridan demonstrated this trait in claiming credit for capturing Missionary Ridge at Chattanooga; and his report of the actions of the Cavalry Corps during Grant's Overland Campaign provides an excellent example of the sort of lies Sheridan regularly told.

Traditional accounts of the capture of Missionary Ridge credit Sheridan's division with driving Bragg's Confederates from the ridge. These claims are false. In fact, Maj. Gen. William B. Hazen's division got there first. However, Sheridan claimed credit for capturing the ridge as well as eighteen pieces of artillery and 380 prisoners. Hazen learned of these claims the next day, and sent Sheridan a note. "Dear Sheridan," Hazen wrote, "I was informed last evening, greatly to my surprise, that you had expressed the opinion that I had claimed and reported a portion of the artillery captured on Missionary Ridge by your command. You know that I would not knowingly do so. Be pleased to give me any facts that you may have in the matter. . . . Please reply by courier." Instead, Sheridan responded in person. He "insisted rather imperiously upon an unquestioning giving up of the guns. I stood upon my written proposition," recalled Hazen, "and as we left for Knoxville the next morning, nothing further was done."[3]

The captured guns had been taken to Hazen's headquarters, and his officers had vehemently opposed giving them up, "upon the grounds that they were not only rightfully our own, but captured long before General Sheridan had any troops on the crest." When he penned his report in February 1864, Sheridan claimed, "General Hazen and his brigade employed themselves in collecting the artillery from which we had driven the enemy, and have claimed it as their own." Years later, Sheridan wrote in his memoirs, "General Hazen took no notice of this report then, though well aware of its existence." However, Hazen wrote that he knew nothing about the existence of the report until twelve years after it was written.[4]

In 1879, Hazen stood for a court-martial when an Arctic expedition under his direct command failed, and Sheridan raised this issue at the trial. When called as a witness, Sheridan was asked, "Did your command reach the crest of Missionary Ridge . . . before that of General Hazen?" Sheridan repeated his claim. "He is mistaken both with regard to the guns and to the priority of reaching the crest," responded Hazen. Sheridan lied incessantly about this episode in an effort to advance his own career. The truth did not matter. As historian James R. Furqueron put it, "The evidence very solidly supports Hazen."[5] However, Sheridan's glory-grabbing prevented Hazen's brave men from receiving the recognition they so richly deserved for capturing Missionary Ridge.

As set forth fully in chapter 2, Sheridan's conduct of the Cavalry Corps during the Overland Campaign was lackluster at best. Instead of an unblemished record of success during the campaign, as he claimed, Sheridan lost nearly all the fights engaged in by his command. When he penned his report of the campaign in 1866, he made a number of astonishing statements. He began by claiming that he had invented a new paradigm for his horsemen. "After carefully studying the topography of the country from the Rapidan to Richmond, which is of a thickly wooded character, its numerous and almost parallel streams nearly all uniting, forming the York River, I took up the idea that our cavalry ought to fight the enemy's cavalry, and our infantry the enemy's infantry," he claimed. "I was strengthened in this impression still more by the consciousness of a want of appreciation on the part of infantry commanders as to the power of a large and well-managed body of horse, but as it was difficult to overcome the established custom of wasting cavalry for the protection of trains, and for the establishment of cordons around a sleeping infantry force, we had to bide our time."[6]

After spelling out the actions of the Cavalry Corps, Sheridan began his mendacious bragging. "It will be seen by the foregoing narrative that the idea advanced by me at the commencement of the campaign, viz, 'that our cavalry ought to fight the enemy's cavalry, and our infantry the enemy's infantry,' was carried into effect immediately after the battle of the Wilderness," he claimed. "The result was constant success and the almost total annihilation of the rebel cavalry. We marched when and where we pleased; were always the attacking party, and always successful."[7]

It did not end there. Sheridan continued, "During the period herein embraced I am led to believe, on information derived from the most reliable sources, that the enemy's cavalry was superior to ours in numbers; but the esprit of our men increased every day, while that of the enemy diminished." The conclusion is, perhaps, the most astonishing part of this report. "It will be seen by this report that we led the advance of the army to the Wilderness; that on the Richmond raid we marked out its line of march to the North Anna, where we found it on our return; that we again led its advance to Hanovertown, and thence to Cold Harbor; that we removed the enemy's cavalry from the south side of the Chickahominy by the Trevilian raid, and thereby materially assisted the army in its successful march to the James River and Petersburg, where it remained until we made the campaign in the valley; marched back to Petersburg, and again took its advance and led it to victory." With a great flourish, Sheridan finished his account. "In all the operations the percentage of cavalry casualties was as great as that of the infantry, and the question which had existed 'Who ever saw a dead cavalryman?' was set at rest."[8]

Many, if not most, of these claims simply were not true. As an example, Sheridan passed up numerous opportunities to give battle during the Overland Campaign. Thus, Sheridan's claims that he was always the aggressor are not true. In particular, the boast that the Cavalry Corps was "always successful" could not have been further from the truth. Wilson, no admirer of Little Phil, analyzed Sheridan's unsuccessful Trevilian Raid. Sheridan's assignment for the raid was to march along the route of the Virginia Central Railroad, break it up at Gordonsville and Charlottesville, link up with Maj. Gen. David Hunter, and then accompany Hunter's army back to join the Army of the Potomac in its move on Petersburg. Wilson pointed out that Sheridan utterly failed in any of his objectives of the raid, and commented wryly, "After striking the railroad at Trevilian's, it is claimed that he broke it up thoroughly, but I think it is a question of doubt whether he succeeded in breaking the track at all." He continued, "Be this as it may, it is certain that, if he did, it was broken in such an inadequate manner that it was repaired in a few hours by an ordinary railroad force, and that consequently for all practical purposes, the raid was a failure."[9]

In stark contrast, Sheridan made an astounding claim about the Battle of Trevilian Station. "At night my command encamped at Trevilian Station, and from prisoners, of which we had captured about 500, I learned that Hunter, instead of coming toward Charlottesville, as I had reason to suppose, was at or near Lexington, moving apparently on Lynchburg; that Ewell's corps was on its way to Lynchburg, on the south side of the James River; and that Breckinridge was at Gordonsville or Charlottesville, having passed up the railroad, as heretofore alluded to," he wrote. Because of the disposition of the Union forces, according to Sheridan, "I, therefore, made up my mind that it was best to give up the attempt to join Hunter, as he was going from me instead of coming toward me, and concluded to return."[10] Considering that Early did not receive orders to lead the Second Corps to the Valley until June 12, it was impossible for word of the move to have reached Sheridan on the night of June 11.

If Sheridan intended to break off the engagement and return to the Army of the Potomac, why did he commit three brigades to a major engagement along the Gordonsville Road the next day? Instead of breaking off the combat, a savage fight broke out along the Gordonsville Road to the west of Trevilian Station on June 12. The Confederate cavalry repulsed seven separate assaults that afternoon, before their own vicious counterattack broke Sheridan's line and sent his troopers flying from the field in a rout. His actions in committing all but one of his brigades to savage combat, in which his command took heavy casualties, are inconsistent with his version of the story. A more likely explanation is that Sheridan believed that Maj. Gen. Wade Hampton had retreated after the close of fighting on June 11, and decided to try to get to Gordonsville after all.

Even though Hampton's gray-clad cavalrymen had soundly beaten Sheridan's two divisions, Little Phil claimed that he had won the Battle of Trevilian Station. He was, at least, a bit more honest in his preliminary report of the engagement, filed on June 18, 1864. After acknowledging that the Confederates had prevented him from linking with Hunter's army, Sheridan wrote, "I regret my inability to carry out your instructions."[11] This preliminary report nevertheless staked a claim to victory. Numerous newspapers carried this report. The editor of the *Pittsburgh Evening Chronicle* inquired, "If he was as successful as he reports, the inquiry arises why did he not, if Gordonsville was unattainable, advance on Charlottesville, or destroy the railroad between that and Gordonsville and then join Hunter, as was his original intention?" The editor concluded, "We fear that Sheridan has not been so successful as was desired or expected, and that his failure to unite with our other forces in that region may lead to serious complications, and preserve to the enemy, not only Gordonsville and Charlottesville, but also Lynchburg. The next reports from there will be awaited with anxiety."[12] The next day, the same editor stated, "From the exceedingly meager reports furnished by the rebel papers it may be inferred that the raid is considered of very little importance, or else that it has met with greater success than the rebels are willing to acknowledge."[13]

Sheridan's report also ran in many of the Southern newspapers, and it met with the predictable result. "We have received a more detailed account of the defeat of Sheridan's forces by our cavalry, under Generals Hampton and Fitz Lee, which not only confirms previous intelligence, but shows that the enemy were thoroughly beaten and demoralized," crowed the *Charleston Mercury.*[14] "The *Philadelphia Inquirer,* like a number of other Yankee papers, pleads very hard to show that Sheridan won a 'great victory.' This was done by one way only—a way the Yankees understand perfectly—*by lying;* infamous, atrocious lying," sneered the editor of the *Richmond Examiner,* who concluded, "If Sheridan won a 'victory'—if the Yankees take delight in such treatment as his men received at the hands of Hampton and his men, we wish them joy, and plenty more of the same sort of comfort."[15]

Sheridan continued to exaggerate in his report on the Shenandoah Valley Campaign. As described in chapter 5, Sheridan intentionally misrepresented the nature of George Crook's contributions to the campaign. He specifically downplayed his old friend's tactical foresight and vision in order to make himself look better regarding the battle plans for both Third Winchester and Fisher's Hill.[16] In describing the aftermath of the Battle of Cedar Creek, Sheridan claimed, "This battle practically ended the campaign in the Shenandoah Valley. When it opened we found our enemy boastful and confident, unwilling to acknowledge that the soldiers of the Union were their equal in courage and manliness; when it closed with Cedar Creek this impression had been removed from his mind, and gave place to good sense and a strong desire to quit fighting." He continued, "The very best troops of the Confederacy had not only been defeated, but had been routed in successive engagements, until their spirit and esprit were destroyed."[17]

While it is true that Sheridan had defeated Early's army on the field of battle, the Confederates remained full of fight after each engagement. As pointed out in chapter 3, Early consistently outfought Sheridan during the campaign, and his men outfought the Federals in two of the three major engagements. The Sixth and Nineteenth Corps infantrymen also left the Valley during the winter of 1864–1865, meaning that Sheridan did not have the offensive power to finish off Early's army. Only Robert E. Lee's ordering all but one division of Early's infantry to return to the siege lines at Petersburg brought the campaign to a close.

Sheridan claimed, "During this campaign I was at times annoyed by guerrilla bands, the most formidable of which was under a partisan chief named Mosby, who made his headquarters east of the Blue Ridge, in the section of country about Upperville. I had constantly refused to operate against these bands, believing them to be, substantially a benefit to me, as they prevented straggling and kept my trains well closed up, and discharged such other duties as would have required a provost guard of at least two regiments of cavalry."[18]

As early as August 16, 1864, Grant had instructed Sheridan to send a division of cavalry into Loudoun County, the heart of what became known as Mosby's Confederacy, "to destroy and carry off the crops, animals, negroes, and all men under fifty years of age capable of carrying arms."[19] Several days earlier, Sheridan ordered Gen. Christopher C. Augur, who commanded the eastern sector of the Middle Military District, to send the 8th Illinois Cavalry to go on a raid deep into Loudoun County "to exterminate as many of Mosby's gang as they can."[20] On August 19, Sheridan candidly admitted to Grant that Mosby's men "give me great annoyance," but claimed that he was quietly disposing of them.[21] Obviously, Sheridan never did dispose of Mosby's tenacious Rangers.

Sheridan also claimed that he developed a strategy to defend against Mosby's guerrillas. The claim was, not surprisingly, false. When George Crook assumed command of the Department of West Virginia in the spring of 1864, he inherited the Mosby problem. In February 1864, he organized a body of picked men from his different regiments, and assigned Capt. Richard Blazer of the 91st Ohio Infantry as their commander. Blazer had a real gift for that sort of work, and "became so efficient that he was not long ridding the district infested with these people." Crook observed that, using the same hit-and-run tactics as Mosby, Blazer's Scouts "had made considerable headway against Mosby's men after the theatre of operations was transferred to the east, but his force was too small to cope with Mosby."[22] According to historian Jeffry D. Wert, "Their leader understood that to engage Mosby successfully he, too, had to strike unexpectedly and swiftly."[23] Crook had intended to enlarge this hunter-killer force, but never got the chance.

Sheridan claimed credit for creating this force, informing Augur, who commanded the Department of Washington, that he had "100 men who will take the contract to clean out Mosby's gang." Sheridan requested one hundred Spencer rifles for them. The request was approved.[24] Historian Wert noted that even though Sheridan gave the order, "the sequence of events in the formation of these Independent Scouts is unclear, but the suggestion for this command came evidently from George Crook."[25] That fall, Mosby dispatched a detachment to wipe out Blazer's command, and Blazer was taken prisoner. Perhaps his capture explains why Sheridan ignored Blazer's contributions in both his official report of the campaign and in his memoirs. Perhaps more importantly, Capt. Blazer had earned the respect of his enemy, Mosby. "He appeared to be ever in the saddle, and was constantly turning up where he was least expected and least desired," noted one of Mosby's Rangers. "Mosby and Blazer could not long inhabit opposite sides of the Blue Ridge Mountain."[26]

Crook's tactics were so effective that Sheridan formed "a similar force for the whole army, after which I was relieved from any further service of that nature," reported Crook. Sheridan placed Maj. Henry H. Young of the 2nd Rhode Island Infantry in command of this force, known as the Jessie Scouts. "Just what they accomplished I don't know," sneered Crook, "but they would dress at times in Confederate uniforms, and at times in our uniform."[27] Sheridan was taken with Young and his Scouts, and praised Young's performance in his memoirs. "I now realized more than I had hitherto how efficient my scouts had become since under Colonel Young; for not only did they bring me almost every day intelligence from within Early's lines, but they also operated efficiently against the guerrillas infesting West Virginia," recounted Little Phil.[28] Not surprisingly, Sheridan did not mention Blazer or his contributions, preferring to claim all of the credit for the concept for himself. Given that Crook had created Blazer's Scouts prior to Sheridan's assignment to command, Little Phil could not have created the concept. The U.S. Army still employs Crook's tactics today, providing a clear testament to their effectiveness.

After Mosby's Rangers killed Sheridan's medical director, Dr. Emil Ohlenschlager, and mortally wounded his quartermaster general, Col. Tolles, on October 12, 1864, Sheridan erupted. In response, Sheridan dispatched Capt. Blazer and a force of one hundred hand-picked men, with the mission of "wiping out" Mosby's "command, or getting wiped out."[29] By mid-November, Mosby's Rangers had thrashed Blazer's command and the captain was a prisoner of war in Richmond's notorious Libby Prison. Before long, two entire regiments of cavalry reinforced Blazer's force, pulling these troopers from the front lines.[30] As the fall wore on, and Mosby's guerrillas became more of an irritant, Sheridan devoted more and more resources to defeating the Rangers and to guarding the army's lines of supply from attack. Each soldier devoted to defeating Mosby decreased the Army of the Shenandoah's effective fighting strength and made the total destruction of Early's army less and less likely.

Mosby's Rangers "caused perhaps more loss than any single body of men in the enemy's service," noted a Federal staff officer.[31] Sheridan had to change his base of operations in order to protect his lines of supply from Mosby's Rangers. As historian Wert noted, "The 43rd Virginia Battalion repulsed all attempts at their elimination, terrorized Union outposts and wagon trains, embarrassed Union soldiers and their military and civilian leaders and cost the North hundreds of thousands of dollars." This was not, however, Mosby's most significant offering to the war effort. Rather, "Mosby's most important contribution might have been instilling in Sheridan the belief that his army could not sustain their supply line for an advance on Charlottesville," continued Wert. "If this were the case, Mosby and his redoubtable band delayed the fall of Petersburg and Richmond."[32]

On a smaller scale, Mosby and his men consistently wreaked havoc on Sheridan's army. The Rangers were fond of striking at night, sneaking up on sleeping Yankees and seizing the groggy men without resistance. Thus, "no Union soldier in northern Virginia or the lower Shenandoah Valley, from general to private, could consider himself safe from Mosby once the sun disappeared," observed historian A. Wilson Greene. "Paranoid pickets constantly sounded alarms, usually false ones, which kept dozens of camps and hundreds of soldiers uneasy throughout the night."[33] An exhausted soldier is an inefficient and demoralized warrior. These tactics took an immeasurable and intangible toll on the Army of the Shenandoah, one that required Sheridan to commit a large amount of resources, including an unsuccessful raid into the Loudoun Valley by an entire cavalry division in November after the campaign had effectively ended.

Lt. Col. Carswell McClellan also spotted the inconsistencies contained in Sheridan's accounts. McClellan quoted the portion of Little Phil's report of the Overland Campaign where he claimed an unending string of glorious victories over the Confederate cavalry. He then concluded with this scathing remark, "It is believed that, unless, perhaps, in the pages of the *Personal Memoirs of P. H. Sheridan,* this paragraph cannot be surpassed in military literature."[34] McClellan was, in fact, correct. If anything, Little Phil's memoirs contain even more prevarications than do his reports of his campaigns.

The lying began on the second page of Sheridan's memoirs, when he wrote about his parents. "Before leaving Ireland they had two children, and on the 6th of March, 1831," he wrote, "I was born in Albany, N.Y., the third child in a family which eventually increased to six—four boys and two girls."[35] In fact, Sheridan was not born in the United States at all. A handsome stone marker stands in front of the simple stone house in Killinkere, Ireland, that reads:

> The birthplace of General Philip H. Sheridan
> General in Chief of U.S. Army
> Born–1831   Died–1888

A neighbor from Killinkere left an account that specifically stated that he had driven the Sheridan family to the ship that carried them to America, and that he distinctly recalled seeing Mary Sheridan carrying baby Philip in her arms as they clattered down the road.[36] Local parish records in County Cavan, Ireland, document the birth of a child named Philip Henry Sheridan in March, 1831.[37] At other times, Sheridan claimed to have been born in either Boston or in Somerset; others believe that he was born on the ship carrying his parents to America. In fact, Mrs. Sheridan told the chairman of the Sheridan Monument Association that Phil had been born at sea on the way over.[38]

There are many reasons why Sheridan would have lied about where he was born, but one, in particular, makes a great deal of sense. Per the provisions of Article II, Section 1 of the U.S. Constitution, only native-born Americans are eligible to be elected president of the United States. In 1905, long after Little Phil's death, an old friend of his said, "There is no longer any dispute as to General Phil Sheridan's birthplace. . . . Now that he is dead and there is no hope of his election to the Presidency, his relatives admit that he was born on the ocean, when his parents were coming from Ireland, but his birth was recorded at Albany, N.Y., where they first settled."[39] There is no record of his birth in Albany, Boston, or Somerset.[40]

Late in life, Sheridan toyed with the idea of running for president. In 1880, he had sent up a trial balloon, exploring the possibility of running for the Republican nomination, and even received a single vote at the party's nominating convention.[41] It had not been a serious effort, but it would not have been possible at all if the public had learned that Sheridan was not a native-born citizen. Nevertheless, the myth of Sheridan having been born in Albany became so ingrained that the State of New York and the city fathers erected a handsome equestrian monument to Little Phil in front of the State Capitol building. All of the published speeches celebrating the dedication of the monument proudly reflected Sheridan's status as a native son of the Empire State.[42]

Sheridan repeated most of his prevarications and half-truths in his memoirs, where he also described his supposed new plan for the use of the cavalry at great length. In his initial meeting with Meade, Sheridan claimed that he laid out his plans. "I told him that if he would let me use the cavalry as I contemplated," claimed Little Phil, "he need have little solicitude in these respects, for, with a mass of ten thousand mounted men, it was my belief that I could make it so lively for the enemy's cavalry that, so far as attacks from it were concerned, the flanks and rear of the Army of the Potomac would require little or no defense, and claimed, further, that moving columns of infantry should take care of their own fronts."[43]

Sheridan then continued, "I also told him that it was my object to defeat the enemy's cavalry in a general combat, if possible, and by such a result establish a feeling of confidence in my own troops that would enable us after a while to march where we pleased, for the purpose of breaking General Lee's communications and destroying the resources from which his army was supplied."[44] However, the prior commander of the Cavalry Corps, Maj. Gen. Alfred Pleasonton, had shaken free of the main body of the Army of the Potomac and had conducted a number of independent actions during 1863. While it had failed, the Kilpatrick-Dahlgren Raid of February 1864 represented a good illustration of just the sort of campaign that Sheridan claimed to invent. In short, Sheridan's proposal was nothing terribly radical, and it was nothing terribly innovative.

Sheridan also addressed the Richmond Raid at length in his memoirs. The raid, which resulted from Sheridan's insubordination to Meade on May 8, left the Army of the Potomac groping blindly for Lee's Army of Northern Virginia. Further, the raid doomed Meade's army to nearly three weeks of slugging it out, with both sides taking massive casualties. The only thing Sheridan's raid accomplished was killing Jeb Stuart. Still, Little Phil claimed victory. "Our return to Chesterfield ended the first independent expedition the Cavalry Corps had undertaken since coming under my command, and our success was commended highly by Generals Grant and Meade, both realizing that our operations in the rear of Lee had disconcerted and alarmed that general so much as aid materially in forcing his retrograde march, and both acknowledged that, by drawing off the enemy's cavalry during the past fortnight, we had enabled them to move the Army of the Potomac and its enormous trains without molestation in the maneuvers that had carried it to the North Anna."[45]

He concluded, "Then, too, great quantities of provisions and munitions of war had been destroyed—stores that the enemy had accumulated at sub-depots from strained resources and by difficult means; the railroads that connected Lee with Richmond broken, the most successful cavalry leader of the South killed, and in addition to all this there had been inflicted on the Confederate mounted troops the most thorough defeat that had yet befallen them in Virginia."[46]

These claims do not stand up under a close reading. Initially, the claim that the Federal trains were left unmolested because Sheridan drew off the Confederate cavalry is untrue. Maj. Gen. Ambrose E. Burnside's Ninth Army Corps stayed behind to guard the train. Further, although Lee did not dispatch his conventional forces to capture the train, Mosby's guerrillas plagued incessantly. Therefore, it is simply not true that the wagon train was able to move about the countryside unmolested because of the actions of Sheridan's cavalry.

The Confederates were accustomed to Union cavalry raids intended to disrupt their lines of communication and supply. The May 1864 raid was the third major cavalry raid toward Richmond during in twelve months. In April 1863, Maj. Gen. Joseph Hooker, then commanding the Union army, ordered Maj. Gen. George Stoneman, the Cavalry Corps commander, to lead his command on a raid deep into the heart of the Confederacy. Hooker wanted to distract Lee's attention from the Army of the Potomac's advance toward its date at the Battle of Chancellorsville. Stoneman's Raid reached the outer defenses of Richmond before the Yankee horsemen broke off and returned to the Army of the Potomac.[47] Then, in the spring of 1864, the Kilpatrick-Dahlgren raid had reached the very outskirts of the Confederate capital. Sheridan's Richmond raid was nothing new.

Sheridan's troopers did destroy supplies and munitions of war. All cavalry raids do. Sheridan made quite a stretch in claiming that these actions made a difference in the outcome of the campaign. He also contended that his troopers had inflicted the worst defeat of the war upon the Confederate horse soldiers during the raid. While it is true that Stuart received a mortal wound during the fighting at Yellow Tavern on May 11, the Union victory was indecisive. Lee's cavalry lived on to fight another day, and Wade Hampton, another extremely effective leader, succeeded Stuart in command of Lee's horsemen. Hampton defeated Little Phil each and every time that they met. Stuart could not make that claim. Further, even by losing, Stuart delayed Sheridan's advance long enough for Gen. Braxton Bragg to shift troops up from the southern defenses of Richmond. Even by losing, Stuart prevented Sheridan from entering Richmond.

Sheridan's claims that his raid somehow induced Lee to retreat are probably the most outrageous of all. In reality, Robert E. Lee made strategic retrograde movements designed to head off the Army of the Potomac's flanking movements. In some instances, Lee anticipated Grant's flanking efforts, and in some instances, Lee responded. Only once, at Spotsylvania Court House, did Grant manage to steal a march on the Army of Northern Virginia. Even then, Lee had anticipated that Grant would attempt to sidle around his flank.

Finally, because Sheridan and the Cavalry Corps were not present, Lee nearly sucked the Army of the Potomac into a trap at Ox Ford on the North Anna.

Lee's army held a nearly impregnable defensive position behind stout earth-works. Had Meade attacked with his whole army at Ox Ford, he would have faced a defeat like the one inflicted upon the Army of the Potomac at Freder-icksburg. "For the third time in the campaign—at the Wilderness, at Spotsylva-nia Court House, and now at the North Anna River—Lee had foiled Grant," commented historian Gordon C. Rhea. "On each occasion Grant had maneu-vered offensively, only to be thwarted by Lee's masterful grasp of terrain, tena-cious fighting, and good luck."[48] When Grant broke the stalemate by sidling to the east again, Lee followed him. The cavalry raid actually did little more than distract Robert E. Lee and was not the major factor in the campaign that Sheri-dan claimed it was.

Had Sheridan been with the army, where he belonged, instead of raiding, Rhea claimed, "it is unlikely . . . that Lee would have slipped past Grant's sleep-ing army on May 21–22 if Sheridan's riders had been available. Good cavalry work would also have brought order to Grant's stumbling approach to the North Anna on May 23 and alerted him to the shape of Lee's line before his abortive—and nearly disastrous—advance on May 24." Rhea saved his harshest words for Little Phil and his horsemen: "Simply put, Sheridan's absence cost Grant dearly."[49]

At best, this presentation of events represents another attempt by Sheridan to make himself look as good as possible under the circumstances. At worst, Sheri-dan was being perfidious, looking to gain glory for himself at the price of the truth. No matter which it was, Sheridan's account does not reflect the truth.

Regardless of whether Phil Sheridan was intentionally untruthful in his ac-counts of events or whether he simply embellished the truth, he was perfidious. A truly great soldier should be prepared to stand on his record and let history judge his performance. Instead, Sheridan insisted on doing all that he could to spin things in as favorable a light as possible, even if it meant that the truth suf-fered as a result. Even giving Sheridan the benefit of the doubt, that he was not intentionally misrepresenting the truth, his misrepresentations cast aspersions on his record and on his character. Sheridan obviously believed that he needed to distort and embellish the truth.

NOTES

1. Frye, "I Resolved to Play a Bold Game," 108.
2. Quoted in McClellan, *Notes,* 24.
3. William B. Hazen, *A Narrative of Military Service* (Boston: Ticknor & Co., 1885), 179–80.
4. Ibid.

5. O.R., vol. 31, part 2, 192; Sheridan, *Personal Memoirs,* 1:320; James R. Furqueron, " 'The Best Hated Man in the Army': Part II: The Remarkable Career of William Babcock Hazen," *North & South,* vol. 4, no. 5 (May 2001): 70.

6. O.R., vol. 36, part 1, 787.

7. Ibid., 801.

8. Ibid., 802.

9. James Harrison Wilson, "The Cavalry of the Army of the Potomac," *Papers of the Military Historical Society of Massachusetts, Civil and Mexican Wars 1861, 1846* 13 (Boston: Military Historical Society of Massachusetts, 1913), 58.

10. O.R., vol. 36, part 1, 796.

11. Ibid., 784.

12. *Pittsburgh Evening Chronicle,* June 20, 1864.

13. Ibid., June 21, 1864.

14. *Charleston Mercury,* June 22, 1864.

15. *Richmond Examiner,* June 24, 1864.

16. O.R., vol. 46, part 1, 47–48.

17. Ibid., 54.

18. Ibid., 55.

19. Ibid., vol. 43, part 2, 679. Sheridan put off obeying this order until November, providing yet another example of his blatant disregard for Grant's orders.

20. Ibid., part 1, 776.

21. Ibid., 841.

22. Schmitt, *General George Crook,* 135.

23. Wert, *From Winchester to Cedar Creek,* 150.

24. O.R., vol. 43, part 1, 860.

25. Wert, *From Winchester to Cedar Creek,* 150. For an interesting study of the role played by Blazer's Scouts, which verifies the fact that Crook came up with the idea for the unit, see Darl L. Stephenson, *Headquarters in the Brush: Blazer's Independent Union Scouts* (Athens: Ohio University Press, 2001).

26. John Scott, *Partisan Life with Colonel John S. Mosby* (Bloomington: University of Indiana Press, 1959), 364–66.

27. Schmitt, *General George Crook,* 135.

28. Sheridan, *Personal Memoirs,* 2:104–5. See also, O.R., vol. 43, part 1, 56.

29. Taylor, *Sketchbook,* 463–64.

30. Ibid., 569.

31. Hagemann, *Fighting Rebels and Redskins,* 261.

32. Wert, *From Winchester to Cedar Creek,* 156.

33. Frye, "I Resolved to Play a Bold Game," 111.

34. McClellan, *Notes,* 25.

35. Sheridan, *Personal Memoirs,* 1:2.

36. "Sheridan Birthplace," article found online at http://cavan.local.ie/content/269shtml/killinkere. A photo of the Sheridan family homestead in Ireland, as well as a photo of the monument to Sheridan's birthplace, may be found in the photograph section of this book.

37. O'Connor, *Sheridan the Inevitable,* 19.
38. *Somerset Press,* October 19, 1905.
39. Ibid. This article reported on the dedication of the equestrian monument to Sheridan that stands in the town square in his childhood hometown, Somerset, Ohio.
40. O'Connor, *Sheridan the Inevitable,* 19.
41. Morris, *Sheridan,* 382.
42. See *Unveiling of the Equestrian Statue of General Philip H. Sheridan.* As an example, "Albany, the birthplace of many citizens who have risen to eminence in the nation and the world, counts among its native sons Philip H. Sheridan, one of the great military heroes of the Civil War" (page 21).
43. Sheridan, *Personal Memoirs,* 2:355–56.
44. Ibid.
45. Ibid., 2:391–92.
46. Ibid.
47. Ironically, William Woods Averell had commanded a division of the Army of the Potomac's Cavalry Corps during the Stoneman Raid. Hooker blamed Averell and Stoneman for his catastrophic defeat at Chancellorsville, and relieved Averell of command without explanation. For additional reading on the Stoneman Raid and its strategic significance within the context of the Battle of Chancellorsville, see A. Wilson Greene, "Stoneman's Raid," in *Chancellorsville: The Battle and Its Aftermath,* ed. Gary W. Gallagher (Chapel Hill: University of North Carolina Press, 1996), 65–106.
48. Rhea, *To the North Anna River,* 358.
49. Ibid., 369–70.

CHAPTER 7

LITTLE PHIL'S FINEST MOMENT: THE PURSUIT OF ROBERT E. LEE, SPRING 1865

Like all men, Philip H. Sheridan had his strengths and weaknesses. This book has explored those weaknesses at great length. In fairness, some assessment of his strengths is needed in order for the reader to have a full picture of the man. Here we will evaluate Little Phil's performance in the Civil War's final campaign. He disobeyed Grant's orders in the spring of 1865, but Sheridan's finest moment resulted because of his insubordination. His relentless quest to bring Robert E. Lee's proud veterans to bay showed Sheridan at his best, just as Five Forks had shown him at his worst. The pursuit of the Army of Northern Virginia in the waning days of the Civil War serves as the centerpiece of this analysis.

After his victory at Five Forks on April 1, 1865, the war's final drama began. With the Union army firmly astride the Boydton Plank Road, Robert E. Lee had no choice but to evacuate the siege lines at Petersburg after a significant skirmish, at Sutherland's Station on the South Side Railroad, cut the final Confederate rail line to the west. With his last remaining route of retreat threatened, Lee had no choice. "I see no prospect of doing more than holding our position here until night," the Confederate commander wrote to Secretary of War John C. Breckinridge. "I am not certain I can do that. If I can I shall withdraw tonight north of the Appomattox, and, if possible, it will be better to withdraw the whole line tonight from the James River. I advise that all preparations be made for leaving Richmond tonight. I will advise you later according to circumstances."[1]

On the night of April 1, after hearing about the important victory at Five Forks, Grant ordered a full-scale assault all along the siege lines at Petersburg. Sheridan commanded the western sector of the battlefield, controlling the Cavalry Corps and most of the Second Corps. He now acted as an independent army commander, answering only to Grant. Little Phil decided "as to the method to be pursued by the cavalry corps was immediate and simple. It was to pursue and attack the left flank of the retreating army at any possible point with the cavalry division that first reached it, and, if possible, compel it to turn and defend its wagon trains and artillery," recalled Sheridan's chief of staff, Col. George A. "Sandy" Forsyth. "Then to send another division beyond and attack the Confederate army again at any possible point, and to follow up this method of attack until at some point the whole army would be obliged to turn and deliver battle."[2]

As the Confederates streamed west, away from the trench lines, Sheridan's troopers led the pursuit. The withdrawal of Lee's army meant that Richmond had to be evacuated. Lee recognized the inevitable. "It is absolutely necessary that we should abandon our position tonight, or run the risk of being cut off in the morning," he wrote. "I have given all the orders to officers on both sides of the river, and have taken every precaution that I can to make the movement successful. It will be a difficult operation, but I hope not impracticable."[3] Confederate President Jefferson Davis and his cabinet fled, leaving the Rebel capital open to capture by the Northern armies.[4]

Lee would try to escape to the west, where he hoped to find desperately needed provisions at Amelia Court House. After resupplying his threadbare army, he would turn south to join Gen. Joseph E. Johnston's Army of Tennessee, fleeing from Sherman's army in North Carolina. Perhaps the combined fragments of armies could then turn on their pursuers and stand a fighting chance. Sheridan, "the Inevitable," as the Confederates called him, would command the left wing and lead the chase across the Virginia countryside, "thundering on with his cavalry."[5]

That morning, Grant instructed Little Phil, "The first object of present movement will be to intercept Lee's army, and the second to secure Burkeville."[6] Sheridan, with the Cavalry Corps and the Fifth Corps, would move in a westerly direction, south of and near the Appomattox River. Little Phil was "to feel Lee's army constantly, and at the same time to strike the Danville Railroad between its crossing of the Appomattox and its crossing of the Lynchburg Railroad at Burke's Junction."[7] With Custer's division leading the way, the Cavalry Corps moved out on the morning of April 3. Little Phil drove his men hard, knowing the stakes involved. That day, he rode the length of his column, "and left a black and withered track behind him like the lightning's path."[8] A brigade of Confederate cavalry, commanded by Brig. Gen. Rufus Barringer, tried to block the Yankee pursuit at Namozine Church, but Custer's troopers defeated the feisty Southerners. "At 11 A.M. the cavalry advance was three miles beyond Namozine Creek, on the main road, pushing forward," Sheridan reported to Grant that afternoon. "The roads are strewn with burning and broken-down caissons, ambulances, wagons, and debris of all descriptions. Up to this hour we have taken about 1,200 prisoners, mostly of A. P. Hill's Corps, and all accounts report the woods filled with deserters and stragglers, principally of this corps."[9] The road now lay wide open, and there was no significant Confederate force to block the pursuit route.

Sheridan spent April 4 marching, trying to get across Lee's line of retreat. Grant and Sheridan tried to guess Lee's intentions. "It was understood that Lee was accompanying his troops and that he was bound for Danville by way of Farmville," instructed the lieutenant general. "Unless you have information more positive of the movements of the enemy push on with all dispatch to Farmville and try to intercept the enemy there." Grant also informed Little Phil that he had sent two divisions of Maj. Gen. E. O. C. Ord's Army of the James to intercept the Army of Northern Virginia at Farmville.[10]

Late that afternoon, one of Sheridan's scouts captured a man riding a mule in the direction of Burkesville. The man was searched, and the scouts found a telegram, signed by Lee's commissary general. "The army is at Amelia Court House, short of provisions," read the telegram. "Send 300,000 rations quickly to Burkville Junction." Sheridan now had proof positive of the state of Lee's army.[11]

Lee's bedraggled veterans pressed on, although they knew not where they went. "They marched along, leaving their fate in the hands of the great leader they knew so well and had trusted so long," recalled a South Carolinian.[12] When he arrived at Amelia Court House on April 5, Lee discovered that the expected provisions were not awaiting his army. The situation grew more desperate with each passing minute. "I have never been in a real retreat before," complained a Virginian, "but this looks like a disorderly one to me."[13] Lee lost a day waiting for the provisions, costing him his lead over Grant's pursuers. "This delay was fatal and could not be retrieved," lamented Lee.[14]

At Painesville, Brig. Gen. Henry Davies' Union cavalry division fell upon Maj. Gen. G. W. Custis Lee's wagon train which was trying to rejoin the Army of Northern Virginia. Custis Lee was the eldest son of the Confederate chieftain. "It is said that the papers of General Robert E. Lee's Headquarters, containing many valuable reports, copies of but few of which are now to be found, were destroyed by the burning of these wagons," observed Gen. Andrew A. Humphreys, "General Fitz Lee says that his own Headquarters' wagons were among those destroyed."[15] The remaining Confederate cavalry was helpless to do much more than watch, as they were too few to stop the Yankee juggernaut. Davies captured the whole wagon train and all the Confederate artillery. Lee's precious lifeline of supplies was even slimmer after this disaster.[16]

After learning of Davies' capture of the wagon train, Sheridan reported his success. "The whole of Lee's army is at or near Amelia Court-House, and on this side of it," he wrote. "General Davies, whom I sent out to Painesville on their right flank, has just captured six pieces of artillery and some wagons. We can capture the Army of Northern Virginia if force enough can be thrown to this point, and then advance upon it. . . . They are out, or nearly out, of rations."[17] Sheridan believed that the likely route of escape lay to the west, and he wanted to attack, "feeling that if time was given, the enemy would get away; but Meade prevented this, preferring to wait till his troops were all up."[18] Later that day, one of Little Phil's scouts captured a letter from a Confederate officer that plainly demonstrated the demoralization of the remnants of the Army of Northern Virginia. Sheridan passed it on to Grant. "I wish you were here yourself," he wrote. "I feel confident of capturing the Army of Northern Virginia if we exert ourselves. I see no escape for Lee."[19]

That night, accompanied by a few staff officers and a small cavalry escort, Grant rode out to have dinner with Sheridan. "We talked over the situation for some little time," recalled Grant, "Sheridan explaining to me what he thought Lee was trying to do, and that Meade's orders, if carried out, moving to the right flank, would give him the coveted opportunity of escaping us and putting us in rear of him."[20] Sylvanus Cadwallader, the newspaper correspondent traveling with Grant's headquarters, accompanied the lieutenant general on this expedition. Sheridan "was enthusiastic, positive and not a little profane in expressing his opinions," he noted. Grant heard Sheridan out, "brimming over with quiet enjoyment of Sheridan's impetuosity." Grant then observed that the Confederate army was in a bad predicament and that it would be compelled to abandon its intended line of retreat. Grant suggested that doing so would further demoralize the Army of Northern Virginia, but that if he was in General Lee's place and thought he could get away with part of his army, that he would do so. Sheridan "didn't believe a single regiment could escape and reiterated the opinion many times." In his quiet, calm way, Grant said that "we were doing splendidly; everything was now in our favor; but we must not expect too much. We would do all in our power, but it was too much to expect to capture the whole Confederate army just then."[21]

About midnight, the two officers then conferred with Meade, who was ill, to plan the next moves in this intricate chess game. The next morning, Sheridan, the cavalry, and Maj. Gen. Horatio G. Wright's Sixth Corps moved southwest, looking to block Lee's route of retreat. Little Phil's troopers "awoke in fine spirits. Never before during their three years or more of service had there been any prospect for an end," an officer of the 1st Maine Cavalry recalled. "All the hard marching and fighting of three summer campaigns, and the long hours on picket and in dull winter quarters, had been with no such encouragement as they now had. . . . Richmond was captured . . . the goal for which they had marched and fought, and for which so many brave boys had died, was reached—the backbone of the rebellion . . . had now been broken . . . and was beyond healing. . . . It was exciting to even think of the situation, that spring morning."[22]

Sheridan's horse soldiers joined in the major battle that raged along the banks of Sailor's Creek on April 6. The combined arms attack by the Union forces shattered the Confederate lines. Sheridan sputtered and fumed while he waited for the infantry to join his cavalry. He was "fuming and raging that he could not do all himself." Brig. Gen. Frank Wheaton's Sixth Corps brigade arrived and reported to Sheridan. Pointing across the creek, Sheridan said, "The enemy are there. I want you to form your brigade in one line, cross the creek, and carry the heights." The brigade commander asked whether Sheridan would cover his flanks as he attacked. "Never mind your flanks," he snapped. "Go through them. They are demoralized as hell."[23]

While the main fight raged, a secondary battle broke out near the double wagon bridges at the confluence of Little & Big Sailor's Creeks. There, Humphreys' Second Corps caught Gordon's corps by surprise and captured 20 percent of the Army of Northern Virginia's wagon train, seventeen hundred Rebels, seventy ambulances, and eleven battle flags.

Sailor's Creek was one of Sheridan's finest moments of the Civil War. His well-executed attacks hammered the small remnant of the Confederate army and drove it from the field in a wild rout. The victorious Yankees swept up thousands of prisoners, including Lt. Gen. Richard S. Ewell, the commander of the forces assigned to the defenses of Richmond, Custis Lee, and six other Southern generals. Gen. Lee lost nearly 20 percent of what remained of the Army of Northern Virginia that day, a crushing blow that he could not hope to overcome. When he learned of the debacle, Lee lamented, "My God! Has the army dissolved?"[24]

Ewell joined Sheridan and his staff for dinner that night. The one-legged Confederate urged Sheridan to send a flag of truce to Lee and "demand his surrender in order to save any further sacrifice." Sheridan informed Ewell that he had no authority to negotiate terms of surrender but promised to pass the suggestion on to Grant.[25] That evening, a jubilant Little Phil reported his success to

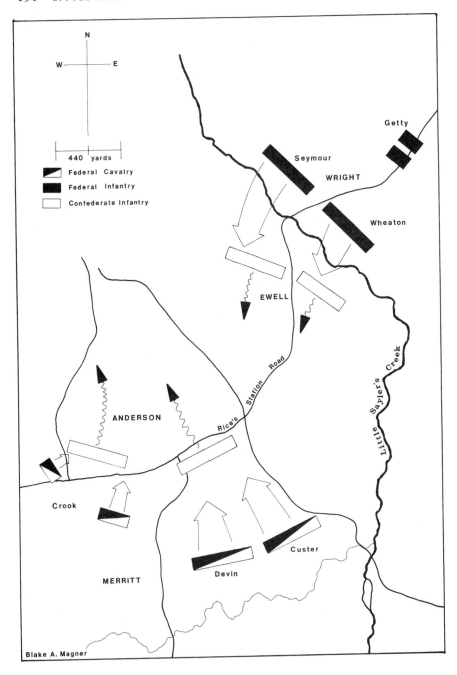

Little Sailor's (Sayler's) Creek, April 6, 1865

the lieutenant general. "I attacked them with two divisions of the Sixth Army Corps and routed them handsomely, making a connection with the cavalry. I am still pressing on with both cavalry and infantry. If the thing is pressed I think Lee will surrender," predicted Little Phil.[26] Grant agreed.

Before the sun rose, Little Phil and the cavalry were already on the road, moving south, "trying to head off the retreating forces—no sleep, no rest, no forage for horses or feed for men," remembered Lt. Charles H. Veil of the 1st U.S. Cavalry. "Everything appeared to be forgotten, save the one object of heading off Lee's army." Little Phil continued to press his men on relentlessly, hoping to cut off the Army of Northern Virginia.[27]

On April 7, the Army of Northern Virginia arrived at Farmville. Four major bridges spanned the Appomattox River there and Lee had to destroy all of them to ensure his safety on the north side of the river. In order to slow the Union pursuit, it was crucial that his army hold the bridges long enough to fire them. The Confederates made a brief stand but failed to burn one of the bridges, which fell intact into the hands of Sheridan's pursuing horse soldiers. Soon, the Southerners counterattacked, and a severe infantry fight broke out, with both sides taking heavy casualties in the close combat near the railroad bridge. The beaten Confederates had to withdraw across the Appomattox. Lee realized he would not be able to shake off Grant's pursuing armies and that the Yankees were now on the same side of the Appomattox as his army. Grant had hemmed in the Southern army, trapping it. The end was now just a matter of time.[28]

That night, Grant sent a message through the lines to Lee. "The result of the last week must convince you of the hopelessness of further resistance on the part of the Army of Northern Virginia in this struggle," wrote the lieutenant general. "I feel that it is so, and regard it as my duty to shift from myself the responsibility of any further effusion of blood by asking of you the surrender of that portion of the C. S. Army known as the Army of Northern Virginia." Although one of his subordinates tried to persuade him to surrender for the good of the army, Lee handed the note to his trusted subordinate, Lt. Gen. James Longstreet, who read it and simply said, "Not yet." Lee then composed his response. "I have received your note of this date. Though not entertaining the opinion you express of the hopelessness of further resistance on the part of the Army of Northern Virginia, I reciprocate your desire to avoid useless effusion of blood, and therefore, before considering your proposition, ask the terms you will offer on condition of its surrender."[29] That night, the Army of Northern Virginia made a stealthy night march, trying to escape Grant's clutches.

Lee's tatterdemalion scarecrows spent April 8 on the road, racing west toward Appomattox Station, where they hoped to find supplies. That morning, Grant responded to Lee's request for terms. "In reply I would say that, peace being my great desire, there is but one condition I would insist upon, that the men and officers surrendered shall be disqualified for taking up arms again against the Government of the United States until properly exchanged." He concluded by offering to meet Lee to discuss the surrender.[30]

Grant informed Little Phil that he had asked for the surrender of the Army of Northern Virginia. In response, Sheridan dispatched Custer's Third Cavalry Division toward Appomattox Station, hoping that the horsemen would get there before the Confederate army. If they did, Lee's route of retreat would be severed, and his surrounded army would have no choice but to surrender. Finding men of the Fifth Corps bogged down, ankle deep in mud, Sheridan cried out, "Boys, boys! You are working hard, I know; but keep it up. I will have Lee and his whole damned army in twenty-four hours!"[31] He then spurred off to lead the pursuit.

After a hard fight with a force of Confederate artillerists fighting as infantry, the hard riding Northern cavalry won the race to Appomattox Station, with the foot soldiers racing along close behind. The Yankee troopers captured a large train of provisions, including more than three hundred thousand rations. As Gen. Joshua L. Chamberlain, commander of a Fifth Corps brigade, recalled, "Sheridan is square across the enemy's front, and with that glorious cavalry alone is holding at bay all that is left of the proudest army of the Confederacy. It has come at last,—the supreme hour. No thought of human wants or weakness now: all for the front; all for the flag, for the final stroke to make its meaning real—these men of the Potomac and James, side by side, at the double in time and column, now one and now the other in the road or the fields beside."[32]

When Lee discovered that his rations had been captured, he held a council of war, which decided that the Army of Northern Virginia would try to break out to the west the next morning if it faced only Yankee cavalry. If it turned out that Union infantry also blocked their route of march, Lee would have no choice but to surrender his army.[33] When the council of war adjourned, Lee penned a response to Grant's dispatch of that morning. Lee responded by saying that he had not proposed a surrender of the Army of Northern Virginia, but rather that he wanted to explore the terms for one. "To be frank, I do not think the emergency has arisen to call for the surrender of this army; but as the restoration of peace should be the sole object of all, I desired to know whether your proposals would lead to that end." Lee offered to meet Grant between the lines the next morning at ten o'clock.[34]

While Lee's council of war met, Sheridan reported on the day's events. After informing Grant of the day's successes, he wrote, "A reconnaissance sent across the Appomattox reports the enemy moving on the Cumberland Road to Appomattox Station, where they expected to get supplies. Custer is still pushing on. If General Gibbon and the Fifth Corps can get up tonight we will perhaps finish the job in the morning." He concluded, "I do not think Lee means to surrender until compelled to do so."[35] Sheridan ordered his command to be ready to march at four o'clock on the morning of April 9. He later wrote, "During the night, although we knew that the remnant of Lee's army was in our front, we held fast with the cavalry to what we had gained, and ran the captured trains back along the railroad to a point where they would be protected by our infantry that was coming up."[36] The cavalry would tighten the noose around Lee's neck, and Maj. Gen. John Gibbon's corps of the Army of the James, rapidly closing on Appomattox Station, would deliver the coup de grace.

The next morning, April 9, Grant replied to Lee's note. "As I have no authority to treat on the subject of peace the meeting proposed for 10 A.M. today could lead to no good," he wrote. "I will state, however, general, that I am equally anxious for peace with yourself, and the whole North entertain the same feeling. The terms upon which peace can be had are well understood. By the South laying down their arms they will hasten that most desirable event, save thousands of human lives, and hundreds of millions of property not yet destroyed."[37]

Lt. Gen. John B. Gordon's Second Corps, supported by Fitz Lee's cavalry division, would spearhead Lee's effort to punch through Sheridan's lines at Appomattox Court House. On the morning of April 9, Gordon's initial volleys drove back the pickets of Brig. Gen. Charles F. Smith's cavalry brigade. "We had nothing to oppose Lee but cavalry and nobly they did their work. We fought them dismounted. They tried hard to break our lines and poured in the shot and shell with their musketry until the air seemed full of it," wrote a Yankee trooper.[38] Spurred by their initial success, the Confederates continued to press the attack, pushing the Federal cavalry back to the next ridge. "It was plain as could be to us that the fighting was drawing nearer, the bullets began every once in a while to crash among the tree-tops overhead," a member of the 19th New York Cavalry wrote. "This made us very anxious, & much speculation was indulged in as to how many and what Infantry were already up, for overestimating as we did Lee's strength . . . & feeling certain that we had all of it to cope with, we felt sure we would be thrashed."[39] Recognizing that his horse soldiers were in danger of breaking in the face of Gordon's fierce attack, Sheridan fretted. He spotted the approaching ranks of the Fifth Corps and sent a staff officer to Gen. Chamberlain, whose brigade led the way. "General Sheridan wishes you to break off from the column and come to his support," cried the breathless aide as he reined in. "The rebel infantry is pressing him hard. Our men are falling back; don't wait for orders through the regular channels, but act on this at once!"[40]

Just as it appeared that the thin line of cavalry pickets would break, Gibbon's infantrymen arrived on the scene. The horse soldiers opened ranks and fell back, so that the advancing Rebels could see the foot soldiers behind them. Gordon realized that further attacks were futile and reported to Lee that Federal infantry had arrived on the scene. "Heard heavy firing in several directions," wrote a Confederate soldier in his diary. "Just before we halted all the firing suddenly ceased. All the men were jubilant as we concluded we had whipped the enemy and put their guns out of commission."[41] Further, Meade's Army of the Potomac was moving to attack Lee's eastern flank, and the Confederates found themselves hopelessly trapped between the pincers of a powerful Union force. Soon, a flag of truce came through the lines.[42] As the cheers of the Yankee soldiers echoed through the valley, Sheridan rode up and down his lines on Rienzi, waving his hat and crying out, "God bless you boys! God bless you boys!"[43]

In spite of the truce, Sheridan prepared a counterattack by the cavalry. A galloper sent by Custer arrived, bearing news of the cease-fire. "Lee has surrendered; do not charge!" exclaimed the courier. "The white flag is up!"

"Damn them," exclaimed Sheridan, "I wish they had held out an hour longer and I would have whipped hell out of them." Brandishing his gloved fist, Little Phil said, "I've got 'em like that!"[44]

Sheridan then rode out to meet with Gordon and the other Confederate officers in that sector. "We have met before. I believe, at Winchester and Cedar Creek in the Valley," Sheridan curtly said.

"I was there," acknowledged the Georgian.

"I had the pleasure of receiving some artillery from your government, consigned to me through your commander, General Early," stated Little Phil. Before Gordon could respond, Sheridan heard shots ring out. The Irishman turned to Gordon, saying, "General, your men fired on me as I was coming over here, and undoubtedly they are treating Merritt and Custer the same way. We might as well let them fight it out."

"There must be some mistake," replied Gordon.

"Why not send a staff officer and have your people cease firing? They are violating the flag," Little Phil said.

Gordon answered, "I have no staff officer to send." Sheridan graciously offered one of his staff officers to carry the message. The staff officer carried Gordon's message to Brig. Gen. Martin W. Gary's cavalry brigade and was made a prisoner. Gary responded, "I do not care for white flags; South Carolinians never surrender." Custer's troopers quickly rescued Sheridan's staff officer from captivity.[45]

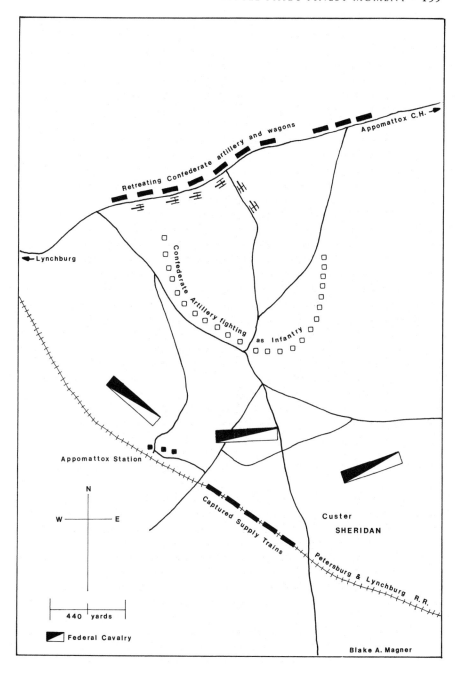

Appomattox Courthouse, April 9, 1865

While waiting for the staff officer to return, Sheridan and Gordon continued their conversation. "General Lee asks for a suspension of hostilities pending the negotiations which he is having with General Grant," said Gordon.

"I have been constantly informed of the progress of the negotiations, and I think it singular that while such discussions are going on, General Lee should have continued his march and attempted to break through my lines this morning," responded Sheridan. "I will entertain no terms except that General Lee shall surrender to General Grant on his arrival here. If these terms are not accepted we will renew hostilities."

"General Lee's army is exhausted," replied Gordon. "There is no doubt of his surrender to General Grant."[46]

Sheridan did not impress Gordon. When Gordon wrote his memoirs years after the end of the war, he reflected on this interview. "I had never seen General Sheridan before, nor received from those who knew him any definite impressions of him as man or soldier. I had seen something of his work in the latter capacity during the campaigns in the Valley of Virginia," the courtly Georgian recalled. "His destruction of barns and mills and farming implements impressed me as in conflict with the laws of war and inconsistent with the enlightened, Christian sentiment of the age, and had prepared me in a measure for his somewhat brusque manners. Truth demands that I say of General Sheridan that his style of conversation and general bearing, while never discourteous, were far less agreeable and pleasing than those of any other officer of the Union army whom it was my fortune to meet. I do not recall a word he said which I could regard as in any degree offensive, but there was an absence of that delicacy and consideration which was exhibited by other Union officers."[47]

General Ord then joined the two officers as they waited for the arrival of Grant and Lee. Soon, Longstreet also rode up. Left with no choice, Lee had agreed to a meeting with Grant.[48] When Grant arrived at Appomattox Court House, Sheridan and Ord awaited him. "How are you Sheridan?" inquired the lieutenant general.

"First-rate, thank you; how are you?" responded Sheridan.

"Is Lee over there?" asked Grant, pointing up the road toward the village.

"Yes," replied Sheridan, "He is in that brick house waiting to surrender to you."

"Well, then, we'll go over," Grant said nonchalantly.[49]

The two commanding generals met in the parlor of Wilmer McLean, and Lee, wearing a magnificent new dress uniform, surrendered the Army of Northern Virginia. A mud-spattered Sheridan attended the meeting, enjoying the fruits of his hard work in pursuing the Confederates across Virginia.

As the meeting wound down, the cheeky Sheridan approached Lee and said that when he had discovered some of the Confederate troops in motion during the morning, it appeared to him to be a violation of the truce. Sheridan then indicated that he had sent a couple of notes to Lee, protesting against the act, and as he had not had time to copy them, he would like to have them back long enough to make copies. Lee pulled the notes from the breast pocket of his coat and handed them over to Sheridan, expressing regret that there had been a misunderstanding leading to the events complained of by Sheridan. After Lee and his staff officers departed, Sheridan purchased the table where the terms of surrender had been drafted from McLean.[50]

Thanks in no small part to Sheridan's aggressive pursuit, the Union had forced Lee to surrender, ending the war in Virginia. A South Carolinian, who hung on until the bitter end, observed, "After a great deal of cautious traveling we got with the remnant of our army and wagon train in full retreat towards Lynchburg. From the 3rd till the 9th we had a fight every day, marching almost constantly day and night. I never was so near worn out in my life."[51] The great national ordeal had ended. On April 12, while Bvt. Maj. Gen. Joshua L. Chamberlain received the formal surrender of the Army of Northern Virginia, Sheridan led the Cavalry Corps off toward Danville in an attempt to join Sherman's army in North Carolina. Because Sheridan did not want to go on this expedition, it started late, made little progress, and produced little in the way of tangible results.[52] He never made it beyond Danville, meaning that Confederate president Jefferson Davis was able to escape into the Deep South via the Danville Railroad. Nevertheless, the final campaign of the war in the East very much bore Phil Sheridan's thumbprint. It was, undoubtedly, Sheridan's finest moment.

"General Lee's army had been literally pounded to pieces after the battle of Five Forks, around Petersburg, which made the evacuation of Richmond and the retreat a necessity," wrote Col. Edward M. Boykin of the 7th South Carolina Cavalry. "When General Longstreet's corps from the north bank joined it, the Army of Northern Virginia, wasted and reduced to skeleton battalions, was still an army of veteran material, powerful yet for attack or defense, all the more dangerous from its desperate condition. And General Grant so recognized and dealt with it, attacking it, as before stated, in detail; letting it wear itself out by straggling and the disorganizing effect of a retreat, breaking down of men and material. The infantry were almost starved."[53] Sheridan's relentless pursuit of Lee, his ruthless driving of the Federal cavalry and infantry, had brought about this result. Col. G. F. R. Henderson, a renowned British military historian and observer of the American Civil War, commented, "There is no finer instance of a pursuit than that of Lee's army by Sheridan in 1865."[54]

Sheridan had demonstrated a true gift for motivating men. He rode his lines, shouting things such as:

- "Take your men in—make your men fight—push on your column!"
- "Go in boys, go in."
- "Ha! The damned scoundrels are running."
- "The cowardly scoundrels can't fight such brave men as mine."[55]

He often drove his men with shocking bursts of creative profanity, raging at them in a voice "that was anything but musical and when exercised under excitement, had a rasping sound, and croaking intonation when in its normal key."[56] Rutherford B. Hayes, who was in the thick of the fighting at Cedar Creek, summed up this trait nicely. Referring to Sheridan's arrival on the battlefield at Cedar Creek, he wrote, "[Sheridan's] enthusiasm, magnetic and contagious. He brought up stragglers. 'We'll whip 'em yet like hell!' he says."[57]

If he found a wounded man, he would say "They've hit you, have they? Don't give it up just yet. Give the bloody rebels a round or two more to remember you by. Down three or four of the rascals before you go to the hospital!"[58] During the fight at Five Forks, one Northern private, after being hit in the neck by a bullet, stumbled to his knees, crying, "I'm killed!" "You're not hurt a bit," replied Little Phil. "Pick up your gun, man and move right on the front." The soldier did as ordered, staggered a few steps and fell over dead.[59] Such was the power of this man's personality, and he demonstrated this trait on many a battlefield.

"If Phil Sheridan had never achieved glorious victories on his own hook; had he fought all his battles as a subordinate under the immediate direction of the commander in chief; had he never attained to high rank as a partial reward for gallant and meritorious services—the fact that Grant loved him would have been sufficient to endear the cavalry commander to the comrades who followed his lead from the Wilderness to Appomattox," a veteran of the 1st Massachusetts Cavalry claimed. "But the troops loved Sheridan for himself. They fairly idolized him. They had the most implicit faith in him as a commander. His presence inspired them to deeds of daring; they were ready to go anywhere—into the jaws of death—if he but said the word."[60]

Sheridan was utterly fearless in combat. Mounted on Winchester—he had renamed Rienzi after his victory at Winchester—"he rolled and bounced upon the back of his steed much as an old salt does when walking up the aisle of a church after a four years' cruise at sea," dodging shot and shell.[61] He often exposed himself to great danger if he believed doing so would change the tide of battle. At Winchester in September 1864, things looked bleak for Sheridan's army. Brig. Gen. Cuvier Grover's demoralized division had taken heavy losses and was falling back. Spotting Grover's men retreating, Sheridan threw "himself into the breech among Grover's half-demoralized troops scattering to the rear, he finally by appeals, threats, and, I must confess it, profanity brought order out of the confusion and got the men faced about to retaliate on [the] graybacks, the author of their discomfiture," recorded correspondent James E. Taylor. With Sheridan's oaths ringing in their ears, Grover's men mounted a successful counterattack, helping to save the day for the Army of the Shenandoah.[62] Later that day, a Southern shell landed under the feet of Sheridan's horse, but failed to explode. Smiling broadly as he rode away, Sheridan proclaimed, "That's all right." He had dodged another bullet.[63]

"He rode up and down the lines under fire for hours," observed Sylvanus Cadwallader of the commander's conduct at Five Forks, "encouraging his men by waving his hat and sword, and exhorting them to seize the opportunity now within their grasp, and to sweep their enemies to destruction."[64] Col. Horace Porter of Grant's staff watched rapt as Sheridan mounted his great black war horse under heavy fire and made for the Confederate barricades. "Sheridan spurred 'Rienzi' up to the angle, and with a bound the animal carried his rider over the earthworks, and landed among a line of prisoners who had thrown down their arms and were crouching close under the breastworks." Sheridan directed the Southerners aside. When the breastworks fell, more than fifteen hundred prisoners were taken. After his victory at Five Forks, Porter rode up to Sheridan and scolded him: "It seems to me that you have exposed yourself in a manner hardly justifiable on the part of a commander of such an important movement." He responded, "I have never in my life taken a command into battle, and had the slightest desire to come out alive unless I won."[65]

"Phil Sheridan never led his men into a ticklish place and left them to get out by themselves," a trooper of the 1st Massachusetts Cavalry wrote. "He never sent his soldiers on a dangerous expedition without arranging to have assistance at hand if there was a suspicion that help would be needed. And he never asked his men to go where he himself was not willing to go himself."[66] To his credit, he demonstrated all of these traits during the Appomattox Campaign.

As the armies raced across the Virginia countryside, Sheridan was seemingly everywhere, indefatigable. "In this campaign . . . he had shown himself possessed of military traits of the highest order," wrote Porter, who was Grant's aide. "Bold in conception, self-reliant, demonstrating by his acts that 'much danger makes great hearts resolute,' fertile in resources, combining the restlessness of a Hotspur with the patience of a Fabius, it is no wonder that he should be looked upon as the wizard of the battlefield." Porter continued, "Wherever blows fell thickest, there was his crest. Despite the valor of the defense, opposing ranks went down before the fierceness of his onsets, never to rise again, and he would not pause till the folds of his banners waved above the strongholds he had wrested from the foe." Porter concluded, "As long as manly courage is talked of or heroic deeds are honored, the hearts of a grateful people will beat responsive to the mention of the talismanic name of Sheridan."[67]

Even though Chamberlain vigorously disagreed with the relief of Warren, he and the other officers of the Fifth Corps also came to respect Sheridan, in part because of the apology he tendered on the night of April 1. "We had had a taste of his style of fighting, and we liked it," wrote Chamberlain, the hero of Round Top. "In some respects it was different from ours; although this was not a case to test all qualities. . . . We could see how this voice and vision, the swing and color, this vivid impression on the senses, carried the pulse and will of men." Chamberlain continued, "Sheridan does not entrench. He pushes on, carrying his flank and rear with him,—rushing, flashing, smashing. He transfuses into his subordinates the vitality and energy of his purpose; transforms them into part of his own mind and will. He shows the power of a commander,—inspiring both confidence and fear. He commanded our admiration, but we could discriminate: we reserved room for question whether he exhibited all the qualities essential to a chief commander in a campaign, or even in the complicated movements of an extensive field of battle."[68]

Cadwallader, the newspaper correspondent who traveled with Grant, observed Sheridan on many battlefields during the final campaign. "Probably no soldier was more terrible in battle than Sheridan," he wrote. "With the first smell of powder he became a blazing meteor, a pillar of fire to guide his own hosts. The rather small short, heavily built man rose to surprising stature in his stirrups, to the sublimity of heroism in action; and infused a like spirit in his troops. I think it no exaggeration to say that America never produced his equal, for inspiring an army with courage and leading them into battle. Absolutely fearless himself, with unwaivering faith in his cause and his plans, he always raised the faith and courage of others, to the level of his own; passed from rank to rank in action, flaming, fiery, omnipresent, and well-nigh omnipotent."[69]

A Federal staff officer, Col. Benjamin Crowninshield of the 1st Massachusetts Cavalry, also had many opportunities to observe Sheridan's conduct throughout the last year of the war. "In one respect Sheridan was especially remarkable: that was in watching the troops in battle, seeing for himself what was done and taking instant advantage of the chances that offered," he wrote.[70] Similarly, a Vermonter who served under Sheridan's command in the Shenandoah Valley asserted that the key to victory "was Sheridan's personal magnetism, and all-conquering energy. He felt no doubt, he would submit to no defeat, and he took his army with him as on a whirlwind."[71]

"Sheridan's stature was far from commensurate with his ability and brain," observed James E. Taylor, the correspondent who so carefully chronicled the Valley Campaign. Taylor described Sheridan as a "little mountain of combative force." He continued, "In that little body there was tremendous energy and untiring vigilance that carried him to victory. To sum up, Sheridan possessed great common sense and based his conduct on its dictates and acquired fame and promotion with phenomenal rapidity."[72]

In particular, during the war's final campaign, Sheridan demonstrated that he could effectively command a combined arms operation. The cavalry, along with infantry corps from two different armies, led the chase across the Virginia countryside. The coordination and logistics of such an effort required skill, and Sheridan demonstrated that skill successfully. Managing a force smaller than the one he commanded in the Shenandoah Valley, Sheridan defeated a large and tenacious Confederate force in his greatest victory of the Civil War. Although his cavalry tactics lacked imagination, and although he had not demonstrated a killer instinct in the Shenandoah Valley, his conduct of the pursuit of Lee's army showed that he had learned from his mistakes in the Valley and that he could be ruthless in bringing his prey to bay.

A British observer commented on Sheridan's performance during the war's final campaign in the *London Pall Mall Gazette* newspaper. "So brilliant was Sheridan's work as a cavalry leader that his name has come to be associated chiefly with that role, but in this injustice has been done him, for he handled all arms with equal skill and enterprise, and in the success of the final and fiercest struggle that culminated in Lee's surrender at Appomattox Court House, he stands out as the principal figure, in whose track of tornado-like energy Grant seems to have followed tamely." The commentator continued, "In the soldierly characteristics of Sheridan and [Russian Gen. Mikhail Dmitriyevich] Skobelev, there was much in common. Both men had innate military genius—both possessed the magnetism which inspired to heroism the men they led, both, when occasion called, became veritable thunderbolts of war, both had their fighting ardor under control, and both were endowed with infinite capacity for taking pains to achieve success."[73]

In spite of his poor performance as commander of the Cavalry Corps, his horse soldiers nevertheless came to love and respect him. "It was evident that he had some regard for the comfort and condition of his men and of the horses; that he did not intend to needlessly tire out either; that he believed men and horses must have rest in order to do the best work and the best fighting," wrote Edward P. Tobie of the 1st Maine Cavalry.[74] Even though the Army of the Potomac's horsemen suffered a nearly unbroken string of defeats under Sheridan's stewardship, his greatest contribution to the successes of the Union cavalry was their newfound confidence, their newfound sense of pride in just being associated with his command.

Phil Sheridan knew only one way to conduct a campaign—his way. If an officer crossed his path—as Averell and Warren did—results were all that mattered. It did not matter to Sheridan whether a man's life or career might be ruined as a result of his single-minded drive. While there is always a human toll to such an attitude, Sheridan's unbending ambition, drive, and aggressiveness definitely put him in a position to accomplish great things, and he did not disappoint during the Appomattox Campaign. Whether the results gained justified the means is not a question for this analysis. Rather, Sheridan deserves credit for having these personality traits. Certainly, a great soldier must lead from the front, but the question lingers as to whether these favorable personality traits offset the many negative aspects that we have already examined in this book. Only the reader can make that decision after analyzing the evidence.

NOTES

1. O.R., vol. 46, part 3, 1378.
2. George A. Forsyth, *Thrilling Days in Army Life* (New York: Harper & Bros., 1900), 175–76.
3. O.R., vol. 46, part 3, 1379. Lt. Gen. A. P. Hill, one of Lee's corps commanders, was killed in action in the fighting that day.
4. Calkins, *The Appomattox Campaign,* 55–59.
5. Horace Porter, *Campaigning with Grant,* 452–53.
6. O.R., vol. 46, part 3, 528.
7. Humphreys, *The Virginia Campaign,* 2:373.
8. Chamberlain, *The Passing of the Armies,* 214.
9. O.R., vol. 46, part 3, 529.
10. Ibid., 557.
11. Sheridan, *Personal Memoirs,* 2:175.
12. Edward M. Boykin, *The Falling Flag: Evacuation of Richmond, Retreat and Surrender at Appomattox* (New York: E. J. Hale & Son, 1874), 18–19.
13. Power, *Lee's Miserables,* 275.
14. O.R., vol. 46, part 1, 1265.
15. Humphreys, *The Virginia Campaign,* 2:377.
16. Calkins, *The Appomattox Campaign,* 85–89.
17. O.R., vol. 46, part 3, 573.
18. Sheridan, *Personal Memoirs,* 2:177; Grant, *Personal Memoirs,* 2:716.
19. O.R., vol. 46, part 3, 582.
20. Grant, *Personal Memoirs,* 2:717.
21. Cadwallader, *Three Years with Grant,* 313.
22. Tobie, *First Maine Cavalry,* 413.

23. Morris Schaff, *The Sunset of the Confederacy* (Boston: John W. Luce & Co., 1912), 104.
24. Ibid., 112; Calkins, *The Appomattox Campaign,* 108–12.
25. Newhall, *With General Sheridan,* 188.
26. O.R., vol. 46, part 3, 610.
27. Charles H. Veil, *The Memoirs of Charles Henry Veil,* ed. Herman J. Viola (New York: Orion Books, 1993), 64.
28. Calkins, *The Appomattox Campaign,* 126–29.
29. O.R., vol. 46, part 3, 619.
30. Ibid., 641.
31. *Unveiling of the Equestrian Statue of General Philip H. Sheridan,* 111.
32. Chamberlain, *The Passing of the Armies,* 231–32.
33. Calkins, *The Appomattox Campaign,* 155–56.
34. O.R., vol. 46, part 3, 641.
35. Ibid., 653.
36. Ibid., part 1, 1109.
37. Ibid., part 3, 664.
38. James McLean, *California Sabers: The 2nd Massachusetts Cavalry in the Civil War* (Bloomington: University of Indiana Press, 2000), 271.
39. Bowen, *First New York Dragoons,* 282.
40. Schaff, *The Sunset of the Confederacy,* 219.
41. Power, *Lee's Miserables,* 280.
42. O.R., vol. 46, part 1, 1109.
43. Edward G. Longacre, *Lincoln's Cavalrymen: A History of the Mounted Forces of the Army of the Potomac* (Mechanicsburg, Pa.: Stackpole, 2000), 332.
44. Morris, *Sheridan,* 256.
45. Boykin, *The Falling Flag,* 59.
46. O'Connor, *Sheridan the Inevitable,* 269; Sheridan, *Personal Memoirs,* 2:196–98.
47. Gordon, *Reminiscences,* 441–42.
48. O'Connor, *Sheridan the Inevitable,* 269; Sheridan, *Personal Memoirs,* 2:196–98.
49. Sheridan, *Personal Memoirs,* 2:200; Horace Porter, *Campaigning with Grant,* 469–70.
50. Horace Porter, *Campaigning with Grant,* 483–84. He gave the table to George Custer and his wife, Elizabeth, as a reward for Custer's yeoman service in spearheading the pursuit of Lee's army across the Virginia countryside. Today, that table is in the collection of the Smithsonian Institution's Museum of American History in Washington, D.C.
51. Power, *Lee's Miserables,* 275.
52. For additional information on the Danville Expedition, which is outside the scope of this work, see Chris M. Calkins, *The Danville Expedition of May and June 1865* (Danville, Va.: Blue & Gray Education Society, 1998), 5–15.
53. Boykin, *The Falling Flag,* 61.
54. G. F. R. Henderson, *The Science of War: A Collection of Essays & Lectures, 1892–1903,* ed. Capt. Neill Malcolm (London: Longmans, Green & Co., 1905), 56.

55. Cadwallader, *Three Years with Grant,* 304.

56. Taylor, *Sketchbook,* 41.

57. Williams, *Rutherford B. Hayes,* 2:527.

58. Cadwallader, *Three Years with Grant,* 304–5.

59. Morris, *Sheridan,* 249.

60. Stanton P. Allen, *Down in Dixie: Life in a Cavalry Regiment in the War Days from the Wilderness to Appomattox* (Boston: D. Lathrop & Co., 1888), 266.

61. Bruce Catton, *A Stillness at Appomattox* (Garden City, N.Y.: Doubleday, 1954), 45.

62. Taylor, *Sketchbook,* 359.

63. Ibid., 361.

64. Cadwallader, *Three Years with Grant,* 304.

65. Horace Porter, *Campaigning with Grant,* 439–41.

66. Allen, *Down in Dixie,* 229.

67. Horace Porter, *Campaigning with Grant,* 469.

68. Chamberlain, *The Passing of the Armies,* 153–54.

69. Cadwallader, *Three Years with Grant,* 305.

70. Benjamin W. Crowninshield, "Sheridan at Winchester," *Atlantic Monthly* 42 (1878): 686.

71. Aldace F. Walker, *The Vermont Brigade in the Shenandoah Valley, 1864* (Burlington, Vt.: The Free Press Association, 1869), 155.

72. Taylor, *Sketchbook,* 41.

73. *London Pall Mall Gazette,* November 26, 1888. Gen. Mikhail Dmitriyevich Skobelev, born September 29, 1843, played prominent roles in Russia's conquest of Turkistan and in the Russo-Turkish War of 1877–1878. Sent to Tashkent (in modern Uzbekistan) in 1868, Skobelev participated in Gen. Konstantin P. Kaufmann's successful campaign (1873) against the Khanate of Khiva in the lower Amu Darya region. Subsequently, when a rebellion in the Khanate of Kokand (1875) resulted in Kaufmann's invasion of that region, Skobelev captured the city of Andizhan (now Andijon) in January 1876, enabling the Russians to occupy the whole khanate. The Russian government then annexed Kokand (February 19, 1876), renamed it the province of Fergana, and appointed Skobelev, who had been promoted to major general, to be its first Russian governor. When war broke out between Russia and Turkey in 1877, Skobelev was transferred to the European front. His forces defeated the Turks in several strategic battles and finally captured Edirne (Adrianople) and San Stefano, thus forcing the Turks to conclude an armistice (January 31, 1878). Because he always appeared in the midst of battle wearing a white uniform and riding a white horse, Skobelev became known by his soldiers as the "White General." Skobelev returned to Turkistan and in 1880 took command of the Russian campaign against the Turkmen living between the Caspian and Aral seas and the Persian province of Khorasan. On January 24, 1881, Skobelev captured Göktepe (now Gökdepe), where he slaughtered the male population in the vicinity. He then forced the region into submission and was proceeding against Ashkhabad

(now Ashgabat) when he was recalled and given command of the Minsk Army Corps. At the beginning of 1882 Skobelev entered the political arena, making speeches in Paris and Moscow in favor of militant pan-Slavism and predicting an inevitable conflict between the German and Slav peoples. Those views, however, clashed with the official policy of the Russian government, which in 1881 had concluded an alliance with Germany and Austria-Hungary. Skobelev therefore was immediately recalled to St. Petersburg, where he suffered a fatal heart ailment and died in June 1882. See "Mikhail Dmitriyevich Skobelev," included in *Encyclopedia Britannica.*

74. Tobie, "Personal Recollections of General Sheridan," 186–87.

SHERIDAN REASSESSED

Having laid out the evidence, the question of whether Philip H. Sheridan deserves the lofty reputation bestowed upon him by history remains to be answered. After thoroughly reviewing the evidence, the following conclusions jump off the page:

Sheridan was not a great commander of cavalry. In fact, his tenure as leader of the Army of the Potomac's Cavalry Corps was lackluster at best. He rarely defeated the Confederate horsemen, and his tactics were unimaginative and not particularly effective. While he deserves some credit for advocating aggressive action against the enemy in the spring and summer of 1864, his insistence on trying to draw Jeb Stuart's cavalry into a decisive battle meant that the Army of the Potomac was doomed to a desperate slugging match against the Army of Northern Virginia in the charnel houses of Spotsylvania Court House and Cold Harbor. In seeking personal glory, Sheridan abrogated the critical role of the cavalry, scouting and screening, and nearly caused the destruction of the Army of the Potomac.

Sheridan's performance in the Shenandoah Valley was also lackluster. Given the tremendous numerical superiority that the Union Army of the Shenandoah enjoyed over Early's Army of the Valley, something would have been dreadfully wrong if Sheridan had not defeated Early. Again, his tactics were unimaginative and, on almost every occasion, Jubal Early displayed superior generalship. One can only conclude that in an even fight, Early would have vanquished Little Phil. Even though Sheridan had a reputation for ruthlessness, he did not demonstrate a killer instinct at any time during the Valley Campaign, and actually prolonged the war by not being more aggressive in his pursuit of Early's dogged little band.

Sheridan had a wide streak of insubordination, and was not dependable in a subordinate role. On more than one occasion, this man refused to obey the lawful orders of a superior officer. Instead of receiving the normal penalty for such conduct—a general court-martial—Sheridan consistently received the reward of being placed in independent command. An insubordinate officer, even if possessed of a brilliant strategic and tactical mind, has little value in a military hierarchy. World War II General George S. Patton Jr. provides a good parallel. Patton's stubborn streak nearly cost him his command, and lost him the lifelong friendship of General Dwight D. Eisenhower.

Because of his insubordination, Little Phil was of almost no use to his commanding officer, Maj. Gen. George G. Meade. That insubordination cost many good men their lives, for no good reason other than to satisfy his enormous ego. Most reprehensible, Sheridan was hypocritical about his insubordination. He consistently and heavy-handedly punished perceived insubordination in those serving under his command but never recognized the hypocrisy of his own conduct. While he could never overlook or forgive that trait in others, he was incapable of seeing it in himself.

Sheridan's inability to recognize his own character flaws meant that others who drew his ire had their lives and careers cavalierly ruined, with no hope of redemption. Sheridan betrayed the trust of his oldest and best friend, George Crook, and took advantage of him to advance his own career. Without even blinking an eye, he destroyed the life of Gouverneur K. Warren for no good reason. Even when faced with the truth—that he had improperly relieved Warren of command—he could not and would not admit it. The same held true of William Woods Averell, who was so devastated by his inexplicable relief from command that he could never speak of it again. Unlike Warren, though, Averell was fortunate enough to find success in other arenas.

Sheridan tended to prevaricate in an effort to improve his standing in the eyes of those reviewing his actions. Some of the lies were relatively harmless, such as the myth of where he was born. Others were far more egregious. As an example, his bald-faced lies about besting the Confederate cavalry in every engagement during the Overland Campaign of 1864 are so blatantly false as to call into question the credibility of everything that he wrote. Even if the lying was not ill intentioned, its effect was to make him appear to be a glory-grabbing, shameless self-promoter who stepped on his lifelong friend in order to advance his own agenda. While the ends may have justified the means, the means nevertheless prove that this man lacked moral fiber.

Little Phil did have some good qualities. The killer instinct, which had been missing during the Valley Campaign, showed up for the Appomattox Campaign. He rightly deserves credit for being the driving force that finally brought Robert E. Lee and his Army of Northern Virginia to bay in the spring of 1865. The Appomattox Campaign demonstrates his gifts for leading a combined arms force in combat and for driving men to the limits of human endurance. He had a real gift for motivating men in battle and for engendering loyalty in them. Most important, this man's very presence gave men confidence that they could do anything. He had an electric personality that charged those who came in contact with him. That trait meant that the Army of the Potomac's Cavalry Corps gained tremendous confidence in its abilities, even in the face of a nearly unbroken streak of defeats in the spring of 1864. That, more than anything, was Phil Sheridan's greatest contribution to the Union victory in the Civil War, a victory that could not have happened without the contributions of the blue-clad horsemen. Their exertions brought Lee to bay and forced the Confederate surrender at Appomattox.

The conclusion can only be that, while Phil Sheridan had a few positive attributes, he does not deserve the lofty reputation bestowed upon him by history. Other than for a period of less than two weeks in 1865, his performance simply does not stand up to scrutiny and simply does not support the conclusion that Sheridan was a great commander of men. Had he not had protective patrons such as William S. Rosecrans, William T. Sherman, and Ulysses S. Grant, he never would have earned the high rank he achieved in the Civil War. In fact, Sheridan's insubordination probably would have been punished by the ending of his military career. That high rank, in turn, led to his achieving even higher rank in the peacetime Regular Army.

Phil Sheridan owed all that he was to Ulysses S. Grant. But for Grant's protection and patience, Sheridan's career would have languished in the Western Theater. While he might have achieved corps command in the West, he never would have eclipsed either Sherman or George H. Thomas. He would be remembered as an aggressive commander of infantry and not as a bold and dashing cavalier. Grant and Sheridan, so unlike in temperament and personality, shared a few common traits—iron will, a belief in their own abilities, and an unwillingness to ever admit defeat. Once Sheridan persuaded Grant of his worth, nothing Sheridan did later, including his blatant insubordination, ever cost Sheridan

Grant's unwavering support. "For this he was rewarded with more promotions, more fame, and more responsibilities, until at last he reached the pinnacle of his soldierly profession," claimed Sheridan's most recent biographer, Roy Morris Jr. "Without Grant, Sheridan would have been merely a good Union divisional commander—all things considered, not a bad legacy—but it is doubtful he would have progressed beyond, at best, command of a corps."[1]

The question remains: Why? Sylvanus Cadwallader, the newspaperman who spent three years at Grant's side, provides a glimpse of the answer. "It was well-known to General Grant's intimates, that he considered Sheridan incomparably the greatest general our civil war produced," Cadwallader observed. "Other generals might be equally good under ordinary circumstances, under the eyes of an able superior commander, and up to the point of a given or limited number of men. Sheridan, he believed, could be more safely trusted with an independent army than any of them; and he often said in private confidential conversation, that no army could ever be raised on this continent so large that Sheridan could not competently command it." The newspaperman concluded, "In this last respect, Grant had unbounded confidence in, and admiration for Sheridan."[2]

It is ironic that someone like Sheridan, who did not deserve the praise and adulation he received, has been enshrined in the pantheon of greats, even though an in-depth review of his military career in the Civil War does not support that reputation. Little Phil's successes should be attributed to his fellow Ohioans. Rosecrans brought Sheridan to prominence. There, he caught Grant's eye. With the support and encouragement of his chief subordinate, Sherman, the lieutenant general coddled Little Phil and, through his patronage, permitted him to reach the pinnacle of military achievement. Crook's tactical and strategic genius provided Sheridan with the impetus to succeed.

Philip Henry Sheridan died in 1889, at the young age of fifty-eight. He had suffered from heart disease for several years, and a series of massive heart attacks claimed his life a few short months after he became only the third member of the U.S. Army to don the four stars of a full general. His meteoric rise from captain to major general in the Regular Army in two short years propelled him over the heads of many officers far more senior than he. His unprecedented climb to the army's highest echelons undoubtedly left many career professional soldiers shaking their heads in wonderment.

Even though the historic record indicates that Sheridan does not deserve the reputation bestowed upon him, he nevertheless continues to loom large over the American landscape more than one hundred years after his death. Six major monuments to this man stand guard over the American landscape. The first, commissioned in 1904 and unveiled in 1905, graces the town square in Sheridan's hometown of Somerset, Ohio. It shows Little Phil atop Rienzi, waving his famous porkpie hat and rallying his troops at Cedar Creek. It occupies the center of the town, which remains proud of its favorite son. The Sheridan family home, a simple wooden house, still stands nearby, its front proudly marked as the boyhood home of Little Phil.

The second, dedicated in Washington, D.C., in November 1908, brought out the glitterati of the era. The handsome equestrian monument, created by the greatest American sculptor Gutzon Borglum, graces Sheridan Circle, in the middle of Massachusetts Avenue in the Embassy Row district of the city's northwest quadrant. The statue portrays Sheridan, mounted on Rienzi, at the moment he rallied his troops in the Winchester Road at Cedar Creek. President Theodore Roosevelt, himself a cavalryman, gave the dedication speech, and Little Phil's son, Lt. Philip H. Sheridan Jr., pulled the cord to unveil it.[3] Borglum then created a second, similar monument that graces Sheridan Road in Chicago. In 1916, an equestrian monument to Sheridan was unveiled in Albany, New York. The last, dedicated in the 1930s, stands in the Greenwich Village section of New York City. It depicts Little Phil standing, directing his troops in the field. Interestingly, monuments to alternative lifestyles flank it in the birthplace of the American gay rights movement. A similar statue, also depicting the critical moment at Cedar Creek also adorns the grounds of Fort Sheridan, Illinois, a few miles northwest of Chicago. Sheridan's sixth likeness, along with those of Grant, Sherman, James Garfield, Salmon P. Chase, and Edwin M. Stanton, graces the lawn of the State House in Columbus, Ohio, in a tribute to that state's great contributions to the Union victory in the Civil War. Rosecrans, another Ohioan, is conspicuous in his absence from that monument, which is called "My Jewels."

In addition to these monuments, at least four cities have been named for Phil Sheridan, and there are countless streets named for him.[4] There is a Sheridan High School in Ohio, which, not surprisingly, has sports teams called the "Little Phils." The U.S. Army, which today mounts its cavalrymen in helicopters and tanks, named an armored vehicle for him. The Sheridan tank was a mainstay of the Army's mechanized force in the 1950s.

Maj. Philip H. Sheridan Jr. rests alongside his father in Arlington National Cemetery, just outside the front doors of Robert E. Lee's Arlington House. Sheridan's grave sits atop the high bluff, with a commanding view of the cemetery, the Potomac River below, and the Lincoln Memorial standing silent guard on the other side of the glittering ribbon of water. Sheridan Avenue winds through the cemetery, and the Sheridan Gate fronted one of the entrances to those hallowed grounds. The resting places of thousands of Civil War veterans surround his grave, many of them in unmarked graves, their identities forever unknown. Undoubtedly, many of those men owed their mortal wounds to Sheridan's presence on the battlefield.

For all of his numerous character flaws and uninspired performance on the battlefield, Philip H. Sheridan still looms large in American lore. It is up to the reader to decide whether he deserves to hold such an exalted place in the annals of American history.

NOTES

1. Morris, *Sheridan,* 385–86.
2. Cadwallader, *Three Years with Grant,* 306.
3. Karen Allamong Jacob, *Testament to Union: Civil War Monuments in Washington, D.C.* (Baltimore: Johns Hopkins University Press, 1998), 134–38. Borglum was the sculptor of Mount Rushmore and the great Confederate monument at Stone Mountain, Georgia. In her book, Jacob sets forth the interesting saga of this monument, which took years and two different sculptors to erect. When Sheridan's widow objected to the concept by the original sculptor, the monument was nearly scratched. A large military parade, led by mounted horse soldiers, celebrated the unveiling of the monument, which was attended by many veterans of Sheridan's commands during the Civil War. It was one of the greatest events of the first decade of the twentieth century, marked by great pomp and circumstance. Little Phil would have been proud. For details on the dedication, see *Washington Evening Star,* November 25, 1908, and *Washington Post,* November 26, 1908.
4. Sheridan, Wyoming; Sheridan, Oregon; Ft. Sheridan, Illinois; and Sheridan, Indiana.

⇌ A P P E N D I X A ⇌

Report of Maj. Gen. Philip H. Sheridan, U.S. Army, Commanding Cavalry Corps, Including Operations April 6–August 4

HEADQUARTERS MILITARY DIVISION OF THE GULF,
New Orleans, La., May 13, 1866

GENERAL:

I have the honor to make the following report of the operations of the Cavalry Corps, Army of the Potomac, from April 6, 1864, to August 4, 1864:

On March 27, 1864, I was relieved from the command of the Second Division, Fourth Corps, Army of the Cumberland, to take command of the Cavalry Corps, Army of the Potomac, and on the 4th of April, in General Orders, No. 144, current series, War Department, I was assigned to that corps, then lying in the vicinity of Brandy Station, Va. The corps consisted of three divisions and twelve batteries of horse artillery, and in a few days after I joined was adjusted as follows: Brig. Gen. A. T. A. Torbert to command the First Division; Brig. Gen. D. McM. Gregg, the Second Division; and Brig. Gen. J. H. Wilson, the Third Division; the artillery being under the command of Captain Robertson, U.S. Army. The officers and men were in pretty good condition, so far as health and equipment were concerned, but their horses were thin and very much worn out by excessive, and, it seemed to me, unnecessary picket duty, the picket-line almost completely encircling the infantry and artillery camps of the army, covering a distance, if stretched out on a continuous line, of nearly 60 miles. The enemy, more wise, had been husbanding the strength and efficiency of his horses by sending them to the rear, in order to bring them out in the spring in good condition for the impending campaign; however, shortly after my taking command, much of the picketing was done away with, and we had about two weeks of leisure time to nurse the horses, on which so much depended; consequently, on the 4th of May, when the campaign opened, I found myself with about 10,000 effective men, and the same number of horses in passable trim. After carefully studying the topography of the country from the Rapidan to Richmond, which is of a thickly wooded character, its numerous and almost parallel streams nearly all uniting, forming the York River, I took up the idea that our cavalry ought to fight the enemy's cavalry, and our infantry the enemy's infantry. I was strengthened in this impression still more by the consciousness of a want of appreciation on the part of infantry commanders as to the power of a large and well-managed body of horse, but as it was difficult to overcome the established custom of wasting cavalry for the protection of trains, and for the establishment of cordons around a sleeping infantry force, we had to bide our time.

On May 4 the army moved; Gregg's division taking the advance to Ely's Ford, on the Rapidan; Wilson's the advance to Germanna Ford, on the same stream; Torbert's covering the trains of the army in rear, holding from Mitchell's Station to Culpeper, and around to Stevensburg, and strongly picketing the fords from Germanna Ford to Rapidan Station. As soon as the Second Corps reached Ely's Ford, Gregg moved to Chancellorsville, and, upon the Fifth Corps reaching Germanna Ford, Wilson made the crossing of the Rapidan, moved through Old Wilderness, and advanced to Parker's Store. On the 5th Torbert joined me at Chancellorsville, and General Meade ordered Wilson in the direction of Craig's Meeting-House, where he was attacked, and, after a sharp engagement, driven back, via Shady Grove Church, to Todd's Tavern. It was necessary for him to take this route, as the enemy's infantry had advanced from the direction of Orange Court-House, and had occupied Parker's Store and the direct road back to our army. When General Meade discovered that Wilson was cut off, he sent word to me, near Chancellorsville, to go to his relief, and I immediately dispatched General Gregg's division in the direction of Todd's Tavern, where he met Wilson, who was still being followed up. The enemy's pursuing force was attacked by Gregg at this place, defeated, and driven to Shady Grove Church, a distance of 3 or 4 miles. It was now well understood that the enemy's cavalry at Hamilton's

Crossing had joined General Lee's forces, and the necessity for my moving to that point, as ordered, was obviated.

As I was held responsible for the left flank of our army and the trains, I made such disposition of the troops under my command as to hold the line of the Brock road beyond the Furnaces, and thence around to Todd's Tavern and Piney Branch Church, but General Meade, on false report, became alarmed about his left, and notified me in the following note that Hancock's left had been turned, and directed me to draw in my forces to protect the trains:

HEADQUARTERS ARMY OF THE POTOMAC,
May 6, 1864—1 p.m.

Major-General SHERIDAN, Commanding Cavalry Corps:
    Your dispatch of 11.45 a.m. received. General Hancock has been heavily pressed, and his left turned. The major-general commanding thinks that you had better draw in your cavalry so as to secure the protection of the trains.
    The order requiring an escort for the wagons to-night has been rescinded.

A. A. HUMPHREYS,

Major-General and Chief of Staff

I obeyed this order, and the enemy took possession of the Furnaces, Todd's Tavern, and Piney Branch Church, the regaining which cost much fighting on the 6th and 7th, and very many gallant officers and men.

On the 6th Custer fought at the Furnaces and defeated the enemy, who left his dead and wounded in our hands. On the 7th the trains of the army, under directions from headquarters Army of the Potomac, were put in motion to go into park at Piney Branch Church. As this point was held by the enemy, I was confident that the order must have been given without fully understanding the condition of affairs, and therefore thought the best way to remedy the trouble was to halt the trains in the vicinity of Alrich's, attack the enemy, and regain the ground. This led to the battle of Todd's Tavern, in which the enemy was defeated. Gregg attacked with one of his brigades on the Catharpin road, and drove the enemy over Corbin's Bridge; Merritt, who was in command of the First Division during the temporary absence of Torbert, attacked with his division, on the Spotsylvania road, driving him toward Spotsylvania, and Davies' brigade, of Gregg's division, made a handsome attack on the Piney Branch Church road, uniting with Merritt on the Spotsylvania road. The pursuit was kept up until dark. Gregg's and Merritt's divisions encamped in open fields, in the vicinity of Todd's Tavern, with orders to move in the morning, at daylight, for the purpose of gaining possession of Snell's Bridge, over the Po River. To accomplish this, Wilson, who was at Alsop's house, was directed to take possession of Spotsylvania early on the morning of the 8th, and thence move into position at Snell's Bridge. Gregg and Merritt were ordered to proceed to the same point, the former via the crossing at Corbin's Bridge, the latter by the Block house. Had these movements been carried out successfully, it would probably have sufficiently delayed the march of the enemy to Spotsylvania Court-House as to enable our infantry to reach that point first, and the battles fought there would have probably occurred elsewhere; but upon the arrival of General Meade at Todd's Tavern the orders were changed, and Gregg was simply directed by him to hold Corbin's Bridge, and Merritt's division ordered in front of the infantry column, marching on the road to Spotsylvania in the darkness of the night, the cavalry and infantry becoming entangled in the advance, causing much confusion and delay. I was not duly advised of these changes, and for a time had fears for the safety of General Wilson's command, which had proceeded, in accordance with my instructions, to Spotsylvania Court-House, capturing and holding it until driven out by the advance of Longstreet's corps.

The time had now come to leave the Wilderness, where we had successfully held the left of the army, and defeated the enemy's cavalry on the 5th at Todd's Tavern and at the Furnaces; again on the 6th at the Furnaces, and on the 7th at Todd's Tavern. During the 8th I received orders to go out and engage the rebel cavalry, and when out of forage, of which we had half rations for one day, I was to proceed to the James River, and replenish from the stores which General Butler had at Bermuda Hundred. Pursuant to this order the three divisions of cavalry, on the evening of this day, were concentrated in the vicinity of Alrich's, on the plank road to Fredericksburg, and on the morning of the 9th commenced the march. It will be seen, upon examination of the map of Virginia, that there was but very little space for a large cavalry force to operate on the left of our army, from Spotsylvania to the Rappahannock, and that we were liable to be shut in. I therefore concluded to march around the right of Lee's army, and put my command, before fighting, south of the North Anna, where I expected to procure grain; where I was confident that while engaging the enemy's cavalry no timely assistance from his infantry could be procured, and whence, if not successful, I could proceed west and rejoin our army, swinging around toward Gordonsville and Orange Court-House. With this view we started, marching out on the plank road to Tabernacle Church; thence to the Telegraph road; thence down through Chilesburg to Anderson's Crossing of the North Anna. This movement was made at a walk, with three divisions on the same road—making a column of about 13 miles in length—marching by the flank of the enemy. I preferred this, however, to the combinations arising from separate roads, combinations rarely working as expected, and generally failing, unless subordinate commanders are prompt and fully understand the situation; besides, an engagement was imminent, and it was necessary that the force be well together. As soon as the Ny, Po, and Ta Rivers, each giving an excellent defensive line to the enemy, were passed, all cause for anxiety was removed, and our ability to cross the North Anna unquestionable.

After passing the Ta River the enemy's cavalry came against the rear of my column, and General Davies, who had the rear brigade, was directed to fight as rear guard, following up the main column. It is with pleasure I say that he and his command performed this responsible and trying duty with courage and good judgment. About dark Merritt crossed the North Anna at Anderson's Ford; Gregg and Wilson encamped on the north side, engaging the enemy up to a late hour at night. After Merritt's division crossed, Custer's brigade was ordered to Beaver Dam Station, on the Virginia Central Railroad, where he recaptured 375 Union prisoners, taken by the enemy in the Wilderness; destroyed the station, 2 locomotives, 3 trains, 100 cars, 90 wagons, from 8 to 10 miles telegraph wire and railroad, 200,000 pounds bacon, and other supplies, amounting in all to about 1,500,000 rations, and nearly all the medical stores of General Lee's army. These stores had been moved from Orange Court-House to this point, either because General Lee wished to have them directly in his rear—the road used for hauling from Orange Court-House to Spotsylvania being on a parallel line to his line of battle—or because he contemplated falling back, or being driven back, to the North Anna. On the morning of the 10th Gregg and Wilson were again attacked, but their crossing was covered by the division on the south side of the North Anna, and was effected without much loss.

An important point of the expedition had now been gained, and we had also obtained forage for our almost famished animals; our next object was to husband their strength and prepare to fight. It now became apparent that the enemy, in following up our rear, had made a great mistake, and he began to see it, for, when we leisurely took the Negro Foot road to Richmond, a doubt arose in his mind as to whether his tactics were good, whereat he immediately hauled off from the rear, and urged his horses to the death so as to get in between Richmond and our column. This he effected, concentrating at Yellow Tavern, 6 miles from the city, on the Brook turnpike; consequently the march on the 10th was without much incident, and we quietly encamped on the south bank of the South Anna, where we procured all necessary forage, marching from 15 to 18 miles. On the night of the 10th and 11th of May Davies' brigade, of Gregg's division, was ordered to Ashland, and arriving before the head of the enemy's column, which had to make a wide detour to reach Yellow Tavern, drove out a force occupying the town; burnt a locomotive with train of cars attached; destroyed the railroad for some distance, and rejoined the main column at Allen's Station, on the Fredericksburg railroad. From Allen's the entire command moved on Yellow Tavern, Merritt in advance, Wilson next, and Gregg in rear. The enemy here again made an error in tactics by sending a large force to attack my rear, thus weakening his force in front, enabling me to throw all my strength on that which opposed my front, and fight this force with a small rear guard.

Merritt gallantly attacked the enemy at Yellow Tavern, and got possession of the Brook turnpike. The enemy, still confident, formed his line a few hundred yards to the east of this pike, enfilading it with his artillery fire, and making Yellow Tavern a hot place; but Gibbs and Devin held fast with their brigades, supported by artillery, and Custer charged the enemy's battery and line, supported by Chapman's brigade, of Wilson's division—in fact, by the whole of Wilson's division, Gregg having one brigade available to support. Custer's charge, with Chapman on his flank, was brilliantly executed; first at a walk, then at a trot, then dashing at the enemy's line and battery, capturing the guns and gunners and breaking the line, which was simple enough to receive the charge in a stationary position. In this assault General J. E. B. Stuart, commanding the enemy's cavalry, was mortally wounded.

Gregg about the same time charged the force in rear with equal success, and ended the engagement. We captured a number of prisoners, and the casualties on both sides were quite severe. After Custer's charge and the enemy's line was broken—one portion of which was driven toward Ashland, the other toward Richmond—a reconnaissance was sent up the Brook turnpike, toward the city, dashed across the south fork of the Chickahominy, drove a small force from the exterior line of the works, and went inside of them. I followed up this party, and found between the two lines of works a road leading to that from Mechanicsville to Richmond. I thought we could go around on this across the Mechanicsville pike, south of the Chickahominy, and encamp next night (12th) at Fair Oaks, and determined to make the movement, being influenced to some extent in doing so by the reports from colored people, during the afternoon, that General Butler's force had reached a small stream about 4 miles south of Richmond, on the south side, and that I possibly could help him by a demonstration. Therefore, after making the wounded as comfortable as possible, we commenced the march about 11 o'clock on the night of the 11th, and massed the command on the plateau south of Meadow Bridge at about daylight; torpedoes planted in the road—many of which exploded, killing several horses—being the only difficulty encountered.

At daylight on the morning of the 12th Wilson encountered the enemy's batteries on, or near, the Mechanicsville pike, and could not pass them. As soon as I was notified of this condition, Custer's brigade was ordered to make the crossing to the north side of the Chickahominy at Meadow Bridge, but as the bridge was found to have been destroyed, and the enemy's cavalry posted on the north side, I ordered Merritt's entire division to repair it, and to make the crossing at all hazards. During the time thus occupied, the enemy gave the working party great annoyance by sweeping the bridge with a section of artillery; and Merritt, to drive away this section and the force supporting it, crossed a small force of two or three regiments, attacked dismounted, and was repulsed: still the work on the bridge continued, and when it was finished, Merritt crossed nearly all his division, dismounted, attacked the enemy, carried his line of temporary breast-works, and continued the pursuit to Gaines' Mill. Meantime the enemy advanced from behind his works at Richmond, and attacked Wilson and Gregg. Wilson was driven back in some confusion, but Gregg was ready, having concealed a heavy line of skirmishers in a bushy ravine, in his front, and when the enemy marched to attack, with more display than grit, this unexpected and concealed line opened a destructive fire with repeating carbines, and some of Wilson's men at the same time turning in on their flank, the line broke in disorder, and went into security behind the breast-works defending the city. The six batteries of regular artillery were used by Captain Robertson, chief of artillery, with great effect, and contributed much to our success. The enemy considered us completely cornered, but such was not the case, for while we were engaged, scouting parties were sent along the Chickahominy, and several fords found by them. This attack and repulse ended the battle; for the balance of the day we collected our wounded, buried our dead, grazed our horses, and read the Richmond papers, two small newsboys having, with commendable enterprise, entered our lines and sold to the officers and men. Between 3 and 4 o'clock in the afternoon the remaining portion of the command crossed the Chickahominy and encamped at and between Walnut Grove and Gaines' Mill.

On the 13th the march was resumed, encamping at Bottom's Bridge. On the 14th we marched through White Oak Swamp, and went into camp between Haxall's Landing and Shirley, on the James River. Our casualties on the march were 425. All transportable wounded and a large number of prisoners were brought along to this point, and the former, through the kindness of General Butler's medical officers, quickly cared for on arrival. From the 14th until the 17th we rested in this camp, sending out scouting parties as far as New Market, in the direction of Richmond. On the night of the 17th we commenced the return march, crossing the Chickahominy at Jones' Bridge, and went into camp on the 18th at Baltimore Cross-Roads and vicinity.

The uncertainty of what had happened to the Army of the Potomac during our absence made the problem of how to get back and where to find it somewhat difficult, particularly so as I knew that re-enforcements had come up from the south to Richmond; I therefore determined to cross the Pamunkey River at the White House, and sent to Fortress Monroe for a pontoon bridge to be used for that purpose. While waiting, I ordered Custer with his brigade to proceed to Hanover Court-House, and, if possible, destroy the railroad bridges over the South Anna; Gregg and Wilson were sent at the same time to Cold Harbor, to demonstrate in the direction of Richmond as far as Mechanicsville, so as to cover Custer's movement; Merritt, with the remaining brigades of his division, held fast at Baltimore Cross-Roads. After Gregg and Custer started it was found on examination that the railroad bridge at the White House had been but partially burned, and could be repaired, and General Merritt was at once put on this duty. By sending mounted parties through the surrounding country, each man bringing back a board, it was made passable in one day, and on the 22d, when Custer and Gregg returned, we crossed, encamping that night at Aylett's, on the Mattapony River. Custer encountered a large force of the enemy apparently moving from the direction of Richmond to Lee's army, and was unable to accomplish his mission. Gregg occupied Cold Harbor and sent scouting parties, which encountered small squads of mounted men, to the vicinity of Mechanicsville, but nothing of great importance occurred.

At Aylett's we learned from citizens, and captives belonging to Lee's army, that the Army of the Potomac was at North Anna River, in the vicinity of Chesterfield Station.

On the 23d the march was resumed, encamping at Reedy Swamp. On the 24th we rejoined the Army of the Potomac in the vicinity of Chesterfield. This ended the first raid, which occupied sixteen days. We lost but few horses, considering their condition when we started. The average distance traveled per day did not exceed 18 miles; the longest march being 30 miles. The horses which failed were shot by the rear guard, as they could have been easily recuperated and made serviceable to the enemy. I think the actual number lost would not exceed 300, perhaps not more than 250.

On the 25th General Wilson, with his division, was transferred to the right of the army, and made a reconnaissance south of the North Anna as far as Little River: the other two divisions remained encamped from the 24th until the 26th, in the vicinity of Pole Cat Station. On the 26th a movement of the army commenced in order to make the crossing of the Pamunkey River at, or near Hanovertown. Torbert's and Gregg's divisions, with Russell's division, of the Sixth Corps, took the advance to secure the crossings, with directions to demonstrate so as to deceive the enemy as much as possible in the movement. To accomplish this end, Torbert was ordered to move to Taylor's Ford, on the Pamunkey, and demonstrate until after dark as if the crossing was to be made at that point, then to leave a small guard, quietly withdraw, and march to Hanovertown ford, where the real crossing was to be made. General Gregg was ordered to Littlepage's crossing of the Pamunkey, to demonstrate in the same manner, to retire quietly after dark, leaving a guard to keep up the demonstration, and march quickly to Hanovertown crossing, taking with him the pontoon bridge. Russell took up the march and followed the cavalry.

On the morning of the 27th Custer's brigade, of Torbert's division, made the crossing, driving from it about 100 of the enemy's cavalry and capturing 30 or 40; the balance of the division followed this brigade, and advanced to Hanovertown, where General Gordon's brigade of rebel cavalry was encountered, routed, and driven in great confusion in the direction of Hanover Court-House, the pursuit being continued to a little stream called Crump's Creek. Gregg was moved up to this line, and Russell encamped near the crossing of the river.

We had been successful in our mission, and, upon the arrival of the army, on the 28th, it crossed the Pamunkey behind our line, unimpeded. I was immediately after ordered to demonstrate in the direction of Mechanicsville, in order to find out the enemy's whereabouts, and therefore directed Gregg's division to move out, via Haw's Shop, on the Mechanicsville road, but when about three-fourths of a mile in advance of Haw's Shop it encountered the enemy's cavalry, which was dismounted and behind a temporary breast-work of rails, &c. Gregg vigorously attacked this force, which appeared to be the rebel cavalry corps, and a brigade of South Carolina troops, reported 4,000 strong, armed with long-range rifles, and commanded by a Colonel Butler; these Carolinians fought very gallantly in this their first fight, judging from the number of their dead and wounded, and prisoners captured. The most determined efforts were made on both sides in this unequal contest, and neither would give way until late in the evening, when Custer's (Michigan) brigade was dismounted, formed in close column of attack, and charged, with Gregg's division, when the enemy was driven back, leaving all his dead and his line of temporary works in our possession. This was a hard contested engagement, with heavy loss, for the number of troops engaged, to both sides, and was fought almost immediately in front of the infantry line of our army, which was busily occupied throwing up breast-works. After dark, our own and the enemy's dead being buried, we moved to the rear of the infantry, and went into camp on the morning of the next day (the 29th) in the vicinity of Old Church.

In the battle at Haw's Shop but one brigade (Custer's) of Torbert's division was engaged; the other two, being posted on the Crump Creek line, could not be gotten up until relieved by the Sixth Corps. They arrived in the afternoon, however, but did not become seriously engaged, only demonstrating on the right of Gregg. After we had taken position at Old Church, Wilson's division was ordered to the right of the army, and Gregg's and Torbert's pickets pushed out in the direction of Cold Harbor, which was occupied by the enemy in some force. As our occupation of this point was essential to secure our lines to the White House, which was to be our base, its possession became a matter of deep interest. The enemy appeared to realize this also, for he, at a very early period, took possession of it, and pushed a force up to Matadequin Creek on the Old Church road, putting his front parallel with the Pamunkey—which was then our line to the White House—in order to make it dangerous for our trains. This force encountered the pickets of the First Division at Matadequin Creek, but they held fast and fought gallantly until re-enforced by their division on the north side of the creek, which took up the contest. The fight then became general and was stubbornly contested, but the enemy finally gave way, and was pursued within 1½ miles of Cold Harbor. In this fight Butler's South Carolinians were again put in to receive the brunt, and many of them were killed and captured. On the morning of the 31st I visited Torbert and Custer, at Custer's head-quarters—Torbert's division having the advance—and found that they had already talked over a plan to attack and capture Cold Harbor, which I indorsed, and on the afternoon of the 31st the attack was made, and, after a hard-fought battle, the town taken. Gregg was immediately moved to the support of Torbert, but the place was captured before any of his troops became engaged.

Cold Harbor was defended by cavalry and infantry, and on the Old Church side the enemy had thrown up temporary breast-works of logs and rails. The fight on the part of our officers and men was very gallant; they were now beginning to accept nothing less than victory. After gaining the town, I notified army headquarters to that effect, but that the enemy in additional numbers were arriving there; that I could not hold it with safety to my command, and that I would move out, and did so; just after we had left, however, a dispatch was received directing that Cold Harbor be held at all hazards, and I therefore immediately ordered its reoccupation, changed the temporary breast-works thrown up by the enemy, so as to make them available for our troops, dismounted the cavalry, placing them behind these works, and distributing the ammunition in boxes along the line, determined to hold the place as directed. While this was being done the enemy could be heard giving commands and making preparations to attack in the morning.

Just after daylight June 1 he marched to the attack, and was permitted to come close in to our little works, when he received the fire of our batteries and repeating carbines, which were used with terrible effect, and was driven back in confusion; still determined to get the place, after reorganizing, he attacked again, but with the same result. About 10 o'clock the Sixth Corps arrived and relieved the cavalry, which moved toward the Chickahominy, and covered the left of the line until relieved by Hancock's corps during the afternoon. While the balance of the cavalry were engaged at Cold Harbor, Wilson's division was posted on the right of the army, near the head waters of the Totopotomoy Creek. On being relieved by the infantry from the Cold Harbor line the two divisions moved down the Chickahominy, encamping for the night of the 1st of June at Prospect Church and vicinity, and on the 2d we moved down the Chickahominy still farther, taking a position on the north side, at Bottom's Bridge: the enemy's cavalry occupying the south side, with artillery in position at the fords. No movements took place on the 3d; the enemy shelled our position at very long range but did no damage.

On the 4th the First Division marched back to Old Church, and on the 6th the Second Division was relieved at Bottom's Bridge by one brigade of Wilson's division, and marched back to the same vicinity: thence both divisions moved to New Castle Ferry, where the trains, which had been sent to White House, reached us, with supplies for a march, since called the Trevilian raid.

While Gregg's and Torbert's divisions were operating on the left of the army, Wilson, who was on the right, engaged the enemy at Mechump's Creek on the 31st of May; at Ashland on the 1st of June, and on the 2d of June at Haw's Shop—the scene of the battle of May 28, and at Totopotomoy Creek. The battle at Ashland was brought about by McIntosh's brigade, which had been ordered to that vicinity for the purpose of covering a movement made to the South Anna to destroy the railroad bridges over that stream, and which was successful.

On the 6th of June I received instructions from General Meade and the lieutenant-general to proceed with two divisions of my corps to Charlottesville, for the purpose of cutting the Virginia Central Railroad, to unite, if possible, with Maj. Gen. D. Hunter, whom I expected to meet at or near Charlottesville, and bring his command over to the Army of the Potomac. There also appeared to be another object, viz, to remove the enemy's cavalry from the south side of the Chickahominy, as, in case we attempted to cross to the James River, this large cavalry force could make such resistance at the difficult crossings as to give the enemy time to transfer his force to oppose the movement. Two divisions being ordered to proceed on this raid, Wilson was detached by the following order, and took the advance of the Army of the Potomac, on its march to the James River:

HEADQUARTERS CAVALRY CORPS, ARMY OF THE POTOMAC,
New Castle Ferry, June 6, 1864

Brig. Gen. J. H. WILSON,
Commanding Third Cavalry Division:

GENERAL: I am directed by the major-general commanding to notify you that he will march from New Castle Ferry at 5 a.m. to-morrow, taking with him the First and Second Cavalry Divisions. During his absence you will report and receive your orders direct from the headquarters Army of the Potomac.

Your division quartermaster and commissary will have to attend to the supplying of your command.

Orders have been issued directing the officers in charge at the White House to send all detachments of cavalry (mounted) belonging to the different cavalry divisions to report temporarily for duty with your command.

Very respectfully, your obedient servant,

JAS. W. FORSYTH,
Lieutenant-Colonel and Chief of Staff

On June 7, the command being prepared with three days' rations in haversacks, to last for five days, two days' forage on the pommel of the saddles, 100 rounds of ammunition, 40 on the person and 60 in wagons, 1 medical wagon, 8 ambulances, and 1 wagon each for division and brigade headquarters, we crossed the Pamunkey at New Castle, and encamped that night between Aylett's and Dunkirk, on the Mattapony River. On the 8th we encamped 2 miles west of Pole Cat Station. It was my intention to march along the north bank of the North Anna, cross it at Carpenter's Ford, strike the railroad at Trevilian Station, and destroy it to Louisa Court-House, march past Gordonsville, strike the railroad again at Cobham Station, and destroy it thence to Charlottesville as we proceeded. We, therefore, on the 9th of June, resumed the march along the Anna—our advance guard skirmishing, as it almost always did, with mounted men of the enemy—and encamped on East Northeast Creek, near Young's Mill. During this day I learned that Breckinridge's division of infantry was passing slowly up the railroad to Gordonsville parallel to me, and that the enemy's cavalry had left their position on the south side of the Chickahominy, and were marching on the old Richmond and Gordonsville road on Gordonsville. This information was confirmed by a party sent to cut the telegraph wires along the railroad during the night. On the 10th the march was resumed; we passed through Twyman's Store, crossed the North Anna at Carpenter's Ford, and encamped on the road leading to Trevilian Station and along the banks of the North Anna. During the night of the 10th the boldness of the enemy's scouting parties, which we had encountered more or less every day, indicated the presence of a large force.

On the morning of the 11th we resumed the march on Trevilian, meeting at once and driving the enemy's advance parties in our front. Torbert had the leading division, and, at a point about 3 or 3½ miles from Trevilian Station, encountered the enemy in full force behind a line of breast-works constructed in dense timber. Custer, with his brigade, was ordered to take a wood road found on our left and get to Trevilian Station, or at least in rear of the enemy, and attack his led horses. In following this road he passed between Fitz Lee's and Hampton's divisions—the former being on the road leading from Louisa Court-House to where the battle commenced, the latter on the direct road from Trevilian to the same point—and on, without opposition, to Trevilian Station, which he took possession of. As soon as I found that Custer had gotten to the rear of the enemy, the remaining two brigades of Torbert's division were dismounted and formed line of battle, assailed the enemy's works, and carried them, driving Hampton's division pell-mell and at a run back on Custer, at Trevilian, who commenced fighting in all directions. So panic-stricken was this division (Hampton's) and so rapidly was it pushed that some of it was driven through Custer's lines, and many captured. While the First Division was thus engaged Gregg attacked Fitz Lee on the Louisa Court-House road, and drove him in the direction of Louisa Court-House; the pursuit was continued until about dark. Hampton's division made its way in the direction of Gordonsville, and was joined during the night by Fitz Lee, who made a detour westward for that purpose. At night my command encamped at Trevilian Station, and from prisoners, of which we had captured about 500, I learned that Hunter, instead of coming toward Charlottesville, as I had reason to suppose, was at or near Lexington, moving apparently on Lynchburg; that Ewell's corps was on its way to Lynchburg, on the south side of James River; and that Breckinridge was at Gordonsville or Charlottesville, having passed up the railroad, as heretofore alluded to. I, therefore, made up my mind that it was best to give up the attempt to join Hunter, as he was going from me instead of coming toward me, and concluded to return. Directions were at once given to collect our own wounded and those of the enemy in hospitals, and to make provision for their transportation back in ammunition wagons and in vehicles collected from the country. I was still further influenced in my decision to return by the burden which these wounded threw upon me, there being over 500 cases of our own, and the additional burden of about 500 prisoners, all of whom must have been abandoned by me in case I proceeded farther; besides, one more engagement would have reduced the supply of ammunition to a very small compass.

On the morning of June 12 we commenced destroying the railroad to Louisa Court-House, and in the afternoon I directed Torbert to make a reconnaissance up the Gordonsville road to secure a by-road leading over Mallory's Ford, on the North Anna, to the Catharpin road, as I proposed taking that route in returning, and proceeding to Spotsylvania Court-House, thence, via Bowling Green and Dunkirk, to the White House. In the reconnaissance Torbert became heavily engaged, first one brigade, then another, then the last, the battle continuing until after dark. Gregg during this time was breaking up the railroad to Louisa Court-House.

The result of Torbert's fighting made it impossible to cross at Mallory's Ford without venturing a battle next day, in which case the remainder of our ammunition would have been consumed, leaving none to get back with; therefore, during the night of the 12th, we moved back on our track, recrossed the North Anna at Carpenter's Ford on the following morning, unsaddled our horses and turned them out to graze, as they were nearly famished, having had no food for two days, and in the afternoon proceeded to the vicinity of Twyman's Store, where we encamped. The enemy, excepting a small party which General Davies dispersed with one of his regiments, did not follow us.

I left near Trevilian three hospitals containing many rebel wounded, and 90 of ours that were non-transportable, with medicines, liquors, some hard-bread, coffee, and sugar. I regret to say that the surgeons left in charge were not well treated by the enemy, and that the hospitals were robbed of liquors and stores. On the 14th the march was continued, and we reached the Catharpin road—upon which it was originally intended to move after crossing Mallory's Ford, and which would have saved much time and distance—and encamped at Shady Grove Church. On the 15th we encamped at Edge Hill, on the Ta River, having passed over the battle-field of Spotsylvania, and on the 16th at Dr. Butler's farm, on the Mattapony, having marched through Bowling Green. Being as yet unable to ascertain the position of the Army of the Potomac, and uncertain whether or not the base at the White House had been discontinued, I did not like to venture between the Mattapony and Pamunkey Rivers, embarrassed as I was with wounded prisoners, and about 2,000 negroes that had joined us, and therefore determined to push down the south bank of the Mattapony far enough to enable me to send them with safety to West Point, where I expected to find gun-boats and transports. Following this plan, we proceeded on the 17th to Walkerton and encamped, and on the 18th resumed the march through King and Queen Court-

House, encamping in its vicinity. I here learned that the base at the White House was not entirely broken up, and that supplies there awaited me; therefore, on the morning of the 19th I sent the wounded, prisoners, and negroes to West Point, escorted by two regiments of cavalry, and turning, marched to Dunkirk, on the Mattapony, a point at which the river was narrow enough for my pontoons to reach across.

On my march from Trevilian to this point we halted at intervals during each day to dress the wounded and refresh them as much as possible. Nothing could exceed the cheerfulness exhibited by them; hauled as they were in old buggies, carts, ammunition wagons, &c., no word of complaint was heard. I saw on the line of march men with wounded legs driving, while those with one disabled arm were using the other to whip up the animals. On the 20th we resumed the march at an early hour, to the sound of artillery, in the direction of the White House, and had proceeded but a short distance when dispatches from General Abercrombie notified me that the place was attacked. I had previously sent an advance party with directions to move swiftly, and to report to me by couriers the condition of affairs; from these I soon learned that there was no occasion to push our jaded animals, as the crisis, if there had been one, was over, and therefore moved leisurely to the banks of the Pamunkey opposite White House, and encamped, the enemy holding the bluffs surrounding the White House farm. On the morning of the 21st Gregg's division was crossed over dismounted, and Torbert's division mounted, and the enemy driven from the bluffs, and also from Tunstall's Station in the evening, after a sharp engagement. I found here orders to break up the White House depot, and to move the trains over to Petersburg, via Jones' Bridge. I immediately commenced breaking up as directed and making my arrangements to carry over and protect a train of over 900 wagons, knowing full well that I would be attacked if the enemy had any spirit left in him. On the morning of the 22d I sent Torbert in advance to secure Jones' Bridge, over the Chickahominy, so that we could make the crossing at that point, and Gregg marched on a road parallel to the one on which the train was moving, and on its right flank, as it was the only flank requiring protection. The train was not attacked, but was safely parked on the south side of the Chickahominy for the night. On the morning after Torbert had secured the crossing, the 23d, the enemy attacked his picket post on the Long Bridge road, with Chambliss's brigade, and drove it in, but on its being reinforced by six companies of colored troops belonging to Getty's command, the enemy was repulsed, and the picket post re-established. This brigade, I was told by the prisoners taken, was the advance of the rebel cavalry corps, and through it Hampton had been advised of our having already secured the crossing of the Chickahominy.

General Getty had relieved General Abercrombie, and was in command of a small infantry force, composed mostly of the odds and ends of regiments and batteries.

On the 24th the march was resumed, with directions to cross the trains at Bermuda Hundred, where there was a pontoon bridge. To reach this point I was obliged to march through Charles City Court-House, thence by Harrison's Landing and Malvern Hill, the latter of which was occupied by the enemy; in fact, he held everything north of the James except the *tete-de-pont* at the crossing. Torbert's division moved out on the Charles City Court-House road as an escort to the trains, and when in the vicinity of the Court-House the advance guard encountered the enemy and drove him across Herring Creek, on the road to Westover Church. As soon as this attack was reported to me, orders were immediately given to park the train—the head of which was far beyond Charles City Court-House at convenient points on the road, and Torbert was directed to push his whole division to the front to meet the enemy, while Gregg, who had marched on the road leading to Saint Mary's Church for the purpose of protecting the right flank of the train, and who had also been attacked, was instructed to hold fast until all the transportation could pass Charles City Court-House. The train was immediately after put in motion, and safely parked in the vicinity of Wilcox's Landing. At Saint Mary's Church Gregg was attacked by the entire cavalry corps of the enemy, and after a stubborn fight, which lasted until after dark, was forced to retire in some confusion, but without any loss in material. This very creditable engagement saved the train, which should never have been left for the cavalry to escort. During the night and next morning the train was moved back through Charles City Court-House to Douthat's Landing, on the James River, where it was ferried over, after which the troops were transported in the same manner.

Before the crossing was completed General Meade notified me to move rapidly to the support of General Wilson, who had been ordered on a raid to break the communication south of Petersburg by destroying the South Side and Danville railroads. General Wilson's expedition had been successful until it reached the left of the army on its return, when it encountered, at Reams' Station, a large force of infantry sent down the Weldon railroad from Petersburg, and being at the same time attacked on the flank by cavalry, the command was routed and obliged to fall back across Nottoway River at Poplar Hill, whence a wide detour was necessary to reach the main army, in consequence of which, as the heat was intense, the loss in animals was great. As soon as the orders from General Meade were received I hastened with Torbert and Gregg, via Prince George Court-House and Lee's Mills, to Reams' Station, where I found the Sixth

Corps, but was too late to render material assistance. I immediately, however, sent out parties to procure information concerning the expedition, and learned from them that it had crossed the Nottoway and was safe.

The results obtained in the destruction of the South Side and Danville rail-roads were considered equivalent to the losses sustained by General Wilson's division. Had an infantry force been sent sooner to Reams' Station, the raid would have been eminently successful.

General Wilson states in his report as follows:

> Foreseeing the probability of having to return northward, I wrote to General Meade the evening before starting that I anticipated no serious difficulty in executing his orders; but unless General Sheridan was required to keep Hampton's cavalry engaged, and our infantry to prevent Lee from making detachments, we should probably experience great difficulty in rejoining the army. In reply to this note, General Humphreys, chief of staff, informed me it was intended the Army of the Potomac should cover the Weldon road the next day, the South Side road the day after, and that Hampton having followed Sheridan toward Gordonsville, I need not fear any trouble from him.

Still no timely relief was sent. As soon as Wilson was found to be safe, I was ordered back to Light-House Point and vicinity to rest my command, which had marched and fought for fifty-six consecutive days, and remained there from the 2d till the 26th of July, refitting and picketing the left of the army. While at this camp I received about 1,500 horses. These, together with about 400 obtained at Old Church by dismounting recruits, were all that were issued to me while personally in command of the Cavalry Corps, from April 6 to August 1, 1864.

On the afternoon of July 26 I moved with the First and Second Divisions of cavalry—Torbert's and Gregg's—for the north side of the James River, in connection with the Second Corps, and was directed, if an opportunity offered, to make a raid on the Virginia Central Railroad and destroy the bridges over the North and South Anna Rivers, and those over Little River. We crossed the Appomattox at Broadway Landing, and on arriving at Deep Bottom, where we were joined by General Kautz's small cavalry division of the Army of the James, the command was massed, to allow the Second Corps to pass and take the advance across the James. Soon after the Second Corps had crossed a small portion of it carried the enemy's works in front of the *tete-de-pont*, and captured four pieces of artillery.

The cavalry moved to the right of the Second Corps, and found the enemy occupying a strong line of works extending across the New Market and Central roads leading to Richmond, the right resting on Four-Mile Creek. His cavalry vedettes, posted in front of Ruffin's house on the New Market road, were discovered by the Second U.S. Cavalry, and driven back on their infantry line of battle, composed of two divisions. The high ground in advance of Ruffin's house thus gained was immediately occupied by the First Division as a line of battle, and the Second Division placed on its right, covering the road from Malvern Hill to Richmond. Immediately upon the formation of our line, the enemy advanced to the attack and drove the cavalry back over the ridge, on the face of which it quickly lay down in line of battle at a distance of about 15 yards from the crest. When the enemy's line reached this crest, a fire from our repeating carbines was opened upon it, whereupon it gave way in disorder, and was followed over the plain beyond by the cavalry, which captured about 250 prisoners, and 2 battle-flags, besides killing and wounding very many. This counter attack against infantry was made by the First and Second Cavalry Divisions simultaneously, and our line re-established. During the engagement, which is called the battle of Darbytown, General Kautz was in support of Gregg on the right of the line.

The enemy, deceived by the long front presented by the Second Corps and cavalry, was undoubtedly impressed with the idea that nearly all of our forces had been moved to the north side of the James, and at once transferred a large body of his troops from the lines at Petersburg to our front at New Market; as I understood, this transfer by the enemy was the object which the lieutenant-general wished to attain, in order that the mine explosion of Petersburg might, to a greater certainty, result in the capture of the city.

On the afternoon of the 28th the Second Corps withdrew to a line near the head of the bridge, and the cavalry was drawn back to a position on its right. In order to deceive the enemy still more, I sent during the night one of my divisions to the opposite side of the James, first covering the bridge with moss and grass to prevent the tramp of the horses being heard, and at daylight marched it back again on foot in full view of the enemy, creating the impression that a large and continuous movement to the north side was still going on. On the 29th nothing occurred during the day on either side, except a skirmish by some of General Kautz's command, in the vicinity of Malvern Hill; but, after dark, the Second Corps was hastily and quietly withdrawn to the south side, to take part in the engagement which was expected to follow the mine explosion. I was directed to follow, and withdrew by brigades from my right, successively, passing them over the bridge. This movement was one involving great anxiety, as, when the Second Corps moved, the space at the mouth of the bridge occupied by me was so circumscribed that an offensive movement in force by the enemy must have resulted in the annihilation of my whole command. Shortly after daylight on the 30th the recrossing had been effected, and by 10 o'clock my advance division was well over to the left of our army in front of Petersburg; but as the mine attack had failed it was not necessary to carry out the part assigned to the cavalry. The movement to the north side of the James for the accomplishment of our part of the plan connected with the mine explosion was well executed, and every point made; but it was attended with such anxiety and sleeplessness as to prostrate almost every officer and man in the command.

On the 1st of August I was relieved from the personal command of the Cavalry Corps, and ordered to the valley of the Shenandoah. Torbert's and Wilson's divisions were directed to join me there.

It will be seen by the foregoing narrative that the idea advanced by me at the commencement of the campaign, viz, "that our cavalry ought to fight the enemy's cavalry, and our infantry the enemy's infantry," was carried into effect immediately after the battle of the Wilderness. The result was constant success and the almost total annihilation of the rebel cavalry. We marched when and where we pleased; were always the attacking party, and always successful.

During the period herein embraced I am led to believe, on information derived from the most reliable sources, that the enemy's cavalry was superior to ours in numbers; but the esprit of our men increased every day, while that of the enemy diminished. In these marches, and in others afterward performed in connection with the Valley and Appomattox campaigns, we were obliged to live to a great extent on the country. Forage had to be thus obtained for our horses and provisions for our men, consequently many hardships were necessarily brought on the people, but no outrages were tolerated. I do not believe war to be simply that lines should engage each other in battle, as that is but the duello part—a part which would be kept up so long as those who live at home in peace and plenty could find the best youth of the country to enlist in their cause (I say the best, for the bravest are always the best), and therefore do not regret the system of living on the enemy's country. These men and women did not care how many were killed or maimed, so long as war did not come to their doors, but as soon as it did come in the shape of loss of property, they earnestly prayed for its termination. As war is a punishment, and death the maximum punishment, if we can, by reducing its advocates to poverty, end it quicker, we are on the side of humanity.

In the foregoing brief sketch I have been unable to give in detail the operations of the cavalry, and will have to trust to the subordinate reports to make up the deficiency. In consequence of our constant activity we were obliged to turn over our wounded and prisoners whenever and wherever opportunity offered, and oftentimes without receipts. I am also, therefore, unable to furnish an accurate list of either my casualties or prisoners captured from the enemy. I think my casualties from May 5 to August 1 will number between 5,000 and 6,000 men, and that the captures in prisoners will exceed 2,000. We sent to the War Department from the 5th of May, 1864, to the 9th of April, 1865, the day on which the Army of Northern Virginia surrendered, 205 battle-flags, captured in open field fighting; it is nearly as many as all the armies of the United States combined sent there during the rebellion. The number of field pieces captured in the same period was between 160 and 170; all in open field fighting. These captures of flags, colors, and artillery were made during the campaign the operations of which I have just related, the Shenandoah campaign, the march from Winchester to Petersburg, and the Appomattox campaign. To the Sixth and Nineteenth Corps, General Crook's command, which, with Merritt's and Custer's divisions of cavalry, composed the Army of the Shenandoah, and to the Fifth and Sixth Corps, which operated with me on the Appomattox campaign, a proportionate share of these captures belong.

It will be seen by this report that we led the advance of the army to the Wilderness; that on the Richmond raid we marked out its line of march to the North Anna, where we found it on our return; that we again led its advance to Hanovertown, and thence to Cold Harbor; that we removed the enemy's cavalry from the south side of the Chickahominy by the Trevilian raid, and thereby materially assisted the army in its successful march to the James River and Petersburg, where it remained until we made the campaign in the valley; marched back to Petersburg, and again took its advance and led it to victory. In all the operations the percentage of cavalry casualties was as great as that of the infantry, and the question which had existed "Who ever saw a dead cavalryman?" was set at rest.

To Generals D. McM. Gregg, Torbert, Wilson, Merritt, Custer, Devin, J. Irvin Gregg, McIntosh, Chapman, Davies, and Gibbs, to the gallant officers and men of their commands, and to the officers of my staff, I return my sincere thanks.

I am, general, very respectfully, your obedient servant,

P. H. SHERIDAN,
Major-General, U.S. Army

Bvt. Maj. Gen. JOHN A. RAWLINS, Chief of Staff,
Headquarters Armies of the United States, Washington, D.C.

Report of Maj. Gen. Philip H. Sheridan,
U.S. Army, commanding Middle Military Division,
including operations August 4, 1864–February 27, 1865

HEADQUARTERS MILITARY DIVISION OF THE GULF,
New Orleans, February 3, 1866

GENERAL:

I have the honor to make the following report of the campaign in the Valley of the Shenandoah, commencing August 4, 1864:

On the evening of the 1st of August I was relieved from the command of the Cavalry Corps of the Army of the Potomac, to take command of the Army of the Shenandoah, and on arriving at Washington, on the 4th instant, I received directions from Maj. Gen. H. W. Halleck, Chief of Staff, to proceed without delay to Monocacy Junction, on the Baltimore and Ohio Railroad, and report in person to the lieutenant-general. At Monocacy the lieutenant-general turned over to me the instructions which he had previously given to Major-General Hunter, commanding the Department of West Virginia, a copy of which is herewith attached. The Army of the Shenandoah at this time consisted of the Sixth Corps, very much reduced in numbers; one division of the Nineteenth Corps; two small infantry divisions, under command of General Crook, afterward designated as the Army of West Virginia; a small division of cavalry under General Averell, which was at that time in pursuit of General McCausland, near Moorefield, McCausland having made a raid into Pennsylvania and burned the town of Chambersburg. There was also one small division of cavalry, then arriving at Washington from my old corps. The infantry portion of these troops had been lying in bivouac in the vicinity of Monocacy Junction and Frederick City, but had been ordered to march the day I reported, with directions to concentrate at Halltown, four miles in front of Harper's Ferry. After my interview with the lieutenant-general I hastened to Harpers Ferry to make preparations for an immediate advance against the enemy, who then occupied Martinsburg, Williamsport, and Shepherdstown, sending occasional, raiding parties as far as Hagerstown, Md. The concentration of my command at Halltown alarmed the enemy and caused him to concentrate at or near Martinsburg, drawing in all his parties from the north side of the Potomac. The indications were that he had intended another raid into Maryland, prompted, perhaps, by the slight success he had gained over General Crook's command at Kernstown a short time before.

The City of Martinsburg, at which the enemy concentrated, is on the Baltimore and Ohio Railroad, at the northern terminus of the Valley pike—a broad macadamized road running up the valley through Winchester and terminating at Staunton. The Shenandoah Valley is a continuation of the Cumberland Valley, south of the Potomac, and is bounded on the east by the Blue Ridge and on the west by the eastern slope of the Allegheny Mountains, the general direction of these chains being southwest. The valley at Martinsburg is about sixty miles broad, at Winchester forty to forty-five, and at Strasburg twenty-five to thirty miles, where an isolated chain, called Massanutten Mountain, rises up, running parallel to the Blue Ridge, and terminates at Harrisonburg. Here the valley again opens out fifty or sixty miles broad. This isolated chain divides the valley for its continuance into two valleys—the one next the Blue Ridge being called the Luray Valley, the one west of it the Strasburg or main valley. The Blue Ridge has many passes through it called gaps. The principal ones, and those which have good wagon roads, are Snicker's, Ashby's, Manassas, Chester, Thoroughfare, Swift Run, Brown's, Rockfish, and two or three others from the latter one up to Lynchburg. Many have macadamized roads through them, and, indeed, are not gaps, but small valleys through the main chain. The general bearing of all these roads is toward Gordonsville, and are excellent for troops to move upon from that point into the valley; in fact, the Blue Ridge can be crossed almost anywhere by infantry or cavalry. The valley itself was rich in grain, cattle, sheep, hogs, and fruit, and was in such a prosperous condition that the rebel army could march down and up it, billetting on the inhabitants. Such, in brief, is the outline and was the condition of the Shenandoah Valley when I entered it August 4, 1864.

Great exertions were made to get the troops in readiness for an advance, and on the morning of August 10, General Torbert's division of cavalry having joined me from Washington, a forward movement was commenced. The enemy while we were making our preparations took position at Bunker Hill and vicinity, twelve miles south of Martinsburg, frequently pushing his scouting parties through Smithfield and up to Charlestown. Torbert was ordered to move on the Berryville pike, through Berryville, and go into position near White Post; the Sixth Corps moved via the Charlestown and Summit Point road to Clifton; the Nineteenth Corps moved on the Berryville pike, to the left of the position of the Sixth Corps at Clifton; General Crook's command, via Kabletown, to the vicinity of Berryville, coming into position on the left of the Nineteenth Corps, and Colonel Lowell, with two small regiments of cavalry, was ordered to Summit Point; so that on the night of August 10 the army occupied a position stretching from Clifton to Berryville, with cavalry at White Post and Summit Point. The enemy moved from vicinity of Bunker Hill, stretching his line from where the Winchester and Potomac Railroad crosses Opequon Creek to where the Berryville and Winchester pike crosses the same stream, occupying the west bank.

On the morning of August 11 the Sixth Corps was ordered to move from Clifton across the country to where the Berryville pike crosses Opequon Creek, carry the crossing, and hold it; the Nineteenth Corps was directed to move through Berryville, on the White Post road, for one mile, file to the right by heads of regiments at deploying distances, and carry and hold the crossing of Opequon Creek at a ford about three fourths of a mile from the left of the Sixth Corps. Crook's command was ordered to move out on the White Post road one mile and a half' beyond Berryville, file to the right and secure the crossing of Opequon Creek at a ford about one mile to the left of the Nineteenth Corps. Torbert was directed to move with Merritt's division of cavalry up the Millwood pike toward Winchester, attack any force he might find, and, if possible, ascertain the movements of the rebel army. Lowell was ordered to close in from Summit Point on the right of the Sixth Corps. My intention in securing these fords was to march on Winchester, at which point, from all my information on the 10th, I thought the enemy would make a stand. In this I was mistaken, as the results of Torbert's reconnaissance proved. Merritt found the enemy's cavalry covering the Millwood pike west of the Opequon, and, attacking it, drove it in the direction of Kernstown and discovered the enemy retreating up the Valley pike. As soon as this information was obtained Torbert was ordered to move quickly via the tollgate on the Front Royal pike to Newtown, to strike the enemy's flank and harass him in his retreat, and Lowell to follow up through Winchester. Crook was turned to the left and ordered to Stony Point, or Nineveh, while Emory and Wright were marched to the left and went into camp between the Millwood and Front Royal pikes, Crook encamping at Stony Point. Torbert met some of the enemy's cavalry at the toll-gate on the Front Royal pike, drove it in the direction of Newtown and behind Gordon's division of infantry, which had been thrown out from Newtown to cover the flank of the main column in its retreat, and, which had put itself behind rail barricades. A portion of Merritt's cavalry attacked this infantry and drove in its skirmish line and, although unable to dislodge the division, held all the ground gained. The rebel division during the night moved off.

Next day Crook moved from Stony Point to Cedar Creek; Emory followed; the cavalry moved to the same point, via Newtown and the Valley pike, and the Sixth Corps followed the cavalry. On the night of the 12th Crook was in position at Cedar Creek, on the left of the Valley pike; Emory on the right of the pike, the Sixth Corps on the right of Emory, and the cavalry on the right and left flanks. A heavy skirmish line was thrown to the heights on the south side of Cedar Creek, which had brisk skirmishing during the evening with the enemy's pickets, his (the enemy's) main force occupying the heights above and north of Strasburg. On the morning of the 13th the cavalry was ordered on a reconnaissance toward Strasburg on the Middle road, which road is two miles and a half to the west of the main pike. Reports of a column of the enemy moving up from Culpeper Court-House and approaching Front Royal through Chester Gap having been received, caused me much anxiety, as any considerable force advanced through Front Royal and down the Front Royal and Winchester pike toward Winchester could be thrown in my rear; or, in case of my driving the enemy to Fisher's Hill and taking position in his front, this same force could be moved along the base of Massanutten Mountain, on the road to Strasburg, with the same result. As my effective line of battle strength at this time was about 18,000 infantry and 3,500 cavalry, I remained quiet during the day—except the activity on the skirmish line—to await further developments. In the evening the enemy retired with his main force to Fisher's Hill. As the rumors of an advancing force from the direction of Culpeper kept increasing, on the morning of the 14th I sent a brigade of cavalry to Front Royal to ascertain definitely, if possible, the truth of such reports, and at the same time crossed the Sixth Corps to the south side of Cedar Creek and occupied the heights above Strasburg. Considerable picket-firing ensued. During the day I received from Colonel Chipman, of the

Adjutant-General's Office, the following dispatch, he having ridden with great haste from Washington, through Snicker's Gap, escorted by a regiment of cavalry, to deliver the same. It at once explained the movement from Culpeper, and on the morning of the 15th the remaining two brigades of Merritt's division of cavalry were ordered to the crossing of the Shenandoah River near Front Royal, and the Sixth Corps withdrawn to the north side of Cedar Creek, holding at Strasburg a strong skirmish line:

CITY POINT, August 12, 1864—9 a.m.

Major-General HALLECK:

Inform Sheridan that it is now certain two divisions of infantry have gone to Early, and some cavalry and twenty pieces of artillery. This movement commenced last Saturday night. He must be cautious and act now on the defensive until movements here force them to this to send this way. Early's force, with this increase, cannot exceed 40,000 men, but this is too much for Sheridan to attack. Send Sheridan the remaining brigade of the Nineteenth Corps. I have ordered to Washington all the 100-days' men. Their time will soon be out, but, for the present, they will do to serve in the defenses.

U. S. GRANT,

Lieutenant-General

The receipt of this dispatch was very important to me, as I possibly would have remained in uncertainty as to the character of the force coming in on my flank and rear until it attacked the cavalry, as it did on the 16th. I at once looked over the map of the Valley for a defensive line—that is, where a smaller number of troops could hold a greater number—and could see but one such. I refer to that at Halltown, in front of Harper's Ferry. Subsequent experience has convinced me that no other really defensive line exists in the Shenandoah Valley. I therefore determined to move back to Halltown, carry out my instructions to destroy forage and subsistence, and increase my strength by Grover's division, of the Nineteenth Corps, and Wilson's division of cavalry, both of which were marching to join me via Snicker's Gap. Emory was ordered to move to Winchester on the night of the 15th, and on the night of the 16th the Sixth Corps and Crook's command were ordered to Clifton via Winchester. In the movement to the rear to Halltown the following orders were given to the cavalry and were executed:

HEADQUARTERS MIDDLE MILITARY DIVISION,
Cedar Creek, Va., August 16, 1864

Brig. Gen. A. T. A. Torbert,
Chief of Cavalry, Middle Military Division:

General: In compliance with instructions of the lieutenant-general commanding, you will make the necessary arrangements and give the necessary orders for the destruction of the wheat and hay south of a line from Millwood to Winchester and Petticoat Gap. You will seize all mules, horses, and cattle that may be useful to our army. Loyal citizens can bring in their claims against the Government for this necessary destruction. No houses will be burned, and officers in charge of this delicate, but necessary, duty must inform the people that the object is to make this Valley untenable for the raiding parties of the rebel army.

Very respectfully,

P. H. SHERIDAN,
Major-General, Commanding

On the afternoon of the 16th I moved my headquarters back to Winchester; while moving back, at Newtown, I heard cannonading at or near Front Royal, and on reaching Winchester, Merritt's couriers brought dispatches from him, stating that he had been attacked at the crossing of the Shenandoah by Kershaw's division, of Longstreet's corps, and two brigades of rebel cavalry, and that he had handsomely repulsed the attack, capturing 2 battle-flags and 300 prisoners. During the night of the 16th and early on the morning of the 17th Emory moved from Winchester to Berryville, and on the morning of the 17th Crook and Wright reached Winchester and resumed the march toward Clifton, Wright, who had the rear guard, getting only as far as the Berryville crossing of the Opequon, where he was ordered to remain, Crook getting to the vicinity of Berryville. Lowell reached Winchester with his two regiments of cavalry on the afternoon of the 17th, where he was joined by General Wilson's division of cavalry. Merritt, after his handsome engagement near Front Royal, was ordered back to the vicinity of White Post, and General Grover's division joined Emory at Berryville. The enemy having a signal station on Three Top Mountain, almost overhanging Strasburg, and from which every movement made by our troops could be seen, was notified early on the morning of the 17th as to this condition of affairs, and without delay followed after us, getting into Winchester about sundown, and driving out General Torbert, who was left there with Wilson and

Lowell, and the Jersey brigade of the Sixth Corps. Wilson and Lowell fell back to Summit Point, and the Jersey brigade joined its corps at the crossing of the Opequon. Kershaw's division and two brigades of Fitz Lee's cavalry division, which was the force at Front Royal, joined Early at Winchester, I think, on the evening of the 17th.

On the 18th the Sixth Corps moved, via Clifton, to Flowing Spring, two miles and a half west of Charlestown, on the Smithfield pike; Emory about two miles and a half south of Charlestown on the Berryville pike; Merritt came back to Berryville; Wilson remained at Summit Point, covering the crossing of Opequon Creek as far north as the bridge at Smithfield, Merritt covering the crossing of the Berryville pike; Crook remained near Clifton, and the next day moved to the left of Emory. This position was maintained until the 21st, when the enemy moved a heavy force across the Opequon at the bridge at Smithfield, driving in the cavalry pickets, which fell back to Summit Point, and advanced rapidly on the position of the Sixth Corps near Flowing Spring, when a very sharp and obstinate skirmish took place with the heavy picket-line of that corps, resulting very much in its favor. The enemy appeared to have thought that I had taken position near Summit Point, and that by moving around rapidly through Smithfield he would get into my rear. In this, however, he was mistaken. During the day Merritt, who had been attacked and held his ground, was recalled from Berryville. Wilson had also been attacked by infantry, and had also held his ground until ordered in. During the night of the 21st the army moved back to Halltown without inconvenience or loss, the cavalry, excepting Lowell's command, which formed on the left, moving early on the morning of the 22d, and going into position on the right of the line.

On the morning of the 22d the enemy moved up to Charlestown, and pushed well up to my position at Halltown, skirmishing with the cavalry vedettes. The dispatches received from the lieutenant-general commanding, from Capt. G. K. Leet, assistant adjutant-general, at Washington, and information derived from my scouts and from prisoners captured, were of so conflicting and contradictory a nature that I determined to ascertain, if possible, while on this defensive line, what re-enforcements had actually been received by the enemy. This could only be done by frequent reconnaissances, and their results convinced me that but one division of infantry (Kershaw's) and one division of cavalry (Fitz Lee's) had joined him. On the 23d I ordered a reconnaissance by Crook, who was on the left, resulting in a small capture and a number of casualties to the enemy. On the 24th another reconnaissance was made, capturing a number of prisoners, our own loss being about thirty men. On the 25th there was a sharp picket-firing during the day on part of the infantry line. The cavalry was ordered to attack the enemy's

cavalry at Kearneysville. This attack was handsomely made, but instead of finding the enemy's cavalry his infantry was encountered, and for a time doubled up
and thrown into the utmost confusion. It was marching toward Shepherdstown.
This engagement was somewhat of a mutual surprise, our cavalry expecting to
meet the enemy's cavalry and his infantry expecting no opposition whatever.
General Torbert, who was in command, finding a large force of the rebel infantry
in his front, came back to our left, and the enemy, believing his (the enemy's)
movement had been discovered and that the force left by him in my front at
Halltown would be attacked, returned in great haste, but before doing so isolated
Custer's brigade, which had to cross to the north side of the Potomac at Shepherdstown and join me via Harper's Ferry. For my own part, I believed Early
meditated a crossing of his cavalry into Maryland at Williamsport, and I sent
Wilson's division around by Harper's Ferry to watch its movements. Averell, in
the meantime, had taken post at Williamsport, on the north side of the Potomac,
and held the crossing against a force of rebel cavalry which made the attempt to
cross.

On the night of the 26th the enemy silently left my front, moving over Opequon Creek at the Smithfield and Summit Point crossings, and concentrating
his force at Brucetown and Bunker Hill, leaving his cavalry at Leetown and
Smithfield. On the 28th I moved in front of Charlestown with the infantry and
directed Merritt to attack the enemy's cavalry at Leetown, which he did, defeating it and pursuing it through Smithfield. Wilson recrossed the Potomac at Shepherdstown and joined the infantry in front of Charlestown. On the 29th Averell
crossed at Williamsport and advanced to Martinsburg. On the same day two
divisions of the enemy's infantry and a small force of cavalry attacked Merritt at
the Smithfield bridge, and after a hard fight drove him through Smithfield and
back toward Charlestown, the cavalry fighting with great obstinacy until I could
re-enforce it with Ricketts' division, of the Sixth Corps, when in turn the enemy
was driven back through Smithfield and over the Opequon, the cavalry again
taking post at the Smithfield bridge. On the 30th Torbert was directed to move
Merritt and Wilson to Berryville, leaving Lowell to guard the Smithfield bridge
and occupy the town. On the 31st Averell was driven back from Martinsburg to
Falling Waters. From the 1st to the 3d of September nothing of importance
occurred. On the 3d Averell, who had returned to Martinsburg, advanced on
Bunker Hill, attacked McCausland's cavalry, defeated it, capturing wagons and
prisoners, and destroying a good deal of property. The infantry moved into position, stretching from Clifton to Berryville, Wright moving by Summit Point,
Crook and Emory by the Berryville pike. Torbert had been ordered to White Post
early in the day, and the enemy, supposing he could cut him off, pushed across

the Opequon toward Berryville, with Kershaw's division in advance; but this division, not expecting infantry, blundered onto Crook's lines about dark, and was vigorously attacked and driven, with heavy loss, back toward the Opequon. This engagement, which was after night-fall, was very spirited, and our own and the enemy's casualties severe. From this time until the 19th of September I occupied the line from Clifton to Berryville, transferring Crook to Summit Point on the 8th to use him as a movable column to protect my right flank and line to Harper's Ferry, while the cavalry threatened the enemy's right flank and his line of communications up the Valley. The difference of strength between the two opposing forces at this time was but little. As I had learned beyond doubt from my scouts that Kershaw's division, which consisted of four brigades, was to be ordered back to Richmond, I had for two weeks patiently awaited its withdrawal before attacking, believing the condition of affairs throughout the country required great prudence on my part, that a defeat of the forces of my command could be ill afforded, and knowing that no interests in the Valley, save those of the Baltimore and Ohio Railroad, were suffering by the delay. In this view I was coinciding with the lieutenant-general commanding.

Although the main force remained without change of position from September 3 to 19, still the cavalry was employed every day in harassing the enemy, its opponents being principally infantry. In these skirmishes the cavalry was becoming educated to attack infantry lines. On the 13th one of these handsome dashes was made by General Mcintosh, of Wilson's division, capturing the Eighth South Carolina Regiment at Abraham's Creek. On the same day Getty's division, of the Sixth Corps, made a reconnaissance to the Opequon, developing a heavy force of the enemy at Edwards' [Gilbert's?] Crossing. The position which I had taken at Clifton was six miles from Opequon Creek, on the west bank of which the enemy was in position. This distance of six miles I determined to hold as my territory by scouting parties, and in holding it in this way, without pushing up the main force, I expected to be able to move on the enemy at the proper time without his obtaining the information, which he would immediately get from his pickets if I was in close proximity. On the night of the 15th I received reliable information that Kershaw's division was moving through Winchester and in the direction of Front Royal. Then our time had come, and I almost made up my mind that I would fight at Newtown, on the Valley pike, give up my line to the rear, and take that of the enemy. From my position at Clifton I could throw my force into Newtown before Early could get information and move to that point. I was a little timid about this movement until the arrival of General Grant, at Charlestown, who indorsed it, and the order for the movement was made out, but in consequence of a report from General Averell on the after-

noon of the 18th of September, that Early had moved two divisions to Martinsburg, I changed this programme and determined to first catch the two divisions,
remaining in vicinity of Stephenson's Depot, and then the two sent to Martinsburg in detail. This information was the cause of the battle of Opequon, instead
of the battle of Newtown.

At 3 o'clock on the morning of the 19th of September the army moved to the
attack. Torbert was directed to advance with Merritt's division of cavalry from
Summit Point, carry the crossings of Opequon Creek, and form a junction, at
some point near Stephenson's Depot, with Averell, who moved from Darkes-
ville. Wilson was ordered to move rapidly up the Berryville pike from Berryville,
carry its crossing of the Opequon, and charge through the gorge or cañon; the
attack to be supported by the Sixth and Nineteenth Corps, both of which moved
across country to the same crossing of the Opequon. Crook moved across country, to be in reserve at the same point. Wilson, with McIntosh's brigade leading,
made a gallant charge through the long cañon, and meeting the advance of Ramseur's rebel infantry division, drove it back and captured the earth-work at the
mouth of the cañon; this movement was immediately followed up by the Sixth
Corps. The Nineteenth Corps was directed for convenience of movement to
report to General Wright on its arrival at Opequon Creek. I followed up the
cavalry attack, and selected the ground for the formation of the Sixth and Nineteenth Corps, which went into line under a heavy artillery fire. A good deal of
time was lost in this movement through the cañon, and it was not till perhaps 9
a.m. that the order for the advance in line was given. I had from early in the
morning become apprised that I would have to engage Early's entire army, instead
of two divisions, and determined to attack with the Sixth and Nineteenth Corps,
holding Crook's command as a turning column to use only when the crisis of
the battle occurred, and that I would put him in on my left and still get the Valley pike. The attack was, therefore, made by the Sixth and Nineteenth Corps, in
a very handsome style and under a heavy fire from the enemy, who held a line
which gave him the cover of slight brushwood and corn-fields. The resistance
during this attack was obstinate, and as there were no earth-works to protect,
deadly to both sides. The enemy, after the contest had been going on for some
time, made a counter-charge, striking the right of the Sixth Corps and left of the
Nineteenth, driving back the center of my line. It was at this juncture that I
ordered a brigade of Russell's division, of the Sixth Corps, to wait till the enemy's
attacking column presented its flank, then to strike it with vigor. This was handsomely done, the brigade being led by General Russell, and its commander,
Upton, in person. The enemy in turn was driven back, our line re-established,
and most of the 2,000 or 3,000 men who had gone to the rear brought back. I

still would not order Crook in, but placed him directly in rear of the line of battle; as the reports, however, that the enemy were attempting to turn my right kept continually increasing, I was obliged to put him in on that flank, instead of on the left as was originally intended. He was directed to act as a turning column, to find the left of the enemy's line, strike it in flank or rear, break it up, and that I would order a left half-wheel of the line of battle to support him. In this attack the enemy was driven in confusion from his position, and simultaneous with it Merritt and Averell, under Torbert, could be distinctly seen sweeping up the Martinsburg pike, driving the enemy's cavalry before them, in a confused mass through the broken infantry. I then rode along the line of the Nineteenth and Sixth Corps, ordered their advance, and directed Wilson, who was on the left flank, to push on and gain the Valley pike, south of Winchester; after which I returned to the right, where the enemy was still fighting with obstinacy in the open ground in front of Winchester, and ordered Torbert to collect his cavalry and charge, which was done simultaneously with the infantry advance, and the enemy routed.

At daylight on the morning of the 20th of September the army moved rapidly up the Valley pike in pursuit of the enemy, who had continued his retreat during the night to Fisher's Hill, south of Strasburg. Fisher's Hill is the bluff immediately south of and over a little stream called Tumbling Run, and is a position which was almost impregnable to a direct assault, and as the valley is but about three miles and a half wide at this point, the enemy considered himself secure on reaching it and commenced erecting breast-works across the valley from Fisher's Hill to North Mountain; so secure, in fact, did he consider himself that the ammunition-boxes were taken from the caissons and placed for convenience behind the breast-work. On the evening of September 20 Wright and Emory went into position on the heights of Strasburg, Crook north of Cedar Creek, the cavalry to the right and rear of Wright and Emory, extending to the Back road. This night I resolved to use a turning column again, and that I would move Crook unperceived, if possible, over onto the face of Little North Mountain and let him strike the left and rear of the enemy's line, and then, if successful, make a left half-wheel of the whole line of battle to his support. To do this required much secrecy, as the enemy had a signal station on Three Top Mountain, from which he could see every movement made by our troops; therefore, during the night of the 20th I concealed Crook in the timber north of Cedar Creek, where he remained during the 21st. On the same day I moved Wright and Emory up in the front of the rebel line, getting into proper position after a severe engagement between a portion of Ricketts' and Getty's divisions, of the Sixth Corps, and a strong force of the enemy. Torbert, with Wilson's and Merritt's cavalry, was ordered down the Luray Valley in pursuit of the enemy's cavalry, and after defeating or driving it, to cross over Luray pike to New Market, and intercept the enemy's infantry should I drive it from the position at Fisher's Hill.

On the night of the 21st Crook was moved to, and concentrated in, the timber near Strasburg, and at daylight on the 22d marched to, and massed in, the timber near Little North Mountain. I did not attempt to cover the long front presented by the enemy, but massed the Sixth and Nineteenth Corps opposite the right center of his line. After Crook had gotten into the position last named, I took out Ricketts' division, of the Sixth Corps, and placed it opposite the enemy's left center, and directed Averell with his cavalry to go up on Ricketts' front and right and drive in the enemy's skirmish line, if possible. This was done, and the enemy's signal officer on Three Top Mountain, mistaking Ricketts' division for my turning column, so notified the enemy and he made his arrangements accordingly, whilst Crook, without being observed, moved on the side of Little North Mountain and struck the enemy's left and rear so suddenly and unexpectedly that he (the enemy), supposing he must have come across the mountains, broke, Crook swinging down behind the line, Ricketts swinging in and joining Crook, and so on the balance of the Sixth and Nineteenth Corps, the rout of the enemy being complete. Unfortunately, the cavalry, which I had sent down the Luray Valley to cross over to New Market, was unsuccessful, and only reached so far as Milford, a point at which the Luray Valley contracts to a gorge, and which was taken possession of by the enemy's cavalry in some force. Had General Torbert driven this cavalry or turned the defile and reached New Market, I have no doubt but that we would have captured the entire rebel army. I feel certain that its rout from Fisher's Hill was such that there was scarcely a con, puny organization held together. New Market being at a converging point in the valley they came together again and, to some extent, reorganized. I did not wait to see the results of this victory, but pushed on during the night of the 22d to Woodstock, although the darkness and consequent confusion made the pursuit slow. On the morning of September 23, General Devin, with his small brigade of cavalry, moved to a point directly north of Mount Jackson, driving the enemy in his front, and there awaited the arrival of General Averell's division, which for some unaccountable reason went into camp immediately after the battle. General Averell reached Devin's command at about 3 p.m., and in the evening returned with all the advance cavalry, of which he was in command, to a creek half a mile north of Hawkinsburg, and there remained until the arrival of the head of the infantry column, which had halted between Edenburg and Woodstock for wagons in order to issue the necessary rations. Early on the morning of the 24th the entire army reached Mount Jackson, a small town on the north bank of the North Fork of the Shenandoah. The enemy had, in the meantime, reorganized and taken position on the bluff south of the river, but had commenced this same morning his retreat toward Harrisonburg; still he held a long and strong line with the troops that were to cover his rear, in a temporary line of rifle-pits on the bluff commanding the plateau. To dislodge him from his strong position, Devin's brigade of cavalry was directed to cross the Shenandoah, work around the base of the Massanutten range, and drive in the cavalry which covered his (the enemy's) right flank, and Powell, who had succeeded Averell, was ordered to move around his left flank, via Timberville, whilst the infantry was pushed across the river by the bridge. The enemy did not wait the full execution of these movements, but withdrew in haste, the cavalry under Devin coming up with him at New Market, and made a bold attempt to hold him until I could push up our infantry, but was unable to do so, as the open, smooth country allowed him (the enemy) to retreat with great rapidity in line of battle, and the 300 or 400 cavalry under Devin was unable to break this line. Our infantry was pushed by heads of columns very hard to overtake and bring on an engagement, but could not succeed, and encamped about six miles south of New Market for the night. Powell meantime had pushed on through Timberville and gained the Valley pike near Lacey's Springs, capturing some prisoners and wagons. This movement of Powell's probably forced the enemy to abandon the road via Harrisonburg, and move over the Keezletown road to Port Republic, to which point the retreat was continued through the night of the 24th and from thence to Brown's Gap in the Blue Ridge.

On the 25th the Sixth and Nineteenth Corps reached Harrisonburg. Crook was ordered to remain at the junction of the Keezletown road with the Valley pike until the movements of the enemy were definitely ascertained. On this day Torbert reached Harrisonburg, having encountered the enemy's cavalry at Luray, defeating it and joining me via New Market, and Powell had proceeded to Mount Crawford. On the 26th Merritt's division of cavalry was ordered to Port Republic, and Torbert to Staunton and Waynesborough to destroy the bridge at the latter place, and in retiring to burn all forage, drive off all cattle, destroy all mills, &c., which would cripple the rebel army or Confederacy. Torbert had with him Wilson's division of cavalry and Lowell's brigade of regulars. On the 27th, while Torbert was making his advance on Waynesborough, I ordered Merritt to make a demonstration on Brown's Gap to cover the movement. This brought out the enemy (who had been re-enforced by Kershaw's division, which came through Swift Run Gap) against the small force of cavalry employed in this demonstration, which he followed up to Port Republic, and, I believe, crossed in some force. Merritt's instructions from me were to resist an attack, but if pressed, to fall back to Cross Keys, in which event I intended to attack with the main force, which was at Harrisonburg, and could be rapidly moved to Cross Keys. The enemy, however, advanced with his main force only to Port

Republic, after which he fell back. Torbert this day took possession of Waynesborough, and partially destroyed the railroad bridge, but about dark on the 28th was attacked by infantry and cavalry, returned to Staunton, and from thence to Bridgewater, via Spring Hill, executing the order for the destruction of subsistence, forage, &c. On the morning of the 28th Merritt was ordered to Port Republic to open communication with General Torbert, but on the same night was directed to leave small forces at Port Republic and Swift Run Gap, and proceed with the balance of his command (his own and Custer's divisions) to Piedmont, swing around from that point to near Staunton, burning forage, mills, and such other property as might be serviceable to the rebel army or Confederacy, and on his return to go into camp on the left of the Sixth and Nineteenth Corps, which were ordered to proceed on the 29th to Mount Crawford in support of this and Torbert's movements. September 29 Torbert reached Bridgewater and Merritt Mount Crawford. On the 1st of October Merritt reoccupied Port Republic, and the Sixth and Nineteenth Corps were moved back to Harrisonburg. The question that now presented itself was, whether or not I should follow the enemy to Brown's Gap, where he still held fast, drive him out, and advance on Charlottesville and Gordonsville. This movement on Gordonsville I was opposed to for many reasons, the most important of which was that it would necessitate the opening of the Orange and Alexandria Railroad from Alexandria, and to protect this road against the numerous guerrilla bands would have required a corps of infantry; besides, I would have been obliged to leave a small force in the Valley to give security to the line of the Potomac. This would probably occupy the whole of Crook's command, leaving me but a small number of fighting men. Then there was the additional reason of the uncertainty as to whether the army in front of Petersburg could hold the entire force of General Lee there, and in case it could not, a sufficient number might be detached and moved rapidly by rail and overwhelm me, quickly returning; I was also confident that my transportation could not supply me farther than Harrisonburg, and therefore advised that the Valley campaign should terminate at Harrisonburg, and that I return, carrying out my original instructions for the destruction of forage; grain, &c., give up the majority of the army I commanded, and order it to the Petersburg line, a line which I thought the lieutenant-general believed, if a successful movement could be made on, would involve the capture of the Army of Northern Virginia. I therefore, on the morning of the 6th of October, commenced moving back, stretching the cavalry across the Valley from the Blue Ridge to the eastern slope of the Alleghenies, with directions to burn all forage and drive off all stock, &c., as they moved to the rear, fully coinciding in the views and instructions of the lieutenant-general, that the Valley should be made a barren waste. The most positive orders were given, however, not to burn dwellings. In this movement the enemy's cavalry followed at a respectful distance until in the vicinity of Woodstock, when they attacked Custer's division and harassed it as far as Tom's Brook, a short distance south of Fisher's Hill. On the night of the 8th I ordered General Torbert to engage the enemy's cavalry at daylight, and notified him that I would halt the army until he had defeated it. In compliance with these instructions Torbert advanced at daylight on the 9th of October, with Custer's division on the Back road and Merritt's division on the Valley pike. At Tom's Brook the heads of the opposing columns came in contact and deployed, and after a short but decisive engagement the enemy was defeated, with the loss of all his artillery excepting one piece, and everything else which was carried on wheels. The rout was complete, and was followed up to Mount Jackson, a distance of some twenty-six miles.

On October 10 the army crossed to the north side of Cedar Creek, the Sixth Corps continuing its march to Front Royal. This was the first day's march of this corps to rejoin Lieutenant-General Grant at Petersburg. It was the intention that it should proceed through Manassas Gap to Piedmont, east of the Blue Ridge, to which point the Manassas Gap Railroad had been completed, and from thence to Alexandria by rail; but on my recommendation that it would be much better to march it, as it was in fine condition, through Ashby's Gap and thence to Washington, the former route was abandoned, and on the 12th the corps moved to the Ashby Gap crossing of the Shenandoah River, but, on the same day, in consequence of the advance of the enemy to Fisher's Hill, it was recalled to await the development of the enemy's new intentions. The question now again arose in reference to the advance on Gordonsville, as suggested in the following dispatch:

WASHINGTON, October 12, 1864—12 m.

Major-General SHERIDAN:
   Lieutenant-General Grant wishes a position taken far enough south to serve as a base for further operations upon Gordonsville and Charlottesville. It must be strongly fortified and provisioned. Some point in the vicinity of Manassas Gap would seem best suited for all purposes. Colonel Alexander, of the Engineers, will be sent to consult with you as soon as you connect with General Augur.

H. W. HALLECK,
Major-General

This plan I would not indorse; but in order to settle it definitely I was called to Washington by the following telegram:

WASHINGTON, October 13, 1864

Major-General Sheridan:
(Through General Augur)
    If you can come here, a consultation on several points is extremely desirable. I propose to visit General Grant, and would like to see you first.

E. M. STANTON,
Secretary of War

On the evening of the 15th I determined to go, believing that the enemy at Fisher's Hill could not accomplish much, and as I had concluded not to attack him at present I ordered the whole of the cavalry force under General Torbert to accompany me to Front Royal, from whence I intended to push it through Chester Gap to the Virginia Central Railroad at Charlottesville, while I passed through Manassas Gap to Piedmont, thence by rail to Washington. Upon my arrival with the cavalry at Front Royal, on the night of the 16th, I received the following dispatch from General Wright, who was left at Cedar Creek in command of the army:

HEADQUARTERS MIDDLE MILITARY DIVISION,
October 16, 1864

Maj. Gen. P. H. SHERIDAN,
Commanding Middle Military Division:
    GENERAL: I inclose you dispatch which explains itself (see copy following). If the enemy should be strongly re-enforced in cavalry, he might, by turning our right, give us a great deal of trouble. I shall hold on here until the enemy's movements are developed, and shall only fear an attack on my right, which I shall make every preparation for guarding against and resisting.
    Very respectfully, your obedient servant,

H. G. WRIGHT,
Major-General, Commanding

Lieutenant-General EARLY:

Be ready to move as soon as my forces join you and we will crush Sheridan.

LONGSTREET,
Lieutenant-General

This message was taken off the rebel signal flag on Three Top Mountain. My first thought was that it was a ruse, but on reflection deemed it best to abandon the cavalry raid and give to General Wright the entire strength of the army. I therefore ordered the cavalry to return and report to him, and addressed the following note on the subject:

HEADQUARTERS MIDDLE MILITARY DIVISION,
Front Royal, October 16, 1864

Maj. Gen. H.G. WRIGHT,

Commanding Sixth Army Corps:

GENERAL: The cavalry is all ordered back to you; make your position strong. If Longstreet's dispatch is true, he is under the impression that we have largely detached. I will go over to Augur, and may get additional news. Close in Colonel Powell, who will be at this point. If the enemy should make an advance I know you will defeat him. Look well to your ground and be well prepared. Get up everything that can be spared. I will bring up all I can, and will be up on Tuesday, if not sooner.

P. H. SHERIDAN,
Major-General

After sending this note I continued through Manassas Gap and on to Piedmont, and from thence by rail to Washington, arriving on the morning of the 17th. At 12 m. I returned by special train to Martinsburg, arriving on the evening of the 18th at Winchester, in company with Colonels Thom and Alexander, of the Engineer Corps, sent with me by General Halleck. During my absence the enemy had gathered all his strength, and, in the night of the 18th and early on the 19th, moved silently from Fisher's Hill, through Strasburg, pushed a heavy turning column across the Shenandoah, on the road from Strasburg to Front Royal, and again recrossed the river at Bowman's Ford, striking Crook, who held the left of our line, in flank and rear, so unexpectedly and forcibly as to drive in his outposts, invade his camp, and turn his position. This surprise was owing, probably, to not closing in Powell, or that the cavalry divisions of Merritt and Custer were placed on the right of our line, where it had always occurred to me there was but little danger of attack. This was followed by a direct attack upon our front, and the result was that the whole army was driven back in confusion to a point about one mile and a half north of Middletown, a very large portion of the infantry not even preserving a company organization. At about 7 o'clock on the morning of the 19th of October an officer on picket at Winchester reported artillery firing, but, supposing it re-suited from a reconnaissance which had been ordered for this morning, I paid no attention to it, and was unconscious of the true condition of affairs until about 9 o'clock, when, having ridden through the town of Winchester, the sound of the artillery made a battle unmistakable, and on reaching Mill Creek, half a mile south of Winchester, the head of the fugitives appeared in sight, trains and men coming to the rear with appalling rapidity. I immediately gave directions to halt and park the trains at Mill Creek, and ordered the brigade at Winchester to stretch across the country and stop all stragglers. Taking twenty men from my escort, I pushed on to the front, leaving the balance under General Forsyth and Colonels Thom and Alexander to do what they could in stemming the torrent of fugitives. I am happy to say that hundreds of the men, when on reflection found they had not done themselves justice, came back with cheers.

On arriving at the front I found Merritt's and Custer's divisions of cavalry, under Torbert, and General Getty's division, of the Sixth Corps, opposing the enemy. I suggested to General Wright that we would fight on Getty's line and to transfer Custer to the right at once, as he (Custer) and Merritt, from being on the right in the morning, had been transferred to the left; that the remaining two divisions of the Sixth Corps, which were to the right and rear of Getty about two miles, should be ordered up, and also that the Nineteenth Corps, which was on the right and rear of these two divisions, should be hastened up before the enemy attacked Getty. I then started out all my staff officers to bring up these troops, and was so convinced that we would soon be attacked that I went back myself to urge them on. Immediately after I returned and assumed command, General Wright returning to his corps, Getty to his division, and the line of battle was formed on the prolongation of General Getty's line, and a temporary breast-work of rails, logs, &c., thrown up hastily. Shortly after this was done the enemy advanced, and from a point on the left of our line of battle I could see his columns moving to the attack, and at once notified corps commanders to be prepared. This assault fell principally on the Nineteenth Corps, and was repulsed. I am pleased to be able to state that the strength of the Sixth and Nineteenth Corps and Crook's command was now being rapidly augmented by the return of those who had gone to the rear early in the day. Reports coming in from the Front Royal pike, on which Powell's division of cavalry was posted, to the effect that a heavy column of infantry was moving on that pike in the direction of Winchester, and that he (Powell) was retiring and would come in at Newtown, caused me great anxiety for the time, and although I could not fully believe that such a movement would be undertaken, still it delayed my general attack. At 4 p.m. I ordered the advance. This attack was brilliantly made, and as the enemy was protected by rail breast-works, and at some portions of his line by stone fences, his resistance was very determined. His line of battle overlapped the right of mine, and by turning with this portion of it on the flank of the Nineteenth Corps caused a slight momentary confusion. This movement was checked, however, by a counter-charge of General McMillan's brigade upon the reentering angle thus formed by the enemy, and his flanking party cut off. It was at this stage of the battle that Custer was ordered to charge with his entire division, but, although the order was promptly obeyed, it was not in time to capture the whole of the force thus cut off, and many escaped across Cedar Creek. Simultaneous with this charge a combined movement of the whole line drove the enemy in confusion to the creek, where, owing to the difficulties of crossing, his army became routed. Custer, finding a ford on Cedar Creek west of the pike, and Devin, of Merritt's division, one to the east of it, they each made the crossing just after dark and pursued the routed mass of the enemy to Fisher's Hill, where this strong position gave him some protection against our cavalry, but the most of his transportation had been captured, the road from Cedar Creek to Fisher's Hill, a distance of over three miles, being literally blockaded by wagons, ambulances, artillery, caissons, &c. The enemy did not halt his main force at Fisher's Hill, but continued the retreat during the night to New Market, where his army had, on a similar previous occasion, come together by means of the numerous roads that converge to this point.

This battle practically ended the campaign in the Shenandoah Valley. When it opened we found our enemy boastful and confident, unwilling to acknowledge that the soldiers of the Union were their equal in courage and manliness; when it closed with Cedar Creek this impression had been removed from his mind, and gave place to good sense and a strong desire to quit fighting. The very best troops of the Confederacy had not only been defeated, but had been routed in successive engagements, until their spirit and esprit were destroyed. In obtaining these results, however, our loss in officers and men was severe. Practically all territory north of the James River now belonged to me, and the holding of the lines about Petersburg and Richmond by the enemy must have been embarrassing, and invited the question of good military judgment.

On entering the Valley it was not my object by flank movements to make the enemy change his base, nor to move as far up as the James River, and thus give him the opportunity of making me change my base, thereby converting it into a race-course as heretofore, but to destroy, to the best of my ability, that which was truly the Confederacy—its armies. In doing this, so far as the opposing army was concerned, our success was such that there was no one connected with the Army of the Shenandoah who did not so fully realize it as to render the issuing of congratulatory orders unnecessary. Every officer and man was made to understand, that when a victory was gained, it was not more than their duty, nor less than their country expected from her gallant sons.

At Winchester, for a moment, the contest was uncertain, but the gallant attack of General Upton's brigade, of the Sixth Corps, restored the line of battle, until the turning column of Crook, and Merritt's and Averell's divisions of cavalry, under Torbert, "sent the enemy whirling through Winchester." In thus particularizing commands and commanders, I only speak in the sense that they were so fortunate as to be available at these important movements. In the above-mentioned attack by Upton's brigade the lamented Russell fell. He had been previously wounded, but refused to leave the field. His death brought sadness to every heart in the army.

It was during a reconnaissance to Fisher's Hill, made on the 13th of October, 1864, that Col. George D. Wells, commanding a brigade in Crook's corps, was killed while gallantly leading his men.

At Fisher's Hill it was again the good fortune of General Crook's command to start the enemy, and of General Ricketts' division, of the Sixth Corps, to first gallantly swing in and more fully initiate the rout.

At Cedar Creek Getty's division, of the Sixth Corps, and Merritt's and Custer's divisions of cavalry, under Torbert, confronted the enemy from the first attack in the morning until the battle was decided, still none behaved more gallantly or exhibited greater courage than those who returned from the rear determined to reoccupy their lost camp. In this engagement, early in the morning, the gallant Colonel Lowell, of the regular brigade, was wounded while in the advance in echelon of Getty's division, but would not leave his command, remaining until the final attack on the enemy was made, in which he was killed. Generals Bidwell, of the Sixth Corps, and Thoburn, of Crook's command, were also killed in the morning while behaving with conspicuous gallantry.

I submit the following list of the corps, division, and brigade commanders who were wounded in the campaign (the killed having already been especially noticed), regretting that the scope of this report will not admit of my specifying by name all the many gallant men who were killed and wounded in the numerous engagements in the Shenandoah Valley, and most respectfully call attention to the accompanying sub-reports for such particulars as will, I trust, do full justice to all: Generals H. G. Wright, J. B. Ricketts, Grover, Duval, E. Upton, R. S. Mackenzie, Kitching (since died of wounds), J. B. Mcintosh, G. H. Chapman, Thomas C. Devin, Penrose; Cols. D. D. Johnson, Daniel Macauley, Jacob Sharpe.

From the 7th of August, the Middle Department, Department of Washington, Department of the Susquehanna, and the Department of West Virginia, were under my command, and I desire to express my gratitude to their respective commanders, Maj. Gens. Lew. Wallace, C. C. Augur, Couch, and Cadwalader, and to Major-Generals Hunter and Crook, who at separate times commanded the latter department, for the assistance given me. General Augur operated very effectively with a small force under his command, the reports of which were forwarded direct to the War Department. After the battle of Cedar Creek nothing of importance occurred in the Valley up to February 27, 1865, the day on which the cavalry moved from Winchester to Petersburg.

On the night of November 11, 1864, General Early moved some of his shattered forces to the north of Cedar Creek, for the purpose of bluster, I suppose, as on the night of the following day he hastily retired. In consequence of contradictory information received from scouts and captured cavalry prisoners, I was unconvinced of any rebel infantry being in my vicinity, until it was too late to overtake it in its galloping retreat, a retreat which was continued until in the vicinity of Lacey's Springs, near Harrisonburg. Powell engaged the rebel cavalry co-operating on the Front Royal pike with this force, and drove it through Front Royal to Milford, capturing two pieces of artillery.

During this campaign I was at times annoyed by guerrilla bands, the most formidable of which was under a partisan chief named Mosby, who made his headquarters east of the Blue Ridge, in the section of country about Upperville. I had constantly refused to operate against these bands, believing them to be, substantially, a benefit to me, as they prevented straggling and kept my trains well closed up, and discharged such other duties as would have required a provost guard of at least two regiments of cavalry. In retaliation for the assistance and sympathy given them, however, by the inhabitants of Loudoun Valley, General Merritt, with two brigades of cavalry, was directed to proceed on the 28th of November, 1864, to that valley, under the following instructions:

HEADQUARTERS MIDDLE MILITARY DIVISION,
November 27, 1864

Bvt. Maj. Gen. WESLEY MERRITT,
Commanding First Cavalry Division:

GENERAL: You are hereby directed to proceed to-morrow morning at 7 o'clock, with the two brigades of your division now in camp, to the east side of the Blue Ridge, via Ashby's Gap, and operate against the guerrillas in the district of country bounded on the south by the line of the Manassas Gap Railroad as far east as White Plains, on the east by the Bull Run range, on the west by the Shenandoah River, and on the north by the Potomac. This section has been the hot-bed of lawless bands, who have from time to time depredated upon small parties on the line of army communications, on safeguards left at houses, and on troops. Their real object is plunder and highway robbery. To clear the country of these parties that are bringing destruction upon the innocent, as well as their guilty supporters, by their cowardly acts, you will consume and destroy all forage and subsistence, burn all barns and mills and their contents, and drive off all stock in the region the boundaries of which are above described. This order must be literally executed, bearing in mind, however, that no dwellings are to be burned, and that no personal violence be offered the citizens. The ultimate results of the guerrilla system of warfare is the total destruction of all private rights in the country occupied by such parties. This destruction may as well commence at once, and the responsibility of it must rest upon the authorities at Richmond, who have acknowledged the legitimacy of guerrilla bands. The injury done this army by them is very slight. The injury they have inflicted upon the people, and upon the rebel army, may be counted by millions. The Reserve Brigade of your division will move to Snickersville on the 29th. Snickersville should be your point of concentration and the point from which you should operate in destroying toward the Potomac. Four days' subsistence will be taken by the command. Forage can be gathered from the country through which you pass. You will return to your present camp at Snickersville on the fifth day.

By command of Maj. Gen. P. H. Sheridan:

JAMES W. FORSYTH,
Lieutenant-Colonel and Chief of Staff

On December 19 General Torbert, with Merritt's and Powell's divisions, was pushed through Chester Gap to strike the Virginia Central Railroad at Charlottesville or Gordonsville. An engagement took place, in which two pieces of artillery were captured, but failing to gain Gordonsville or strike the railroad he returned to Winchester, via Warrenton. Custer, with his division, was at the same time pushed up the Valley to make a diversion in favor of Torbert, but encountering the enemy near Harrisonburg, who attacked his camp at daylight on the ensuing day, he was obliged, in consequence of superior force, to retire. The weather was so intensely cold during these raids that horses and men suffered most severely, and many of the latter were badly frostbitten.

On the 5th of February Harry Gilmor, who appeared to be the last link between Maryland and the Confederacy, and whose person I desired in order that this link might be severed, was made prisoner near Moorefield, his capture being very skillfully made by Colonel Young, my chief of scouts, and a party under Lieutenant-Colonel Whitaker, First Connecticut Cavalry, sent to support him. Gilmor and Mosby carried on the same style of warfare, running trains off railways, robbing the passengers, &c.

In closing this report it gives me great pleasure to speak of the skill, energy, and gallantry displayed by my corps and division commanders, and I take this opportunity of acknowledging the assistance given me by them at all times. To the members of my staff, who so cheerfully on all occasions gave me their valuable assistance, who so industriously labored to execute every duty promptly, and who always behaved with gallantry, I return my sincere thanks. They all joined with me in the deep grief felt at the loss sustained by the army, and the friendly ties broken by the death of their fellow staff officers, Colonel Tolles, chief quartermaster, and Assistant Surgeon Ohlenschlager, medical inspector, who were killed while on their way from Martinsburg to Cedar Creek in October, 1864, and in that of the death of the gallant Lieutenant Meigs, my chief engineer, who was killed while examining and mapping the country near Bridgewater, just above Harrisonburg. This young officer was endeared to me on account of his invaluable knowledge of the country, his rapid sketching, his great intelligence, and his manly and soldierly qualities. I would also here especially mention the loss of two of my most efficient staff officers, Lieutenant-Colonels Kellogg and O'Keeffe, both of whom died after having passed through the dangers and privations of years of warfare, the former of fever, consequent upon excessive labor during the campaign from Petersburg to Appomattox, the latter from wounds received at the battle of Five Forks.

The report of the march from Winchester to Petersburg, to engage in the final campaign, has heretofore been furnished, but I consider it in fact a sequel to this.

I attach hereto an abstract of ordnance and ordnance stores captured from the enemy during the campaign (the 101 pieces of artillery being exclusive of the twenty-four pieces recaptured in the afternoon at Cedar Creek), also a detailed report of my casualties, which are, in the aggregate, as follows: Killed, 1,938; wounded, 11,893; missing, 3,121; total, 16,952.

The records of the provost-marshal, Middle Military Division, show about 13,000 prisoners (as per annexed certificate) to have been received by him, and receipts are among the records of the assistant adjutant-general, Middle Military Division, for forty-nine battle-flags, forwarded to the honorable the Secretary of War.

I am, sir, very respectfully, your obedient servant,

P. H. SHERIDAN,
Major-General, U.S. Army

Bvt. Maj. Gen. JOHN A. RAWLINS,
Chief of Staff, Washington, D.C.

➤ APPENDIX C ➤

MARCH 29–APRIL 9, 1865.—The Appomattox (Virginia) Campaign.
Report of Maj. Gen. Philip H. Sheridan, U.S. Army,
commanding Cavalry

CAVALRY HEADQUARTERS,
May 16, 1865

GENERAL:

I have the honor to submit the following narrative of the operations of my command during the recent campaign in front of Petersburg and Richmond, terminating with the surrender of the rebel Army of Northern Virginia at Appomattox Court House, Va., on April 9, 1865:

On March 26 my command, consisting of the First and Third Cavalry Divisions, under the immediate command of Bvt. Maj. Gen. Wesley Merritt, crossed the James River by the bridge at Jones' Landing, having marched from Winchester, in the Shenandoah Valley, via White House, on the Pamunkey River.

On March 27 this command went into camp near Hancock's Station, on the military railroad, in front of Petersburg, and on the same day the Second Cavalry

Division, which had been serving with the Army of the Potomac, reported to me, under the command of Maj. Gen. George Crook.

The effective force of these three divisions of cavalry was as follows: General Merritt's command, First and Third Divisions, 5,700; General Crook's command, Second Division, 3,300; total effective force, 9,000.

With this force I moved out on the 29th of March, in conjunction with the armies operating against Richmond, and in the subsequent operations I was under the immediate orders of the lieutenant-general commanding. I moved by the way of Reams' Station, on the Weldon railroad, and Malone's Crossing, on the Rowanty Creek, where we were obliged to construct a bridge. At this point our advance encountered a small picket of the rebel cavalry, and drove it to the left across Stony Creek, capturing a few prisoners, from whom and from my scouts I learned that the enemy's cavalry was at or near Stony Creek Depot, on the Weldon railroad, on our left flank and rear. Believing that it would not attack me, and that by pushing on to Dinwiddie Court-House I could force it to make a wide detour, we continued the march, reaching the Court-House about 5 p.m., encountering only a small picket of the enemy, which was driven away by our advance.

It was found necessary to order General Custer's division, which was marching in rear, to remain near Malone's Crossing, on the Rowanty Creek, to assist and protect our trains, which were greatly retarded by the almost impassable roads of that miry section.

The First and Second Divisions went into camp, covering the Vaughan, Flat Foot, Boydton plank, and Five Forks roads, which all intersect at Dinwiddie Court-House, rendering this an important point, and from which I was expected to make a cavalry raid on the South Side Railroad, and thence join General Sherman or return to Petersburg, as circumstances might dictate. However, during the night the lieutenant-general sent me instructions to abandon the contemplated raid and act in concert with the infantry, under his immediate command, and turn the right flank of Lee's army if possible.

Early on the morning of the 30th of March I directed General Merritt to send the First Division, Brigadier-General Devin commanding, to gain possession of the Five Forks, on the White Oak road, and directed General Crook to send General Davies' brigade of his division to the support of General Devin. Gregg's brigade, of Crook's division, was held on the Boydton plank road, and guarded the crossing of Stony Creek, forcing the enemy's cavalry, that was moving from Stony Creek Depot to form a connection with the right of their army, to make a wide detour, as I had anticipated, on the roads south of Stony Creek and west of Chamberlain's Bed—a very fatiguing march in the bad condition of the roads. A very heavy rain fell during this day, aggravating the swampy nature of the ground, and rendering the movements of troops almost impossible. General Merritt's reconnaissance developed the enemy in strong force on the White Oak road, in the vicinity of the Five Forks, and there was some heavy skirmishing throughout the day.

Next morning, March 31, General Merritt advanced toward the Five Forks with the First Division, and, meeting with considerable opposition, General Davies' brigade, of Crook's division, was ordered to join him, while General Crook, advancing on the left with the two other brigades of his division, encountered the enemy's cavalry at Chamberlain's Creek, at a point a little north and west of Dinwiddie, making demonstrations to cross. Smith's brigade was ordered to hold them in check, and Gregg's brigade to a position on his right. The advance of the First Division got possession of the Five Forks, but in the meantime the Fifth Army Corps, which had advanced toward the White Oak road from the Vaughan road, was attacked and driven back, and withdrawing from that point, this force of the enemy marched rapidly from the front of the Fifth Corps to the Five Forks, driving in our cavalry advance, and moving down on roads west of Chamberlain's Creek, attacked General Smith's brigade, but were unable to force his position. Abandoning the attempt to cross in his front, this force of the enemy's infantry succeeded in effecting a crossing higher up the creek, striking General Davies' brigade, of the Second Division, which, after a gallant fight, was forced back upon the left flank of the First Division, thus partially isolating all this force from my main line covering Dinwiddie Court-House. Orders were at once given to General Merritt to cross this detached force over to the Boydton plank road and march down to Dinwiddie Court-House and come into the line of battle. The enemy, deceived by this movement, followed it up rapidly, making a left wheel and presenting his rear to my line of battle. When his line was nearly parallel to mine, General Gibbs' brigade, of the First Division, and General Irvin Gregg's brigade, of the Second Division, were ordered to attack at once, and General Custer was directed to bring up two of his brigades rapidly, leaving one brigade of his division with the trains, that had not yet reached Dinwiddie Court-House. In the gallant attack made by Gibbs and Gregg the enemy's wounded fell into our hands, and he was forced to face by the rear rank and give up his movement, which, if continued, would have taken in flank and rear the infantry line of the Army of the Potomac. When the enemy had faced to meet this attack, a very obstinate and handsomely contested battle ensued, in which, with all his cavalry and two divisions of infantry, the enemy was unable to drive five brigades of our cavalry, dismounted, from an open plain in front of Dinwiddie Court-House. The brunt of their cavalry attack was borne by General Smith's brigade, which had so gallantly held the crossing of Chamberlain's Creek in the morning. His command again held the enemy in check with determined bravery, but the heavy force brought against his right flank finally compelled him to abandon his position on the creek and fall back to the main line immediately in front of Dinwiddie Court-House. As the enemy's infantry advanced to the attack, our cavalry threw up slight breast-works of rails at some points along our lines, and when the enemy attempted to force this position, they were handsomely repulsed and gave up the attempt to gain possession of the Court-House. It was after dark when the firing ceased, and the enemy lay on their arms that night not more than 100 yards in front of our lines.

The commands of Generals Devin and Davies reached Dinwiddie Court-House without opposition by way of the Boydton plank road, but did not participate in the final action of the day.

In this well-contested battle the most obstinate gallantry was displayed by my entire command. The brigades commanded by General Gibbs and Colonels Stagg and Fitzhugh, in the First Division, Generals Davies, Gregg, and Smith, in the Second Division, Colonels Pennington and Capehart, in the Third Division, vied with each other in their determined efforts to hold in check the superior force of the enemy, and the skillful management of their troops in this peculiarly difficult country entitles the brigade commanders to the highest commendation.

Generals Crook, Merritt, Custer, and Devin, by their courage and ability, sustained their commands and executed the rapid movements of the day with promptness and without confusion.

During the night of the 31st of March my headquarters were at Dinwiddie Court-House, and the lieutenant-general notified me that the Fifth Corps would report to me and should reach me by midnight. This corps had been offered to me on the 30th instant, but very much desiring the Sixth Corps, which had been with me in the Shenandoah Valley, I asked for it, but on account of the delay which would occur in moving that corps from its position in the lines in front of Petersburg it could not be sent me. I respectfully submit herewith my brief account of the operations of the day, the response to which was the ordering of the Fifth Corps to my support and my command, as also the dispatch of the lieutenant-general notifying me of his action. I understood that the Fifth Corps, when ordered to report to me, was in position near S. Dabney's house, in the angle between the Boydton Plank road and the Five Forks road. Had General Warren moved according to the expectations of the lieutenant-general, there would appear to have been but little chance for the escape of the enemy's infantry in front of Dinwiddie Court-House. Ayres' division moved down the Boydton plank road during the night, and in the morning moved west by R. Boisseau's house, striking the Five Forks road about two miles and a half north of Dinwiddie Court-House. General Warren, with Griffin's and Crawford's divisions, moved down the road by Crump's house, coming into the Five Forks road near J. Boisseau's house between 7 and 8 o'clock on the morning of the 1st of April. Meantime I moved my cavalry force at daylight against the enemy's lines in my front, which gave way rapidly, moving off by the right flank, and crossing Chamberlain's Creek. This hasty movement was accelerated by the discovery that two divisions of the Fifth Corps were in their rear, and that one division was moving toward their left and rear.

The following were the instructions sent to General Warren:

CAVALRY HEADQUARTERS,
Dinwiddie Court-House, April 1, 1865—3 a.m.

Maj. Gen. WARREN,
Commanding Fifth Army Corps:

I am holding in front of Dinwiddie Court-House, on the road leading to Five Forks, for three-quarters of a mile, with General Custer's division. The enemy are in his immediate front, lying so as to cover the road just this side of A. Adams' house, which leads out across Chamberlain's bed or run. I understand you have a division at J. Boisseau's; if so, you are in rear of the enemy's line and almost on his flanks. I will hold on here. Possibly they may attack Custer at daylight; if so, attack instantly and in full force. Attack at daylight anyhow, and I will make an effort to get the road this side of Adams' house, and if I do you can capture the whole of them. Any force moving down the road I am holding, or on the White Oak road, will be in the enemy's rear, and in all probability get any force that may escape you by a flank attack. Do not fear my leaving here. If the enemy remains I shall fight at daylight.

P. H. SHERIDAN,
Major-General

As they fell back the enemy was rapidly followed by General Merritt's two divisions—General Devin on the right and General Custer on the left; General Crook in rear. During the remainder of the day General Crook's division held the extreme left and rear and was not seriously engaged.

I then determined that I would drive the enemy with the cavalry to the Five Forks, press them inside of their works, and make a feint to turn their right flank, and meanwhile quietly move up the Fifth Corps with a view to attacking their left flank, crush the whole force, if possible, and drive westward those who might escape, thus isolating them from their army at Petersburg. Happily, this conception was successfully executed. About this time General Mackenzie's division of cavalry, from the Army of the James, reported to me, and consisted of about 1,000 effective men. I directed General Warren to hold fast at J. Boisseau's house, refresh his men, and be ready to move to the front when required; and General Mackenzie was ordered to rest in front of Dinwiddie Court-House until further orders. Meantime General Merritt's command continued to press the enemy, and by impetuous charges drove them from two lines of temporary works, General Custer guiding his advance on the Widow Gilliam's house and General Devin on the main Five Forks road. The courage displayed by the cavalry officers and men was superb, and about 2 o'clock the enemy was behind his works on the White Oak road, and his skirmish line drawn in. I then ordered up the Fifth Corps on the main road, and sent Brevet Major Gillespie, of the Engineers, to turn the head of the column off on the Gravelly Church road, and put the corps in position on this road obliquely to and at a point but a short distance from the White Oak road and about one mile from the Five Forks. Two divisions of the corps were to form the front line, and one division was to be held in reserve, in column of regiments, opposite the center. I then directed General Merritt to demonstrate as though he was attempting to turn the enemy's right flank, and notified him that the Fifth Corps would strike the enemy's left flank, and ordered that the cavalry should assault the enemy's works as soon as the Fifth Corps became engaged, and that would be determined by the volleys of musketry. I then rode over to where the Fifth Corps was going into position, and found them coming up very slowly. I was exceedingly anxious to attack at once, for the sun was getting low, and we had to fight or go back. It was no place to intrench, and it would have been shameful to have gone back with no results to compensate for the loss of the brave men who had fallen during the day.

In this connection I will say that General Warren did not exert himself to get up his corps as rapidly as he might have done, and his manner gave me the impression that he wished the sun to go down before dispositions for the attack could be completed. As soon as the corps was in position I ordered an advance in the following formation: Ayres' division on the left, in double lines; Crawford's division on the right, in double lines; and Griffin's division in reserve, behind Crawford; and the White Oak road was reached without opposition.

While General Warren was getting into position I learned that the left of the Second Corps of the Army of the Potomac, on my right, had been swung around from the direction of its line of battle until it fronted on the Boydton Plank road and parallel to it, which afforded an opportunity to the enemy to march down the White Oak road and attack me in right and rear. General Mackenzie was therefore sent up the Crump road with directions to gain the White Oak road if possible, but to attack at all hazards any enemy found, and if successful then march down that road and join me. General Mackenzie executed then with courage and skill, attacking a force of the enemy on the White Oak road and driving it toward Petersburg. He then countermarched and joined me on the White Oak road just as the Fifth Corps advanced to the attack, and I directed him to swing round with the right of the infantry and gain possession of the Ford road at the crossing of Hatcher's Run. The Fifth Corps on reaching the White Oak road made a left wheel and burst on the enemy's left flank and rear like a tornado, and pushed rapidly on, orders having been given that if the enemy was routed there should be no halt to reform broken lines. As stated before, the firing of the Fifth Corps was the signal to General Merritt to assault, which was promptly responded to, and the works of the enemy were soon carried at several points by our brave cavalrymen. The enemy were driven from their strong line of works and completely routed, the Fifth Corps doubling up their left flank in confusion, and the cavalry of General Merritt dashing on to the White Oak road, capturing their artillery, and turning it upon them and riding into their broken ranks so demoralized them that they made no serious stand after their line was carried, but took to flight in disorder. Between 5,000 and 6,000 prisoners fell into our hands, and the fugitives were driven westward, and were pursued until long after dark by Merritt's and Mackenzie's cavalry for a distance of six miles.

During this attack I again became dissatisfied with General Warren. During the engagement portions of his line gave way when not exposed to a heavy fire, and simply from want of confidence on the part of the troops, which General Warren did not exert himself to inspire. I therefore relieved him from the command of the Fifth Corps, authority for this action having been sent to me before the battle, unsolicited.

When the pursuit was given up I directed General Griffin, who had been ordered to assume command of the Fifth Corps, to collect his corps at once, march two divisions back to Gravelly Church, and put them into position at right angles to the White Oak road, facing toward Petersburg, while Bartlett's division (Griffin's old) covered the Ford road to Hatcher's Run. General Merritt's cavalry went into camp on the Widow Gilliam's plantation, and General Mackenzie took position on the Ford road at the crossing of Hatcher's Run.

I cannot speak too highly of the conduct of the troops in this battle and of the gallantry of their commanding officers, who appeared to realize that the success of the campaign and fate of Lee's army depended upon it. They merit the thanks of the country and reward of the Government. To Generals Griffin, Ayres,

Bartlett, and Crawford, of the Fifth Corps, and to Generals Merritt, Custer, Devin, and Mackenzie, of the cavalry, great credit is due, and to their subordinate commanders they will undoubtedly award the praise which is due to them for the hearty co-operation, bravery, and ability which were everywhere displayed.

At daylight on the morning of April 2 General Miles' division, of the Second Corps, reported to me, coming over from the Boydton plank road. I ordered it to move up the White Oak road toward Petersburg and attack the enemy at the intersection of that road with the Claiborne road, where he was in position in heavy force, and I followed General Miles immediately with two divisions of the Fifth Corps. Miles forced the enemy from this position and pursued with great zeal, pushing him across Hatcher's Run and following him up on the road to Sutherland's Depot. On the north side of the run I overtook Miles, who was anxious to attack, and had a very fine and spirited division. I gave him permission, but about this time General Humphreys came up, and receiving notice from General Meade that General Humphreys would take command of Miles' division, I relinquished it at once, and facing the Fifth Corps by the rear (I afterward regretted giving up this division, as I believe the enemy could at that time have been clashed at Sutherland's Depot) I returned to Five Forks and marched out the Ford road toward Hatcher's Run.

The cavalry had in the meantime been sent westward to cross Hatcher's Run and break up the enemy's cavalry, which had collected in considerable force north of that stream, but they would not stand to fight, and our cavalry pursued them in a direction due north to the Namozine road.

Crossing Hatcher's Run with the Fifth Corps, the South Side Railroad was struck at Ford's Depot, meeting no opposition, and the Fifth Corps marched rapidly toward Sutherland's Depot, in flank and rear of the enemy opposing Miles as he approached that point. The force of the enemy fled before the Fifth Corps could reach them, retreating along the main road by the Appomattox River, the cavalry and Crawford's division, of the Fifth Corps, engaging them slightly about dusk.

On the morning of the 3d our cavalry took up the pursuit, routing the enemy's cavalry and capturing many prisoners. The enemy's infantry was encountered at Deep Creek, where a severe fight took place. The Fifth Corps followed up the cavalry rapidly, picking up many prisoners and five pieces of abandoned artillery, and a number of wagons. The Fifth Corps, with Crook's division of cavalry, encamped that night (the 4th) at Deep Creek, on the Namozine road, neither of these commands having been engaged during the day.

On the morning of the 4th General Crook was ordered to strike the Danville railroad between Jetersville and Burke's Station, and then move up toward

Jetersville. The Fifth Corps moved rapidly to that point, as I had learned from my scouts that the enemy was at Amelia Court-House, and everything indicated that they were collecting at that point. On arriving at Jetersville, about 5 p.m., I learned without doubt that Lee and his armor were at Amelia Court-House.

The Fifth Corps was at once ordered to intrench, with a view to holding Jetersville until the main army could come up.

It seems to me that this was the only chance the Army of Northern Virginia had to save itself, which might have been done had General Lee promptly attacked and driven back the comparatively small force opposed to him and pursued his march to Burkeville Junction. A dispatch from General Lee's chief commissary to the commissary at Danville and Lynchburg, requiring 200,000 rations to be sent to meet the army at Burkeville, was here intercepted.

So soon as I found that the entire army of the enemy was concentrated at Amelia Court-House, I forwarded promptly all the information I obtained to General Meade and the lieutenant-general.

On the morning of April 5 General Crook was directed to send General Davies' brigade to make a reconnaissance to Paine's Cross-Roads on our left and front, and ascertain if the enemy was making any movement toward that flank to escape. General Davies struck a train of 180 wagons, escorted by a considerable force of the enemy's cavalry, which he defeated, capturing five pieces of artillery. He destroyed the wagons and brought in a large number of prisoners. Gregg's and Smith's brigades, of the Second Division, were sent out to support Davies, and some heavy fighting ensued, the enemy having sent a strong force of infantry to attack and cut off Davies' brigade, which attempt was unsuccessful.

During the afternoon, and after the arrival of the Second Corps at Jetersville (which General Meade requested me to put in position, he being ill), the enemy demonstrated strongly in front of Jetersville against Smith's and Gregg's brigades, of Crook's division of cavalry, but no serious attack was made.

Early on the morning of April 6 General Crook was ordered to move to the left to Deatonsville, followed by Custer's and Devin's divisions, of General Merritt's command. The Fifth Corps had been returned to the command of General Meade at his request. I afterward regretted giving up the corps.

When near Deatonsville the enemy's trains were discovered moving in the direction of Burkeville or Farmville, escorted by heavy masses of infantry and cavalry, and it soon became evident that the whole of Lee's army was attempting to make its escape. Crook was at once ordered to attack the trains, and if the enemy was too strong one of the divisions would pass him, while he held fast and pressed the enemy and attack at a point farther on, and this division was ordered to do the same, and so on, alternating, and this system of attack would enable us finally to strike some weak point. This result was obtained just south of Sailor's Creek and on the high ground over that stream. Custer took the road, and Crook and Devin coming up to his support, 16 pieces of artillery were captured and about 400 wagons destroyed and many prisoners taken, and three divisions of the enemy's infantry were cut off from the line of retreat.

Meantime Colonel Stagg, commanding the Michigan brigade, of the First Division, was held at a point about two and a half miles south of Deatonsville, and with this force and a section of Miller's battery, which shelled the trains with excellent effect while Colonel Stagg demonstrated to attack them, thus keeping a large force of the enemy from moving against the rest of the cavalry and holding them until the arrival of the Sixth Corps, which was marching to report to me. I felt so strongly the necessity of holding this large force of the enemy that I gave permission to General Merritt to order Colonel Stagg's brigade to make a mounted charge against their lines, which was most gallantly done, the men leaving many of their horses dead almost up to the enemy's works.

On the arrival of the head of the Sixth Corps the enemy commenced withdrawing. Major-General Wright was ordered to put Seymour's division into position at once, and advance and carry the road, which was done at a point about two miles or two miles and a half from Deatonsville. As soon as the road was in our possession Wright was directed to push General Seymour on, the enemy falling back, skirmishing briskly. Their resistance growing stubborn a halt was called to get up Wheaton's division, of the Sixth Corps, which went into position on the left of the road, Seymour being on the right. Wheaton was ordered to guide right, with his right connecting with Seymour's left and resting on the road. I still felt the great importance of pushing the enemy, and was unwilling to wait for Getty's division, of the Sixth Corps, to get up. I therefore ordered an advance, sending to General Humphreys, who was on the road to our right, requesting him to push on, as I felt confident we could break up the enemy. It was apparent, from the absence of artillery fire and the manner in which they gave way when pressed, that the force of the enemy opposed to us was a heavy rear guard. The enemy was driven until our lines reached Sailor's Creek, and from the north bank I could see our cavalry on the high ground above the creek and south of it, and the long line of smoke from the burning wagons. A cavalryman, who in a charge cleared the enemy's works and came through their lines, reported to me what was in front. I regret that I have forgotten the name of this gallant young soldier.

As soon as General Wright could get his artillery into position I ordered the attack to be made on the left, and sent Colonel Stagg's brigade of cavalry to strike and flank the extreme right of the enemy's line. The attack by the infantry was not executed exactly as I had directed, and a portion of our line in the open ground was broken by the terrible fire of the enemy, who were in position on commanding ground south of the creek. This attack by Wheaton's and Seymour's divisions was splendid, but no more than I had reason to expect from the gallant Sixth Corps. The cavalry in rear of the enemy attacked simultaneously, and the enemy, after a gallant resistance, were completely surrounded and nearly all threw down their arms and surrendered. General Ewell, commanding the enemy's forces, and a number of other general officers fell into our hands, and a very large number of prisoners. I have never ascertained exactly how many prisoners were taken in this battle. Most of them fell into the hands of the cavalry, but they are no more entitled to claim them than the Sixth Corps, to which command equal credit is due for the good results of this engagement.

Both the cavalry and the Sixth Corps encamped south of Sailor's Creek that night, having followed up the small remnant of the enemy's forces for several miles.

In reference to the participation of the Sixth Corps in this action, desire to add that the lieutenant-general had notified me that this corps would report to me. Major McClellan and Lieutenant-Colonel Franklin, of General Wright's staff, had successively been sent forward to report the progress of the corps in coming up; and on the arrival of Major-General Wright he reported his corps to me, and from that time until after the battle received my orders and obeyed them; but after the engagement was over, and General Meade had communicated with General Wright, the latter declined to make his report to me until directed to do so by the lieutenant-general.

On the 7th instant the pursuit was continued early in the morning by the cavalry, General Crook in the advance. It was discovered that the enemy had not been cut off by the Army of the James, and under the belief that he would attempt to escape on the Danville road through Prince Edward Court-House, General Merritt was ordered to move his two divisions to that point, passing around the left of the Army of the James. General Crook continued the direct pursuit, encountering the main body of the enemy at Farmville and again on the north side of the Appomattox, where the enemy's trains were attacked by General Gregg, and a sharp fight with the enemy's infantry ensued, in which General Gregg was unfortunately captured. On arriving at Prince Edward Court-House I found General Mackenzie, with his division of cavalry from the Army of the James, and ordered him to cross the bridge on the Buffalo River, and make a reconnaissance to Prospect Station, on the Lynchburg railroad, and ascertain if the enemy were moving past that point. Meantime I heard from General Crook that the enemy had crossed to the north side of the Appomattox, and General Merritt was then moved on and encamped at Buffalo Creek, and General Crook was ordered to recross the Appomattox and encamp at Prospect Station.

On the morning of the 8th Merritt and Mackenzie continued the march to Prospect Station, and Merritt's and Crook's commands then moved on to Appomattox Depot, a point on the Lynchburg railroad, five miles south of Appomattox Court-House. Shortly after the march commenced, Sergeant White, one of my scouts, notified me that there were four trains of cars at Appomattox Depot loaded with supplies for General Lee's army. Generals Merritt and Crook were at once notified, and the command pushed on briskly for twenty-eight miles. General Custer had the advance, and, on nearing the depot, skillfully threw a force in rear of the trains and captured them. Without halting a moment he pushed on, driving the enemy (who had reached the depot about the same time as our cavalry) in the direction of Appomattox Court-House, capturing many prisoners and twenty-five pieces of artillery, a hospital train, and a large park of wagons. General Devin coming up went in on the right of Custer. The fighting continued till after dark, and the enemy being driven to Appomattox Court-House I at once notified the lieutenant-general, and sent word to Generals Ord and Gibbon, of the Army of the James, and General Griffin, commanding the Fifth Corps, who were in rear, that if they pressed on, there was now no means of escape for the enemy, who had reached " the last ditch."

During the night, although we knew that the remnant of Lee's army was in our front, we held fast with the cavalry to what we had gained, and ran the captured trains back along the railroad to a point where they would be protected by our infantry that was coming up.

The Twenty-fourth and Fifth Corps and one division of the Twenty-fifth Corps arrived about daylight on the 9th at Appomattox Depot. After consulting with General Ord, who was in command of these corps, I rode to the front, near Appomattox Court-House, and just as the enemy in heavy force was attacking the cavalry with the intention of breaking through our lines, I directed the cavalry, which was dismounted, to fall back gradually, resisting the enemy, so as to give time for the infantry to form its lines and march to the attack, and when this was done to move off to the right flank and mount. This was done, and the enemy discontinued his attack as soon as he caught sight of our infantry. I moved briskly around the left of the enemy's line of battle, which was falling back rapidly, heavily pressed by the advance of the infantry, and was about to charge the trains and the confused mass of the enemy, when a white flag was presented to General Custer, who had the advance, and who sent the information to me at once that the enemy desired to surrender.

Riding over to the left at Appomattox Court-House I met Major-General Gordon, of the rebel service, and Major-General Wilcox. General Gordon requested a suspension of hostilities pending negotiations for a surrender then being held between Lieutenant-General Grant and General Lee. I notified him that I desired to prevent the unnecessary effusion of blood, but as there was nothing definitely settled in the correspondence, and as an attack had been made on my lines with the view to escape, under the impression our force was only cavalry, I must have some assurance of an intended surrender. This General Gordon gave, by saying that there was no doubt of the surrender of General Lee's army. I then separated from him, with an agreement to meet these officers again in half an hour, at Appomattox Court-House. At the specified time, in company with General Ord, who commanded the infantry, I again met this officer, also Lieutenant-General Longstreet, and received from them the same assurance, and hostilities ceased until the arrival of Lieutenant-General Grant.

I am, sir, very respectfully, your obedient servant,

P. H. SHERIDAN,
Major-General

Bvt. Maj. Gen. JOHN A. RAWLINS,
Chief of Staff

✢ BIBLIOGRAPHY ✢

PRIMARY SOURCES

Newspapers
Charleston Mercury
Ionia (Michigan) Sentinel
London Pall Mall Gazette
New York Herald
New York Times
Philadelphia Press
Pittsburgh Evening Chronicle
Richmond Examiner
Richmond Sentinel
Somerset Press

Unpublished Sources
Bentley Historical Library, University of Michigan, Ann Arbor:
    James H. Kidd Papers
    J. W. Monaghan Diary

Clements Library, University of Michigan, Ann Arbor:
    Schoff Civil War Collection
        Diary of Nathan Webb

Manuscripts Division, Library of Congress, Washington, D.C.:
Diary of William G. Hills
Philip H. Sheridan Papers

Maryland Historical Society, Baltimore, Maryland:
Charles E. Phelps Papers

Museum of the Confederacy, Richmond, Virginia:
John D. Imboden Papers

The National Archives, Washington, D.C.:
Medal of Honor Files

New York State Library, Albany, New York:
William Woods Averell Papers

Archives, U.S. Army Military History Institute, Carlisle, Pennsylvania:
Lewis Leigh Collection

Southern Historical Collections, University of North Carolina, Chapel Hill:
Bryan Grimes Papers

Alderman Library, University of Virginia, Charlottesville, Virginia:
Beverly Whittle Diary

Virginia State Archives, Richmond, Virginia:
John C. Donohoe Diary

Published Works

Agassiz, George R., ed. *Meade's Headquarters, 1863–1865: Letters of Colonel Theodore Lyman from the Wilderness to Appomattox.* Boston: Atlantic Monthly Press, 1922.

Alexander, Edward Porter. *Fighting for the Confederacy: The Personal Recollections of General Edward Porter Alexander.* Edited by Gary W. Gallagher. Chapel Hill: University of North Carolina Press, 1989.

Allen, Stanton P. *Down in Dixie: Life in a Cavalry Regiment in the War Days from the Wilderness to Appomattox.* Boston: D. Lothrop & Co., 1888.

Beale, George W. *A Lieutenant of Cavalry in Lee's Army.* Boston: Gorham Press, 1918.

Bonaparte, Napoleon. *Napoleon's Art of War.* Translated by Lt. Gen. Sir G. C. D'Aguilar. New York: Barnes & Noble, 1995.

Bowen, James R. *Regimental History of the First New York Dragoons.* Privately published, 1900.

Boykin, Edward M. *The Falling Flag: Evacuation of Richmond, Retreat and Surrender at Appomattox.* New York: E. J. Hale & Son, 1874.

Brooks, Ulysses R. *Butler and His Cavalry in the War of Secession.* Columbia, S.C.: State Publishing Co., 1912.

Butler, Matthew C. "The Cavalry Fight at Trevilian Station." In eds. Robert U. Johnson and Clarence C. Buel. *Battles and Leaders of the Civil War,* 4 vols., (vol. 4, pp. 237–39). New York: Century Publishing Co., 1884–1888.

Cadwallader, Sylvanus. *Three Years with Grant, as Recalled by War Correspondent Sylvanus Cadwallader.* Edited by Benjamin P. Thomas. New York: Alfred A. Knopf Inc., 1955.

Carpenter, Louis H. "Sheridan's Expedition around Richmond, May 9–25, 1864." *Journal of the United States Cavalry Association* 1 (1888): 1–32.

Chamberlain, Joshua L. *The Passing of the Armies.* Dayton, Ohio: Morningside House, 1989.

Conrad, Thomas Nelson. *The Rebel Scout: A Thrilling History of Scouting Life in the Southern Army.* Washington, D.C.: The National Publishing Co., 1904.

Crowninshield, Benjamin W. *A History of the First Regiment of Massachusetts Volunteer Cavalry.* Boston: Houghton-Mifflin Co., 1891.

———. "Sheridan at Winchester." *Atlantic Monthly* 42 (1878): 684–90.

Douglas, Henry Kyd. *I Rode with Stonewall.* Chapel Hill: University of North Carolina Press, 1940.

DuPont, Henry A. *The Campaign of 1864 in the Valley of Virginia and the Expedition to Lynchburg.* New York: National Americana Society, 1925.

Early, Jubal A. *Autobiographical Sketch and Narrative of the War between the States.* Philadelphia: J. B. Lippincott & Co., 1912.

Eckert, Edward K., and Nicholas J. Amato, eds. *Ten Years in the Saddle: The Memoir of William Woods Averell, 1851–1862.* San Rafael, Calif.: Presidio Press, 1978.

Forsyth, George A. *Thrilling Days in Army Life.* New York: Harper & Bros., 1900.

Foster, Alonzo V. *Reminiscences and Record of the 6th New York V.V. Cavalry.* Brooklyn: privately published, 1892.

Gilbert, Charles. "On the Field of Perryville" In *Battles and Leaders of the Civil War,* 4 vols., edited by Robert U. Johnson and Clarence C. Buel (vol. 3, pp. 52–59). New York: Century Publishing Co., 1884–1888.

Gordon, John B. *Reminiscences of the Civil War.* New York: Charles Scribner's Sons, 1903.

Grant, Ulysses S. "Chattanooga." In *Battles and Leaders of the Civil War,* 4 vols., edited by Robert U. Johnson and Clarence C. Buel (vol. 3, pp. 679–711). New York: Century Publishing Co., 1884-1888.

———. *Personal Memoirs of U. S. Grant.* 2 vols. New York: Charles L. Webster & Co., 1885.

Hagemann, E. R., ed. *Fighting Rebels and Redskins: Forty Years of Army Life.* Norman: University of Oklahoma Press, 1968.

Harris, Moses. "The Union Cavalry." *War Papers Read before the Commandery of the State of Wisconsin, Military Order of the Loyal Legion of the United States* 1 (1891): 340–73.

Harris, Samuel. *Personal Reminiscences of Samuel Harris.* Chicago: The Robinson Press, 1897.

Hazen, William B. *A Narrative of Military Service.* Boston: Ticknor & Co., 1885.

Humphreys, Andrew A. *The Virginia Campaign of 1864 and 1865.* 2 vols. New York: Charles Scribner's Sons, 1881.

Hyndman, William. *History of a Cavalry Company: A Complete Record of Company A, Fourth Pennsylvania Cavalry.* Philadelphia: James B. Rogers Co., 1870.

Ide, Horace K. *History of the First Vermont Cavalry Volunteers in the War of the Great Rebellion.* Edited by Elliott W. Hoffman. Baltimore: Butternut & Blue, 2000.

Isham, Asa B. "The Cavalry of the Army of the Potomac." *Sketches of War History, 1861–1865: Papers Prepared for the Ohio Commandery of the Military Order of the Loyal Legion of the United States* 5 (1903): 301–27.

Kennon, L. W. V. "The Valley Campaign of 1864: A Military Study." *The Shenandoah Campaigns of 1862 and 1864 and the Appomattox Campaign of 1865: Papers of the Military Historical Society of Massachusetts* 6: 31–57. Boston: The Military Historical Society of Massachusetts, 1907.

Kidd, James H. *Personal Recollections of a Cavalryman in Custer's Michigan Brigade.* Ionia, Mich.: Sentinel Printing Co., 1908.

Lee, William O., comp. *Personal and Historical Sketches and Facial History of and by Members of the Seventh Regiment Michigan Volunteer Cavalry, 1862–1865.* Detroit: Ralston Co., 1901.

Lloyd, William P. *History of the First Regiment Pennsylvania Reserve Cavalry, from Its Organization, August 1861, to September 1864, with List of Names of All Officers and Enlisted Men Who Have Ever Belonged to the Regiment, and Remarks Attached to Each Name, Noting Change.* Philadelphia: King & Baird, 1864.

Longstreet, James. *From Manassas to Appomattox: Memoirs of the Civil War in America.* Philadelphia: J. B. Lippincott, 1896.

Lowden, J. K. "A Gallant Record: Michigan's 5th Cav. In the Latter Period of the War." In three parts, *National Tribune*, 16, 23, and 30 July 1896.

Mahan, Dennis Hart. *An Elementary Treatise on Advanced-Guard, Out-Post, and Detachment Service of Troops, and the Manner of Posting and Handling Them in the Presence of an Enemy.* New York: J. Wiley, 1861.

McDonald, Carlos. "Diary." In *Report of the Forty-Sixth Annual Reunion of the Sixth Ohio Veteran Volunteer Cavalry Association.* Warren, Ohio: Wm. Ritezel & Co., 1911.

Meade, George, ed. *The Life and Letters of General George Gordon Meade.* 2 vols. New York: Charles Scribner's Sons, 1913.

Merington, Marguerite, ed. *The Custer Story: The Life and Letters of General George A. Custer and His Wife Elizabeth.* New York: Devin-Adair Co., 1950.

Merritt, Wesley. "Sheridan in the Shenandoah Valley." In *Battles and Leaders of the*

Civil War, 4 vols., edited by Robert U. Johnson and Clarence C. Buel (vol. 4, pp. 500–21). New York: Century Publishing Co., 1884–1888.

Mohr, James C., ed. *The Cormany Diaries: A Northern Family in the Civil War.* Pittsburgh: University of Pittsburgh Press, 1982.

Mosby, John S. *The Memoirs of Colonel John S. Mosby.* New York: Little, Brown & Co., 1917.

————. "Retaliation." *Southern Historical Society Papers* 27 (1899): 314–22.

Neese, George M. *Three Years in the Confederate Horse Artillery.* New York: Neale Publishing Co., 1911.

Nevins, Alan, ed. *A Diary of Battle: The Personal Journals of Colonel Charles S. Wainwright, 1861–1865.* New York: Harcourt, Brace & World, 1962.

Newhall, Frederick C. *With General Sheridan in Lee's Last Campaign.* Philadelphia: J. B. Lippincott, 1866.

Opie, John N. *A Rebel Cavalryman with Lee, Stuart, and Jackson.* Chicago: W. B. Conkey Co., 1899.

Pond, George E. *The Shenandoah Valley in 1864.* New York: Charles Scribner's Sons, 1883.

Porter, Charles H. "Operations of the Fifth Corps on the Left, March 29 to Nightfall March 31, 1865; Gravelly Run." *Papers of the Military Historical Society of Massachusetts* 6:209–34. Boston: Military Historical Society of Massachusetts, 1907.

Porter, Horace. *Campaigning with Grant.* Bloomington: University of Indiana Press, 1961.

————. "Five Forks and the Pursuit of Lee." In *Battles and Leaders of the Civil War,* 4 vols., edited by Robert U. Johnson and Clarence C. Buel (vol. 4, 708–22). New York: Century Publishing Co., 1884–1888.

Pyne, Henry. *Ride to War: The History of the First New Jersey Cavalry.* New Brunswick, N.J.: Rutgers University Press, 1961.

Reader, Francis Smith. *History of the Fifth West Virginia Cavalry, Formerly the Second Virginia, and Battery G First West Virginia Light Artillery.* New Brighton, Pa.: Daily News, 1890.

Rockwell, Alonzo D., M.D. *Rambling Recollections: An Autobiography.* New York: Paul B. Hoeber, 1920.

Rodenbough, Theophilus F. "Sheridan's Richmond Raid." In *Battles and Leaders of the Civil War,* 4 vols., edited by Robert U. Johnson and Clarence C. Buel (vol. 4, pp. 188–93). New York: Century Publishing Co., 1884–1888.

————. "Some Cavalry Leaders." In *The Photographic History of the Civil War,* 10 vols., edited by Francis Trevelyan Miller (vol. 4: 262–88). New York: Review of Reviews Co., 1911

Rosser, Thomas L. *Addresses of Gen'l T. L. Rosser at the Seventh Annual Reunion of the Association of the Maryland Line.* New York: L. A. Williams Printing Co., 1889.

Rosser, Thomas L. *Riding with Rosser.* Edited by S. Roger Keller. Chambersburg, Pa.: Burd Street Press, 1998.

Schaff, Morris. *The Sunset of the Confederacy.* Boston: John W. Luce & Co., 1912.

Schmitt, Martin F., ed. *General George Crook: His Autobiography.* Norman: University of Oklahoma Press, 1946.

Scott, John. *Partisan Life with Colonel John S. Mosby.* Bloomington: University of Indiana Press, 1959.

Sheridan, Philip H. *Personal Memoirs of P. H. Sheridan.* 2 vols. New York: Charles L. Webster & Co., 1888.

Stevens, Hazard. "The Battle of Cedar Creek." *The Shenandoah Campaigns of 1864–1865, Personal Memoirs of the Military History Society of Massachusetts* 6: 89–140. Boston: Military History Society of Massachusetts, 1907.

Strang, Edgar B. *Sunshine and Shadows of the Late Civil War.* Privately published, 1898.

Summers, Festus P., ed. *A Borderland Confederate.* Pittsburgh: University of Pittsburgh Press, 1962.

Sumner, Merlin E., comp. *The Diary of Cyrus B. Comstock.* Dayton, Ohio: Morningside House, 1987.

Sun Tzu. *The Art of War.* Translated by Samuel B. Griffith. London: Oxford University Press, 1963.

Supplement to the Official Records of the Union and Confederate Armies. 100 vols. Wilmington, N.C.: Broadfoot Publishing, 1995.

Swinton, William. *Campaigns of the Army of the Potomac.* New York: Charles Scribner's Sons, 1882.

Taylor, James E. *The James E. Taylor Sketchbook—With Sheridan Up the Shenandoah Valley in 1864: Leaves from a Special Artist's Sketchbook and Diary.* Dayton, Ohio: Morningside House, 1989.

The War of the Rebellion: A Compilation of the Official Records of the Union and Confederate Armies. 128 volumes in 3 series. Washington, D.C.: U.S. Government Printing Office, 1880–1891.

Thomas, Hampton S. *Personal Reminiscences of Service in the Cavalry of the Army of the Potomac.* Philadelphia: L. R. Hamersly & Co., 1889.

Tobie, Edward P. *History of the First Maine Cavalry.* Boston: Press of Emery & Hughes, 1887.

———. "Personal Recollections of General Sheridan." *Personal Narratives of Events in the War of the Rebellion, Being Papers Read before the Rhode Island Soldiers and Sailors Historical Society* 6: 183–218. Providence: Rhode Island Soldiers and Sailors Historical Society, 1889.

Veil, Charles H. *The Memoirs of Charles Henry Veil.* Edited by Herman J. Viola. New York: Orion Books, 1993.

Walker, Aldace F. *The Vermont Brigade in the Shenandoah Valley, 1864.* Burlington, Vt.: The Free Press Association, 1869.

Wallace, Robert C. *A Few Memories of a Long Life.* Fairfield, Wash.: Ye Galleon Press, 1988.

Wells, Edward L. *Hampton and His Cavalry in '64.* Richmond, Va.: B. F. Johnson Co., 1899.

Williams, Charles Richard, ed. *The Diary and Letters of Rutherford B. Hayes, Nineteenth President of the United States.* 5 vols. Columbus: Ohio Historical Society, 1922.

Wilson, James Harrison. "The Cavalry of the Army of the Potomac." *Papers of the Military Historical Society of Massachusetts, Civil and Mexican Wars 1861, 1846* 13: 33–88. Boston: Military Historical Society of Massachusetts, 1913.

Wittenberg, Eric J., ed. *At Custer's Side: The Civil War Writings of James H. Kidd.* Kent, Ohio: Kent State University Press, 2001.

———. *One of Custer's Wolverines: The Civil War Letters of Brevet Brigadier General James H. Kidd, Sixth Michigan Cavalry.* Kent, Ohio: Kent State University Press, 2000.

SECONDARY SOURCES

Alberts, Don E. *Brandy Station to Manila Bay: A Biography of General Wesley Merritt.* Austin, Texas.: Presidial Press, 1980.

Bates, Samuel P. *Martial Deeds of Pennsylvania.* Philadelphia: T. H. Davis & Co., 1875.

Bearss, Edwin C., and Chris M. Calkins. *The Battle of Five Forks.* Lynchburg, Va.: H. E. Howard Co., 1985.

Burgess, Milton V. *David Gregg: Pennsylvania Cavalryman.* Privately published, 1984.

Burr, Frank A., and Richard J. Hinton. *"Little Phil" and His Troopers: The Life of Gen. Philip H. Sheridan.* Providence, R.I.: J. A. & R. A. Reid, 1888.

Calkins, Chris M. *The Appomattox Campaign, March 29–April 9, 1865.* Conshohocken, Pa.: Combined Publishing, 1999.

———. *The Danville Expedition of May and June 1865.* Danville, Va.: Blue & Gray Education Society, 1998.

Catton, Bruce. *A Stillness at Appomattox.* Garden City, N.Y.: Doubleday, 1954.

———. *Grant Takes Command.* Boston: Little, Brown, 1968.

Collins, Darrell L. *General William Averell's Salem Raid.* Shippensburg, Pa.: Burd Street Press, 1998.

"David McMurtrie Gregg," Circular No. 6, Series of 1917, Military Order of the Loyal Legion of the United States, Commandery of Pennsylvania, May 3, 1917.

Davies, Henry E. *General Sheridan.* New York: D. Appleton, 1895.

Duncan, Richard R. *Lee's Endangered Left: The Civil War in Western Virginia, Spring of 1864.* Baton Rouge: Louisiana State University Press, 1998.

Eanes, Capt. Greg. *Wilson-Kautz Raid: Battle for the Staunton River Bridge.* Lynchburg, Va.: H. E. Howard Co., 1999.

Fordney, Ben F. *Stoneman at Chancellorsville: The Coming of Age of the Union Cavalry.* Shippensburg, Pa.: White Mane, 1998.

Frye, Dennis E. " 'I Resolved to Play a Bold Game': John S. Mosby as a Factor in the 1864 Valley Campaign." In *Struggle for the Shenandoah: Essays on the 1864 Valley Campaign,* edited by Gary W. Gallagher (pp. 107–26). Kent, Ohio: Kent State University Press, 1991.

Furqueron, James R. " 'The Best Hated Man in the Army': Part II—The Remarkable Career of William Babcock Hazen." *North & South,* vol. 4, no. 5 (May 2001): 66–79.

Greene, A. Wilson. "Stoneman's Raid." In *Chancellorsville: The Battle and Its Aftermath,* edited by Gary W. Gallagher (pp. 65–106). Chapel Hill: University of North Carolina Press, 1996.

———. "Union Generalship in the 1864 Valley Campaign." In *Struggle for the Shenandoah: Essays on the 1864 Valley Campaign,* edited by Gary W. Gallagher (pp. 41–76). Kent, Ohio: Kent State University Press, 1991.

Heatwole, John L. *The Burning: Sheridan in the Shenandoah Valley.* Charlottesville, Va.: Rockbridge Publishing, 1998.

Henderson, G. F. R. *The Science of War: A Collection of Essays & Lectures, 1892–1903.* Edited by Capt. Neill Malcolm. London: Longmans, Green & Co., 1905.

Hergesheimer, Joseph. *Sheridan: A Military Narrative.* Boston: Houghton-Mifflin Co., 1931.

Holmes, Torlief S. *Horse Soldiers in Blue: First Maine Cavalry.* Gaithersburg, Md.: Butternut Press, 1985.

Jacob, Karen Allamong. *Testament to Union: Civil War Monuments in Washington, D.C.* Baltimore: Johns Hopkins University Press, 1998.

Jones, Virgil Carrington. *Gray Ghosts and Rebel Raiders.* New York: Henry Holt & Co., 1956.

Longacre, Edward G. *The Cavalry at Gettysburg: A Tactical Study of Mounted Operations During the Civil War's Pivotal Campaign, 9 June–14 July 1863.* Rutherford, N. J.: Rutgers University Press, 1986.

———. *Custer and His Wolverines: The Michigan Cavalry Brigade 1861–1865.* Conshohocken, Pa.: Combined Books, 1997.

———. *Lincoln's Cavalrymen: A History of the Mounted Forces of the Army of the Potomac.* Mechanicsburg, Pa.: Stackpole, 2000.

Mahr, Theodore C. *The Battle of Cedar Creek: Showdown in the Shenandoah, October 1–30, 1864.* Lynchburg, Va.: H. E. Howard Co., 1992.

Mayhew, David R. "Sheridan and Crook: Anatomy of a Failed Friendship." *Civil War* 70 (October 1998): 22–35.

McClellan, Carswell. *Notes on the Personal Memoirs of P. H. Sheridan.* St. Paul, Minn.: Press of William S. Banning, Jr., 1889.

McDonough, James Lee. *War in Kentucky: From Shiloh to Perryville.* Knoxville: University of Tennessee Press, 1994.

McFeely, William S. *Grant: A Biography.* New York: Norton, 1982.

McLean, James. *California Sabers: The History of the 2nd Massachusetts Cavalry in the Civil War.* Bloomington: University of Indiana, 2000.

Morris, Roy, Jr. *Sheridan: The Life and Wars of General Phil Sheridan.* New York: Crown Publishing, 1992.

Naroll, Raoul S. "Sheridan and Cedar Creek—A Reappraisal." *Military Analysis of the Civil War: An Anthology by the Editors of Military Affairs* (pp. 153–68). Millwood, N.Y.: KTO Press, 1977.

O'Connor, Richard. *Sheridan the Inevitable.* Indianapolis: Bobbs-Merrill Co., 1953.

Power, Tracy. *Lee's Miserables: Life in the Army of Northern Virginia from the Wilderness to Appomattox.* Chapel Hill: University of North Carolina Press, 1998.

Ramage, James A. *Gray Ghost: The Life of Col. John Singleton Mosby.* Lexington: University of Kentucky Press, 1999.

Rhea, Gordon C. *The Battles for Spotsylvania Court House and the Road to Yellow Tavern, May 7–12.* Baton Rouge: Louisiana State University Press, 1997.

———. *The Battle of the Wilderness, May 5–6, 1864.* Baton Rouge: Louisiana State University Press, 1994.

———. *To the North Anna: Grant and Lee, May 13–25, 1864.* Baton Rouge: Louisiana State University Press, 2000.

Sheridan Monument Commission. *Unveiling of the Equestrian Statue of General Philip H. Sheridan.* Albany, N.Y.: Sheridan Monument Commission, 1916.

Stackpole, Edward J. *Sheridan in the Shenandoah.* 2nd ed. Harrisburg, Pa.: Stackpole Books, 1992.

Starr, Stephen Z. *The Union Cavalry in the Civil War.* 3 vols. Baton Rouge: Louisiana State University Press, 1981.

Stephenson, Darl L. *Headquarters in the Brush: Blazer's Independent Union Scouts.* Athens, Ohio: Ohio University Press, 2001.

Suderow, Bryce A. "Glory Denied: The First Battle of Deep Bottom, July 27th–29th, 1864." *North & South* 3, no. 7 (September 2000): 17–33.

Taylor, Emerson Gifford. *Gouverneur Kemble Warren: The Life and Letters of an American Soldier.* Boston: Houghton-Mifflin Co., 1932.

Thomas, Emory M. *Bold Dragoon: The Life of J. E. B. Stuart.* New York: Random House, 1986.

Tsouras, Peter G., ed. *Military Quotations from the Civil War.* New York: Sterling Publishing, 1998.

Urwin, Gregory J. W. *Custer Victorious: The Civil War Battles of George Armstrong Custer.* East Brunswick, N.J.: Associated University Presses, 1983.

Warner, Ezra J. *Generals in Blue: The Lives of the Union Commanders.* Baton Rouge: Louisiana State University Press, 1964.

Weigley, Russell. "Philip H. Sheridan: A Personality Profile." *Civil War Times Illustrated,* no. 7 (July 1968): 4–9, 46–48.

Wert, Jeffry D. *Custer: The Controversial Life of George Armstrong Custer.* New York: Simon & Schuster, 1996.

———. *From Winchester to Cedar Creek: The Shenandoah Campaign of 1864.* Carlisle, Pa.: South Mountain Press, 1987.

———. *Mosby's Rangers: The True Adventures of the Most Famous Command of the Civil War.* New York: Simon & Schuster, 1990.

Wheeler, Richard. *Witness to Appomattox.* New York: Harper and Row, 1989.

Whittaker, Frederick. *A Complete Life of Gen. George A. Custer, Major-General of Volunteers, Brevet Major-General U.S. Army, and Lieutenant-Colonel Seventh U.S. Cavalry.* New York: Sheldon & Co., 1876.

Wittenberg, Eric J. *Glory Enough for All: Sheridan's Second Raid and the Battle of Trevilian Station.* Washington, D.C.: Brassey's Inc., 2001.

tanooga, 13; command of Department of the Mississippi, 6; credit to Sheridan by, 14; dependence on cavalry, 20; Five Forks orders, 100, 221; friendship with Sheridan, 5, 162; as general in chief of Union armies, 14, 16; Lee's defeats of, 146; Lee's surrender to (*see* surrender); military rank, 14; monument to, 174; orders for final campaign, 99–100; raids ordered by, 51; Richmond capture strategy, 36; Shenandoah Valley assignment to Sheridan, 59–60; Shenandoah Valley campaign, 59–61; Shenandoah Valley strategy, 61, 63, 72, 85; support of Sheridan, 3, 92, 95, 96, 102, 126, 172–73; view of cavalry commanders, 17; views of, 16; Warren and, 117, 124, 125

Greene, A. Wilson, 142

Gregg, David M., 17, 18, 19–20, 22 n.44; Appomattox campaign, 230; Cavalry Corps division command, 36, 176; Cold Harbor assignment, 183; Haw's Shop battle, 184; North Anna River engagements, 180; orders to, 27, 92–93; rear-guard defense, 181; Samaria Church battle, 42–44, 46; Stony Creek assignment, 221–22; Todd's Tavern battle, 178

Gregg, Irvin, 222

Griffin, Charles, 123, 124, 125, 130; commendation of, 226–27; Five Forks battle, 224

Grimes, Bryan, 61, 72

Grover, Cuvier, 64, 162–63, 201, 216

guerilla/scout groups, 140–42

guns: captured, 13–14, 78; Spencer repeating carbine, 18, 20, 141. *See also* weapons

Halleck, Henry W., 4–5, 17, 59; as general in chief of Union armies, 6; Shenandoah Valley campaign strategy, 61, 196

Halltown, 61, 200, 202

Hampton, Wade, 28, 31, 53; command succession, 145; defeat of Sheridan, 50; pursuit of Sheridan's cavalry, 39, 41, 42; Samaria Church battle, 44, 46; Trevilian Station battle, 39, 188

Hancock, Winfield Scott, 49, 117

hangings, 70, 79–80

Harney, William S., 117

Harpers Ferry, 59

Haw's Shop battle, 33, 34, 35, 50; Sheridan's report of, 184–85

Haxall's Landing, 28

Hayes, Rutherford B., 61, 107, 127

Hazen, William B., 136

Henderson, G. F. R., 161

Hill, A. P., 151, 166 n.3

Hoke, Robert, 35

Hooker, Joseph, 110, 148 n.47

horses, 20; condition of, 24, 31, 33, 177; killed, 37, 183; new, 192; Sheridan's (*see* Rienzi)

Hotchkiss, Jedediah, 74

Humphreys, Andrew A., 51, 125, 227; in Appomattox campaign, 153; on supply train destruction, 152

Hunter, David ("Black Dave"), 33, 36, 196; command declined, 59; as department commander, 59; Lynchburg assignment, 37, 47, 58; Sheridan's orders to join, 138

Hupp's Hill engagement, 74

hypocrisy, 130, 171. *See also* mendacity

Imboden, John D., 33

infantry, subordination of cavalry to, 24–25

Ingalls, Rufus, 16

insubordination. *See* disobedience

Jackson, Thomas J. ("Stonewall"), 58, 91

James River, 28, 186–87

James River Canal, 36–37, 98, 99

Jetersville, 227, 228

Johnson, D. D., 216

Johnston, Joseph E., 16, 100, 150

Jones, William E. ("Grumble"), 36

Kautz, August V., 42, 47, 49. *See also* Wilson-Kautz raid

Kellogg, [Lt. Col.], 218

Kelly's Ford battle, 110

Kelton, John, 4

Kernstown, 58, 197

Kershaw, Joseph, 60, 61, 70, 201, 204

Kidd, James H., 2, 61, 66; on Cedar Creek battle, 77–78

Kilpatrick, Judson, 17, 18, 144, 145

Kitching, [General], 216

Knoxville siege, 111

Laurel Brigade, 25, 72, 88 n.54

Lee, Custis, 153

Lee, Fitzhugh, 25, 27, 28; cavalry commands, 28–29; friendship with Averell, 109; Kelly's Ford battle, 110; Old Cold Harbor engagement, 35; pursuit of Trevilian Station raiders, 39; Samaria Church battle, 44; Trevilian Station battle, 188; Union strategy against, 36

Lee, G. W. Curtis, 151

Lee, Robert E., 16, 17, 31; at Amelia Court House, 228; Appomattox campaign. *See* Appomattox campaign; cavalry, 36; defense of Richmond, 58; delay for provisioning, 151; Early's army with, 78; final retreat, 149–50; generalship of, 145–46; North Anna River trap, 51; papers of, 151–52; pursuit of Hunter's army, 47; Sheridan actions' influence on, 145, 172; on Sheridan's defeat, 46; surrender by. *See* surrender; as West Point commandant, 109

Lee, W. H. F., 42

ABOUT THE AUTHOR

Eric J. Wittenberg has spent much of his adult life studying Union cavalry operations in the Civil War. A practicing lawyer, Mr. Wittenberg is a graduate of Dickinson College and the University of Pittsburgh School of Law. He is the editor of *Under Custer's Command* and *One of Custer's Wolverines.* In addition, he has authored *Glory Enough for All: Sheridan's Second Raid and the Battle of Trevilian Station, Gettysburg's Forgotten Cavalry Actions,* which won the Bachelder-Coddington Literary Award as 1998's best new work interpreting the Battle of Gettysburg, and *We Have It Damn Hard Out Here.* He has also written numerous articles for national Civil War magazines. He and his wife, Susan, live in Columbus, Ohio.